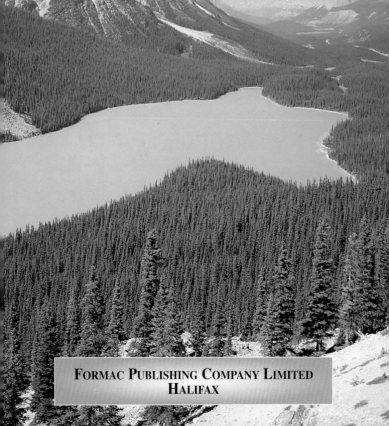

THE CANADIAN ROCKIES

SECOND EDITION
A Colourguide

Edited by Brian Brennan

FORMAC PUBLISHING COMPANY LIMITED
HALIFAX

CONTENTS

Welcome to the Canadian Rockies!	5

CALGARY 7

Exploring Calgary	8
A Short History	12
Top Attractions	16
Entertainment	21
Shopping	25
Dining	28
Museums	31
Festivals	35
Calgary Stampede	37

KANANASKIS 41

Kananaskis Country	42
Outdoor Recreation	44
Canmore	49

BANFF NATIONAL PARK 51

Exploring Banff	53
A Short History	55
Hiking and Climbing	58
Skiing and Other Winter Sports	61
Summer Recreation	65
Exploring the Town of Banff	68
Lake Louise	83
Kootenay, Yoho and More	91

CONTENTS

COLUMBIA ICEFIELD 99
The Icefields Parkway 100
The Columbia Icefield 105

JASPER NATIONAL PARK 109
A Short History 111
Exploring the Town of Jasper 115
Hiking and Camping 123
Skiing Jasper 127
Miette Hot Springs 129
Jasper Excursions 131

EDMONTON 135
Exploring Edmonton 136
A Fur Trading Post Grows Up 139
Shopping 141
Top Attractions 143
Dining 148
City of Festivals 151
Excursions from Edmonton 154

DRUMHELLER & WATERTON 157
Drumheller & The Badlands 158
Waterton Lakes National Park 165

LISTINGS 169

INDEX 204

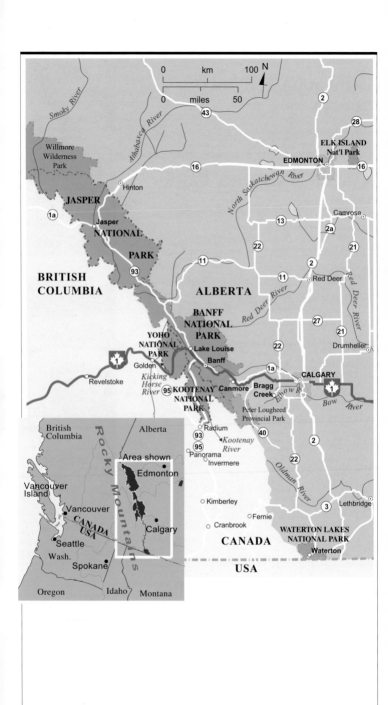

WELCOME TO THE CANADIAN ROCKIES!

BRIAN BRENNAN

MORAINE LAKE

This guide, completely revised and updated, is designed to help you derive maximum benefit from your visit to Canada's mountain playground. It will enrich your visit to Alberta — and parts of southeastern British Columbia — by directing you to major attractions, places to go and things to see and do. This guide can be used in many ways, but will work particularly well for those who fly into Calgary, explore the city and then set out on a driving holiday across the province. Using Calgary as a launching pad, visitors have easy access to such featured destinations as Kananaskis Country, Banff National Park, Jasper National Park, Edmonton, Drumheller and Waterton Lakes National Park — all within three driving hours or less.

All sections of the guide are written by people who live and work in Alberta or British Columbia. They lead you to the best of everything from shopping to dining to indoor entertainment and outdoor recreation, with plenty of colourful local history to enhance the experience for you.

Turn to the listings at the end of the guide for addresses, telephone numbers, websites, e-mails, hours of operation and other useful information to help you enjoy your visit. Remember, though, that things do change over time. While every effort has been made to ensure the information in this guide is up to date, it is always prudent to call ahead to confirm details.

Like the other books in the Colourguide series, this is an independent publication. No payments or contributions have been solicited or accepted by the creators or publishers of the guide.

This book is the work of an especially talented team of writers, editors and photographers, most with deep roots in Alberta:

BRIAN BRENNAN is the Calgary-based author of five books about the colourful personalities and social history of Alberta. His latest title is *Romancing the Rockies: Mountaineers, Missionaries, Marilyn & More*.

BOB BERGEN is a Calgary writer with a PhD in strategic studies from the University of Calgary. He specialized in covering Canadian military affairs over a 25-year journalism career at the *Albertan* and *Calgary Herald* newspapers. For 23 of those years he also covered the Calgary Exhibition and Stampede.

Born and raised in Western Canada, FERN BROOKS has worked as a writer/editor around B.C. and Alberta for more than 20 years. She calls Calgary home, but heads for the Rockies whenever she can.

CINDA CHAVICH has been a food, travel and features writer in Calgary for 20 years. A contributor to *The Globe and Mail* and such magazines as *Wine Spectator* and *Chatelaine*, she has authored *The Girl Can't Cook* and the award-winning *High Plains: The Joy of Alberta Cuisine*.

Born in Banff and raised in Edmonton, JANICE MACDONALD has published non-fiction about the Edmonton area and the fur trade (*The Northwest Fort, Canoeing Alberta*) and mysteries set in the Edmonton area (*The Next Margaret, Sticks and Stones, The Monitor*). She also has written children's books and a college textbook and is a member of the Northern Alberta Old-Timers Association.

SUSAN MATE is a Calgary-based freelance writer and editor who specializes in travel. A proud lifetime Albertan, she has written for numerous publications including *Business Edge, Alberta Parent, The Globe and Mail, Spa Life* and *Horizon Airlines* magazine.

CHRIS MORRISON has been writing about Waterton for 20 years from her summer residence in this national park. She is co-author of three books about the area: *Waterton and Glacier In a Snap!, View with a Room* and *M. V. International* as well as being contributing editor for other park books.

DARLENE BARRY QUAIFE has lived on the doorstep of Kananaskis Country, outside Priddis, Alberta, for 25 years. Her novel *Bone Bird* won a Commonwealth Writers Prize. Her latest title, *Polar Circus*, is a thriller set at a remote polar bear research site.

HARRY M. SANDERS is a Calgary-based historical consultant and freelance writer. He is the author of *The Story Behind Alberta Names* and *Historic Walks of Calgary* and is a frequent contributor to *Avenue* magazine.

GILLIAN STEWARD is a Calgary-based journalist who has lived in Alberta for more than 30 years. She has written for newspapers, magazines, books and CBC radio and travelled to almost every corner of the province.

MONTE STEWART is a Vancouver-based journalist and author who lived in Calgary for many years and still spends much of his spare time camping, golfing and fishing in the Rockies.

RANDY WILLIAMS is an Edmonton-based writer, editor and elementary school teacher. Married with two daughters, he whisks the family off to Jasper as often as possible.

CALGARY

EXPLORING CALGARY

BRIAN BRENNAN

CALGARY SKYLINE

Jammed like a restless teenager between the prairie and the foothills of the Canadian Rockies, Calgary is a brash young city of constant change. Over the course of its century-old history, it has been a cowtown, an oil town, a garrison town and now an oil town again — with just enough briefcase-carrying cowboys around to prove that it hasn't completely forgotten its ranching roots.

It's also a city of chinooks — those sun-kissed, snow-melting winds that cascade over the eastern slopes of the Rocky Mountains, softening winter's bite and creating spring-like conditions for up to 35 days annually. While snow can fall in any month, including July and August, in winter the chinooks turn the weather prognostications completely upside down by raising the temperature as much as 30ºC in half an hour. Seven winters out of eight produce at least

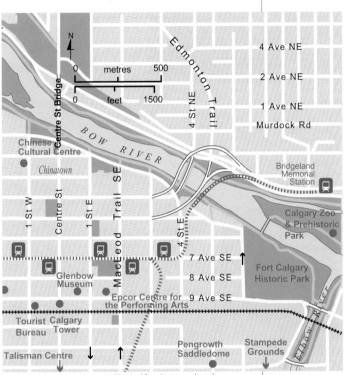

one notable chinook; usually, half a dozen raise the temperature 10 or 15°C and linger for days.

So, the weather is unpredictable — but usually it's dry and sunny. Among Canadian cities, Calgary holds the record for driest air (relative humidity: 6 per cent) and boasts the most sunny days: 329 per year, on average. Against this elemental backdrop, and with a highly educated, mostly white-collar population of more than 933,000, Calgary has emerged in recent decades as one of the most dynamic and fastest-growing cities in Canada — now growing at the more leisurely rate of 1.8 percent annually, compared to the 3.1 percent average recorded in 1998–2002.

In 1968, the tallest building in the city after the recently opened 190-metre Calgary Tower was the 20-storey Elveden House. Today, the downtown is a head-office haven — nine of the *Financial Post's* Top 50 companies are headquartered in Calgary — a gleaming, steel-and-glass cityscape in which the tallest

OUTDOOR SCULPTURE, DOWNTOWN

THE CALGARY
STAMPEDERS

BRONCO RIDER AT
THE STAMPEDE
(BELOW); HERITAGE
PARK (BOTTOM)

skyscraper, Petro-Canada's 52-storey west tower, is challenged by competitive neighbours.

ENTERTAINMENT AND RECREATION

Nestled among the office towers are state-of-the-art entertainment and recreation facilities: the Epcor Centre for the Performing Arts, where close to 300,000 people enjoy more than 1,700 live performances annually in its four theatres and 1,800-seat concert hall; the 17,000-seat Pengrowth Saddledome, which provides a venue for big-ticket concerts, rodeos, ice shows and circuses, and a home for the NHL's Calgary Flames, the WHL's Calgary Hitmen and the NLL's Calgary Roughnecks; and the Talisman Centre for Sport and Wellness, which offers everything from kick-boxing to synchronized swimming and attracts more than 1.5 million visits each year, making it the most widely used sports facility in Canada.

All of these can be reached by public transit, which includes both buses and an above-ground, light-rail transit system called the C-Train. But make no mistake: Calgary belongs to the Age of the Automobile, and it rewards those who rent cars at the airport and follow the signs into town.

CALGARY TOWER

First opened in June 1968 and endowed in 2005 with a new outside observation gallery featuring a glass floor that gives visitors the sensation of stepping into space, the iconic tower is Calgary's most famous and distinctive landmark. It attracts more than half a million visitors annually, boasts an elegant 150-seat revolving restaurant at the top, and on special occasions — from Canada Day to those rare times when the Calgary Flames make a serious run for the Stanley Cup — it turns into the world's tallest torch, with a celebratory gas-fired flame burning up top.

PLUS-15 WALKWAY SYSTEM

Designed by architect Harold Hanen in the 1960s and immortalized in the Canadian independent film

waydowntown, the Plus-15 system is downtown Calgary's innovative response to winter: a heated indoor skywalk development that — at more than 12 kilometres in length — is one of the most extensive above-ground pedestrian networks in the world. More than 400 shops and services are linked through a maze of glassed-in bridges. The main branches of the city's banks connect to corporate head offices, libraries, museums, theatres, exercise facilities, private clubs, municipal buildings, parking garages, hotels, restaurants, shopping centres and even apartment buildings, giving rise to the surrealistic notion that a person could live, work and play in downtown Calgary without ever having to step outside!

PENNY LANE ENTERTAINMENT DISTRICT

Visitors to downtown Calgary will discover a diverse mix of clubs, pubs and restaurants including Ceili's, Indulge and Cowboys. The area of Eighth Avenue and Fifth Street is home to retro movie houses and retail stores such as The Globe Theatre, Uptown Screen and Stage and Sears. There are some unique life-size fiberglass cows on display in the Plus-15 section of the Centennial Parkade. These sculpted bovines are a rare spectacle and are part of the 2000 Udderly Art project, one of the largest displays of street art in Calgary's history.

CHRIS CRAN
SCULPTURE (ABOVE);
DOWNTOWN
CALGARY (TOP AND
BOTTOM)

CHINATOWN

When the $6-million Chinese Cultural Centre rose in 1992, like the Temple of Heaven from the heart of Chinatown's motley village of wonton houses, herb centres and video rental stores, it demonstrated how far the Chinese community in Calgary had come since the dark days of 1910 when the *Calgary Herald* editorialized that a proposed Chinatown would be a "menace to our white city." A magnificent building at the corner of Daqing Ave. and 1st St. SW, it is the largest centre of its kind in North America. It stands today in marked contrast to the rundown laundry shacks and grocery stores that dotted the neighbourhood at the turn of the 20th century.

11

A SHORT HISTORY

HARRY M. SANDERS

FORT CALGARY

INTERPRETER AT
FORT CALGARY

For more than ten thousand years, the area at the confluence of the Bow and Elbow rivers offered abundant fresh water and excellent hunting to prehistoric and aboriginal inhabitants of the Rocky Mountain foothills. Then, in the mid-1870s, the arrival from the east of Roman Catholic missionaries and the NorthWest Mounted Police (NWMP) led to the establishment of Calgary. The mission developed into a largely Roman Catholic, Irish-French village named Rouleauville. Immediately to its north, Fort Calgary — briefly named Fort Brisebois by the unpopular NWMP commander Insp. Ephrem Brisebois and renamed by his superiors — became the nucleus of a settlement. The city is named after Calgary Bay, Isle of Mull, Scotland. Long misinterpreted as "clear, running water," the original Gaelic name for Calgary actually means "bay farm."

As the vanguard of Canadian law and order, the NWMP ended the illicit whiskey traffic that had devastated native society. They won the confidence of aboriginal chiefs such as Crowfoot and Red Crow, and Col. James F. Macleod negotiated Treaty #7 with these and other leaders in 1877. The treaty established separate reserves for the Stoneys, Sarcee (now known as Tsuu T'ina), Blackfoot (now Siksika), Blood (Kainai) and Peigan tribes, including one reserve (Tsuu T'ina) which borders present-day Calgary. Southern Alberta now lay open to railway construction and large-scale settlement.

HISTORIC POLICE BARRACKS, HERITAGE PARK

CANADA'S WILD WEST

The transcontinental Canadian Pacific Railway (CPR), whose right-of-way still shapes the city's development, reached the tent-and-shack community of Calgary in August 1883. As was its pattern across the prairies, the CPR bypassed the existing settlement and built its station nearby, on a section of land that the railway company already owned. The CPR subdivided the townsite, naming its principal streets after corporate officers such as company president George Stephen (later Lord Mount Stephen). Settlers pulled up stakes, sledded their buildings across the frozen Elbow River and relocated nearer the station (now the site of the Calgary Tower).

Though in the 1880s Calgary was a law-abiding town, it resembled the "wild west" to the south in one aspect: bootlegging. Despite a prohibitory law that lasted until 1892, Calgary boasted dozens of saloons open to anyone who knew the secret knock. In 1885, magistrate Jeremiah Travis identified a powerful "whiskey ring" that included Mayor Murdoch and members of his council. Travis interfered in Calgary's second election, disqualifying the mayor and appointing his opponent to the position. The result was a ten-month deadlock, in which two competing councils claimed legitimacy, but neither had the power to act.

THE GRAIN EXCHANGE

Every city worth a guidebook has its great fire, and Calgary's came on November 7, 1886. Most of the town was built of wood, and the conflagration destroyed a large part of what is now the downtown. (A souvenir shop at 131 Stephen Avenue occupies the only building that survived the fire.) As the city was rebuilt, locally quarried sandstone figured in most substantial construction over the next quarter century, giving Calgary a distinct appearance and the nickname "Sandstone City." Calgary was incorporated as a city — the first in what was still the Northwest Territories — on January 1, 1894.

For southern Alberta, the 1880s and 1890s were the golden age of ranching.

RANCHING IN 1880	Both wealthy ranchers and the cowboys who worked for them frequented Calgary's hotels and enjoyed the city's delights. Another familiar figure in pioneer Calgary was the remittance man — often the younger son of a titled English family sent to the "colonies" to make good and sometimes to avoid embarrassment at home.

BOOM AND BUST

Between 1901 and 1913, Calgary enjoyed phenomenal economic, physical and population growth. Hundreds of thousands of agricultural settlers poured into the Canadian west and, as a hub of north-south and east-west railway traffic, Calgary quickly became a regional distribution and manufacturing centre. Its population grew ten-fold between 1901 and 1911. The city limits expanded, taking in a vast area that included the villages of Rouleauville to the south and Crescent Heights to the north. A streetcar system, established in 1909, allowed the development of distant suburbs and industrial areas. Towering new landmarks such as the Grain Exchange Building, the Palliser Hotel and the Robin Hood Flour Mills demonstrated confidence in the city's future. The first Calgary Stampede coincided with the peak of the boom in 1912.

PALLISER HOTEL, 1910

The city's first downturn arrived with the collapse of the real estate market in 1913 and the outbreak of the First

World War the following year (although the Turner Valley oil boom of 1914 offered some relief). The economy grew little over the next thirty years and the population, expected during the boom to reach 100,000 by 1921, did not do so until 1947. Still, many key elements of Calgary's identity were formed during that period. The Centre Street Bridge, with its stately lion figures was probably the largest single municipal undertaking during the First World War. Memorial Drive, which skirts the north bank of the Bow River, was designated in 1922 to remember the fallen of that conflict. The Calgary Zoo was founded in 1929. The federal government financed the development of Calgary's army

base, Currie Barracks, in the mid-1930s. The barracks —which was officially closed in 1998 after the army units transferred to Edmonton — served as an infantry training centre during the Second World War, and the adjacent Lincoln Park was developed as a Royal Canadian Air Force base. The Provincial Institute of Technology and Art (known as the "Tech" until 1962, when it was renamed the Southern Alberta Institute of Technology or SAIT), became a centre for the British Commonwealth Air Training Plan.

Further oil discoveries in 1924 and 1936 proved the value of the Turner Valley field and solidified Calgary's growing position as the oil industry's administrative headquarters. But it took the 1947 Leduc discovery to ignite Calgary's lasting petroleum-based prosperity. Oil and gas quickly replaced agriculture as the city's leading industry. The Leduc gusher, paired with the Calgary Stampeders' 1948 Grey Cup victory in Toronto, signalled that the "Foothills City" had arrived on the national scene. Throughout the 1950s, Mayor Don Mackay and the iconic white stetson he promoted became symbolic of Calgary's new confidence. The city's population doubled between 1948 and 1958, and doubled again by 1971. The future University of Calgary was established in 1946.

By the time the oil boom peaked in the 1970s, the city had been thoroughly transformed. Landmark buildings fell before the wrecker's ball, to be replaced by gleaming skyscrapers. The recession of 1981 temporarily put the brakes on Calgary's growth, but the city's winning bid that year for the 1988 Olympic Winter Games softened the blow. Calgarians also finally recognized the value of their historic buildings, and many of Stephen Avenue's sandstone gems have been restored.

Calgary's economy diversified in the 1980s and 1990s, expanding its high technology sector, in particular, from oil and gas and energy services, to medical research, computer technology and telecommunications. Attracted by this vibrant economic climate, many major corporations made Calgary their headquarters in the 1990s. In the first decade of the third millennium, Calgarians could reflect on their history with pride and on their future with confidence.

SANDSTONE BUILDING, STEPHEN AVENUE WALK

OIL PUMPJACK

TOP ATTRACTIONS

SUSAN MATE

THE RCMP IN HERITAGE PARK	**FORT CALGARY HISTORIC PARK**

FORT CALGARY HISTORIC PARK

Close your eyes and let your mind travel back in time to 1875, when Canada's North West Mounted Police set up the city's first outpost at the convergence of the Bow and the Elbow rivers. Calgary was then little more than a rollicking frontier settlement where the moonshine flowed freely. The 50 Mounties who arrived in late summer were among hundreds of mounted police sent to outposts throughout the region to staunch the whiskey trade and bring law and order to the Wild West. It took six back-breaking weeks to build the new fort with supplies brought in by bull train from Montana, and the accommodations were dismal, to say the least. The mud and clay used to build the fort's log-beam walls were no match for the rain and, seven years later, the fort had to be torn down and rebuilt. The bare-bones men's barracks was gutted by fire in 1887 and replaced by a two-storey structure. In 1914, the land was sold to the Grand Trunk Pacific Railway, which demolished all of the buildings except the pretty Deane House. It still lies across the Elbow from the site of the main fort and is now a restaurant. The land was used for industrial purposes until 1975, when the city reclaimed and excavated it, uncovering the remains of the original fort and other buildings. Now designated a national and provincial historic site, the fort recently gained a new addition — a two-storey clapboard replica of one of the original structures. The tale of the city's founding fort is brought to life

VISITING FORT CALGARY

today at the 16-hectare park through exhibits, interpretive programs and hands-on activities.

HERITAGE PARK

History buffs can continue their time-travel at Western Canada's largest living historical village, situated along the bluffs of the Glenmore Reservoir in the city's southwest. An authentic re-creation of life in the early 1900s, Heritage Park includes an antique midway, steam-train ride and turn-of-the-century exhibits such as ice cream making and horseshoeing. The 26-hectare park boasts more than 150 buildings, many of them antique structures moved to the park from Alberta towns, plus a stately paddlewheeler boat that plies the reservoir waters through one of the city's prettiest areas. Stroll up the boardwalk of the gorgeous Wainwright Hotel for a classy Sunday brunch, or swagger into the old-style saloon and pretend you're John Wayne. Special events such as the Festival of Quilts, Railway Days, Old Time Fall Fair and the Twelve Days of Christmas add to its widespread appeal. You can't find this much old-fashioned fun anywhere else, pardner.

FORT CALGARY (ABOVE); PREHISTORIC PARK AND DESTINATION AFRICA (BELOW)

CALGARY ZOO AND PREHISTORIC PARK

First-time Calgary visitors should have no trouble finding the city zoo as long as they watch for dinosaurs from the car. Life-sized and life-like replicas and iron sculptures of the ancient beasts in the zoo's 6.5-hectare Prehistoric Park can be seen as you hurtle past with the high-speed traffic on Memorial Drive. These mammoth beasts are even more impressive when you're standing in the zoo's Jurassic-style dinosaur kingdom, especially at the foot of a *Tyrannosaurus rex* that's bigger than your house. This park

is just one of many clever facets of this forward-thinking zoo, which has captured international acclaim for its conservation efforts, wildlife rehabilitation initiatives and interpretive programs such as the endangered species breeding program. Calgary's zoo has gone to great lengths to replicate the natural environment of animals that include rare Siberian tigers, snow leopards, whooping cranes and red pandas. In 2003, the wildly acclaimed Destination Africa exhibit opened to eager crowds, expected to push annual guest visits to more than one million a year. The $31.5-million exhibit is designed to give visitors the sense of being in Africa, from a steamy rainforest or an African village to the country's vast savannahs, teeming with wildlife. The Botanical Gardens can occupy a nature-loving visitor for hours, especially the indoor conservatory, a

CANADA OLYMPIC PARK

year-round tropical Valhalla crammed with exotic plants, goldfish ponds, waterfalls and free-flying birds. At the outdoor Dorothy Harvie Garden, more than 4,000 ornamental plant species are cultivated to test their hardiness in Calgary's sometimes-erratic climate, providing a valuable resource for city green thumbs. Ongoing initiatives such as Zoofari eco-trips, the master gardener program, kids' camps, sleepovers and zoo study programs have earned the zoo its place among the city's best-loved local attractions.

OLYMPIC PLAZA

This popular plaza, built for medal presentations at the 1988 Winter Olympic Games, has injected a sense of life into the east downtown. Even during a busy lunch hour, when the office crowd descends on the plaza, the soothing fountains and lapping pools offer a welcome oasis in an urban jungle. In the winter the area is strung with a canopy of lights, and Calgarians flock there to ice skate and listen to seasonal music. The outdoor amphitheatre plays host to many events each year, including the International Children's Festival each spring. Situated along the main east-west LRT artery, the plaza is also within walking distance of most downtown attractions such as the Glenbow Museum and Calgary Centre for Performing Arts.

CANADA OLYMPIC PARK (COP)

It's better to wait until well after lunch before climbing aboard the Road Rocket, a popular attraction at COP. Even the hardiest thrill-seekers will experience butterflies on this one-minute ride as they hurtle 95 kilometres an hour down a concrete chute aboard a modified bobsled on wheels.

OLYMPIC PLAZA

Built in 2000, the Road Rocket is the only ride of its kind in Canada and the thrill of choice for summer visitors to the park, situated on Calgary's western edge. Blast down a 123-metre vertical drop, navigating 14 corners at ever-increasing speeds — why not? The four-season park also boasts mountain biking, mini-golf, beach volleyball and softball; winter activities include downhill skiing, snowboarding, bobsleigh and luge. COP is also home to the 90-metre ski-jump tower (the highest point in Calgary), the Olympic Hall of Fame and Museum, the luge/bobsleigh track and the Flag of Nations concourse.

OLYMPIC OVAL

There aren't many professional sports where you can share facilities with elite

athletes and soak up Olympic ambience at the same time. Rental speed skates are available at the University of Calgary Olympic Oval, where the pros practice. Okay, the real skaters have probably already finished practice, but that's just as well because your first time on speed skates will be sufficiently memorable. In winter, when the mercury sinks to inhuman depths, fitness-loving Calgarians flock to the cushy half-kilometre indoor track that encircles the ice (fringe benefit: watching professional speed skaters is a fine distraction as you run or walk around the track in mind-numbing circles). The Oval plays host to several major national and international events each winter.

SPRUCE MEADOWS EQUESTRIAN CENTRE

There are few outdoor entertainment activities in Calgary that can hold a candle to this world-renowned show-jumping facility just southwest of the city limits off Highway 22X. Even if you're not a member of the "horsy" set, it's hard to have a bad day when the sun illuminates the manicured show-jumping arena and the view to the west features the snow-capped Rocky Mountains. Even if the weather isn't perfect, Calgarians flock to Spruce Meadows on summer long weekends for such events as the Spruce Meadows National (featuring the world-famous RCMP Musical Ride) or the Masters (a prestigious international competition held each September). Aside from the equestrian events, the equestrian centre is loaded with other activities such as international food kiosks, craft booths, entertainers and livestock displays.

PRINCE'S ISLAND PARK

It's a gloriously sunny summer day and Blue Rodeo is delivering yet another perfect set to the cheering of thousands of fans in downtown Calgary. Such is the joy of life on a sunny summer day during the Calgary Folk Music Festival, one of the biggest events each year at this downtown oasis. Flanked by office skyscrapers and trendy high-rise condos, the park is blanketed by a canopy of trees and ringed by red shale pathways and a lush, duck-filled lagoon. Situated just off the expansive Bow River pathway system at the east end of downtown, the park is a beloved year-round recreation hub for

Calgarians and host to cultural, musical or sporting events on most summer weekends. In July and August, head for the park with a picnic supper and stick around for free outdoor theatre, known as Shakespeare in the Park. Visitors can reserve a seat on the flower-ringed patio at the gorgeous River Café and watch the world zoom by across the lagoon. In recent winters, the park's ponds have been turned into cleared ice for skaters.

CALGARY FARMER'S MARKET (CURRIE BARRACKS)

The best place to buy just-picked produce, gourmet grub-to-go, organic fare, cool candy or Simple Simon's famous savoury and sweet pies is situated on a former military base in the city's southwest. It's not the only market in town (the once-trendy Eau Claire Market has a few produce vendors and some artisans, restaurants and stores, but it's no farmer's market, to be sure). Crossroads Market east of the Stampede grounds has lots of fresh produce and homemade goods, as does the on-again-off-again summertime Blackfoot Market off Glenmore Trail and Deerfoot. But the totally enclosed, all-season Calgary Farmer's Market, which opened in 2004 in an abandoned army warehouse, is chock-full of everything along with ample parking and easy access off Crowchild Trail and Flanders Avenue SW.

SHAW MILLENNIUM SKATEBOARD PARK

If you're young and skateboard-savvy (or have kids who are), this popular 88,000-sq.-ft. facility just west of downtown near the Bow River is the place to be — especially when school's out. Billed as the world's largest free outdoor skate park, the $1.8-million park attracts more than 1,000 skaters and scores of spectators each summer day, as well as occasional concerts and other events. The city-run facility, built in 2000, is also equipped for beach volleyball and basketball and is staffed seven days a week during peak months. Situated next to the Telus World of Science (formerly the Calgary Science Centre), the all-hours park includes three distinct areas — an intro park for

beginners, a central park and an expert park, along with connecting bridges and walkways. Lessons are also available to help you learn the tricks of the trade — from ramp riding to half-pipe basics to ramp rail slides, kick flips and other tricks. Safety gear is recommended.

ENTERTAINMENT

BRIAN BRENNAN

The hub of Calgary's vibrant and eclectic performing arts scene is the Olympic Plaza Cultural District, anchored by the Epcor Centre for the Performing Arts — a 3,300-seat complex that offers more than 1,700 performances and draws close to 300,000 patrons annually. Built at a cost of $80 million in 1985 and situated just west of City Hall in the heart of downtown, the Epcor Centre houses four theatres — the Max Bell, Martha Cohen, Engineered Air and Big Secret — as well as the acoustically impressive 1,800-seat Jack Singer Concert Hall.

Calgary's other major performance venue is the 2,700-seat Jubilee Auditorium, reopened in September 2005 after being closed for more than a year for renovations. This is where Alberta Ballet and Calgary Opera perform their seasons, and international touring shows such as *Chicago!*, *The Producers* and *Mamma Mia!* are staged. Transit access to the Jubilee is excellent — the C-Train stops on the doorstep — but if you drive, allow extra time because the parking lineups move like molasses.

DREAM MACHINE **BY ONE YELLOW RABBIT**

FIGARO **BY CALGARY OPERA**

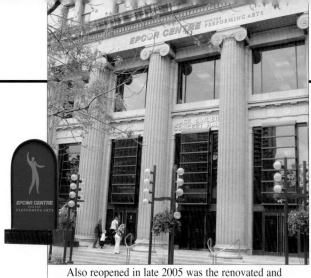

Also reopened in late 2005 was the renovated and renamed Grand Culturehouse, first opened in 1912 as a 1,500-seat vaudeville house playing host to such major stars of early 20th-century show business as Sarah Bernhardt, Dame Nellie Melba, George Arliss and Sophie Tucker. In its new incarnation it is a more intimate 250- to 400-seat performing space and the home of Calgary's Theatre Junction.

MUSIC AND OPERA

The Calgary Philharmonic Orchestra is one of Canada's most respected ensembles. Under the direction of music director Roberto Minczuk, the orchestra presents classic, baroque, light classic, pops and young people's series. In today's more fiscally cautious times, the guest artists tend to be prominent Canadian soloists.

One of Calgary's musical claims to fame is the Carthy Organ, a magnificent pipe organ installed in Jack Singer Hall in 1987. In summer, free Organ à la Carte concerts demonstrate its majestic sound.

A more intimate recital venue is the Eckhardt-Gramatté Hall in the Rozsa Centre at the University of Calgary. Notable presenters of concerts here and around town include the University of Calgary Department of Music, Calgary Pro Musica Society, Kensington Sinfonia, Millennium Music Foundation and Foothills Brass. The renowned Mount Royal College Conservatory is also a hotbed of musical talent; concerts are usually held in the Leacock Theatre on campus.

Like many regional opera companies, the Calgary Opera is a producing shell that imports singers, a stage director and a conductor — usually Canadians — for each production. It stages three operas per season at the Jubilee, accompanied by the CPO. While the company's programming is dominated by popular classics, it occasionally tackles 20th-century operas and musicals such as *Lakmé, Dead Man Walking* and *Sweeney Todd.* Calgary Opera also presents concerts and recitals by major singing stars such as Valdine Anderson, Kimberly Barber, Laura Whalen and John Tessier.

THEATRE

The city's two largest theatre companies reside in the Centre for the Performing Arts. Theatre Calgary is the more conservative of the two, with a philosophy of presenting "plays of enduring value." Typical offerings are Shakespearean and Shavian classics, musicals such as *West Side Story* or *Guys & Dolls*, or sure box-office bets such as *The Miracle Worker* and *Wingfield's Inferno*. The company's annual December production of *A Christmas Carol* is guaranteed to put you in the plum-pudding mood.

Alberta Theatre Projects (ATP) is slightly more daring. With a mission to present "the best in contemporary theatre," the company mounts recent Canadian or international hits such as *The Syringa Tree*, *The Clean House* and *Vincent in Brixton*. ATP is also home to the Enbridge playRites Festival of New Canadian Plays.

One of Calgary's unique exports to the international stage is One Yellow Rabbit Performance Theatre, also resident in the centre. This avant-garde troupe offers such wildly inventive shows as *Ilsa, Queen of the Nazi Love Camp* and *Doing Leonard Cohen*.

In recent years so many small, spunky theatre companies have sprung up that Calgary can now give drama-drenched Edmonton a run for its money. Theatre Junction, Sage Theatre and Ground Zero Theatre are all worthwhile bets for modestly priced professional theatre. Families can try Quest Theatre.

If the concept of staying in one place for dinner and a play appeals to you, Stage West Theatre Restaurant has a long track record of serving up a filling buffet along with a farce or musical. Jubilations Dinner Theatre does the same, offering "entertainment lighter than the meals." You can also combine lunch with a play at Lunchbox Theatre, on the second level of downtown's Bow Valley Square mall, where you can brown-bag it while enjoying a 50-minute comedy or drama.

Another special-to-Calgary company is Vertigo Mystery Theatre, which bills itself as Canada's only professional mystery theatre. It mounts a popular five-play season of murder and mayhem at its theatre in Palliser Square, by the base of the Calgary Tower. Agatha Christie works are a staple.

HAY FEVER AT THEATRE CALGARY

THE DIARY OF ANNE FRANK AT THEATRE CALGARY

THE ALBERTA
BALLET

BLUES MUSICIAN
TIM WILLIAMS
(BELOW); COWBOYS
DANCE HALL
(BOTTOM)

DANCE

Calgary is home to Alberta Ballet, Canada's fourth-largest ballet company, which pursues a contemporary direction under artistic director Jean Grand-Maître. It typically presents a fall program in October, a spring program in April and a glittering traditional *Nutcracker* just prior to Christmas (all with live accompaniment by the Calgary Philharmonic). Alberta Ballet also presents touring companies such as the Royal Winnipeg Ballet. All performances are at the Jubilee.

Then there's Decidedly Jazz Danceworks (DJD), the only troupe in Canada with a mission to perform rhythmically complex jazz choreography to authentic jazz music. In early June, you can catch DJD's annual run at the Jack Singer Concert Hall.

CLUBS

No trip to Calgary would be complete without a visit to a genuine honky-tonk. Ranchman's, a Calgary institution frequented by real cowboys, is as authentic as a western watering hole gets (and worth the rather long cab ride from downtown). More trendy western types line up to party at Cowboys Dance Hall, a cavernous downtown bar featuring live country bands, and also at Outlaws and Coyotes.

Calgary's hottest dance clubs include the Hifi Club, Cherry Lounge, Tequila Nightclub and the intimate Bamboo Tiki Room. For rock, pop and soul, try The Underground, Bruno's Hideout and Trappers Pub. For alternative acts, check out The Night Gallery. Another favourite meeting spot for alternative types is the patio at the funky Ship & Anchor Pub.

The University of Calgary's MacEwan Hall Ballroom has all the charm of a legion hall, but it presents some of the hottest touring bands. Of the numerous Celtic pubs offering

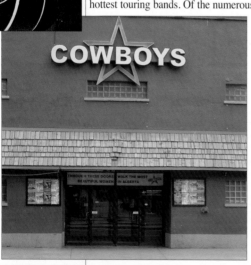

live music, the most popular is the downtown James Joyce, followed by Céilís and the Joyce on Fourth. For live folk music, try the Ironwood Stage and Grill in the trendy Inglewood district.

For blues, the suitably grungy Shamrock Hotel has replaced the previously grungy and now defunct King Eddy (King Edward Hotel) as the venue of choice. For jazz, the intimate Beat Niq has the best reputation.

SHOPPING

CINDA CHAVICH

COWBOY BOOTS AT
RILEY &
MCCORMICK

Like most big cities, Calgary has its complement of chainstores, shopping malls and big-box stores. But there are eclectic shopping districts and unique spots to haunt within walking distance of the downtown core. The fact that Alberta is the only place in the country with no provincial sales tax makes many things a bargain here. With the country's only privatized liquor system, selection and prices, especially for luxury products such as champagne and cognac, are often better than in many places in the world.

DOWNTOWN
Calgary's downtown claim to fame is its so-called Plus-15, a system of enclosed walkways 15 feet above street level that links office towers and shopping centres so that you can cruise the malls in comfort even if the weather outside is frightful. Start at The Bay and continue through the Scotia Centre to the Calgary Eaton Centre/TD Square and Bankers Hall, and you'll find 400 stores, all under one roof.

   The Bay has great Canadiana such as its own Hudson's Bay blankets, tons of clothing and a good culinary shop on the lower level. If you want designer labels and luxuries, Holt Renfrew, an upscale clothing store, anchors the Calgary Eaton Centre.

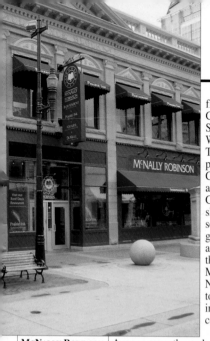

Moving into Bankers Hall, you'll find great kitchen equipment at The Compleat Cook, gourmet goodies at Sunterra Market, chic styles at Blu's Womens Wear and designer bags at Taschen. Stroll the Stephen Avenue pedestrian mall and check out La Cache for retro-hippie-chic clothing and home fashions, and Arnold Churgin Shoes (don't miss the sale shop next door) for an amazing selection of designer footwear. A good place for local history books and quality crafts is the gift store on the main level of the Glenbow Museum, or nearby Micah Gallery of Native Arts. McNally Robinson is a top-notch bookstore that specializes in local and Canadian content, with a comfy café for lunch upstairs.

McNALLY ROBINSON BOOKSTORE

Riley & McCormick on Stephen Avenue carry the real cowboy duds. Across the tracks at Alberta Boot, Canada's largest cowboy boot store, visitors can slip into the appropriate wild western footwear, or find a custom cowboy hat at Smithbilt Hats.

UPTOWN 17TH AVENUE

This is the best place to stroll on a summer afternoon. Everything awaits, from upscale fashions and spas to bakeries, coffee shops, restaurants and galleries. Shop for designer shoes at Mount Royal Village or relax at The Oasis Spa, then head up the street to Park Avenue Boutique and Focus Clothing. Rubaiyat sells collectible handcrafts from stained glass to raku and jewelry, while The Muse is the place for fun, trendy gifts. For cool new and vintage clothing shop at Blue Light Special and Purr, or go stylish and contemporary at Smyth & Kang. Don't miss Gravity Pope for unique, funky footwear and Lululemon for comfy, Canadian-made yoga and exercise wear.

Foodies will want to check out Bernard Callebaut Chocolates, Eiffel Tower Bakery, Rustic Sourdough Bakery and Janice Beaton Fine Cheese. Or go up to 11th Avenue for The Cookbook Co. and the city's best selection of cookbooks and other gourmet goodies, with MetroVino wine shop next door.

KENSINGTON

Kensington is another people-watching paradise — a trendy, inner-city neighborhood that takes its informal name from its main thoroughfare, Kensington Road. Splash of Fashion has cool clothing; there are wonderful reproduction tin toys at Livingstone & Cavell and if you can't find a swimsuit at Swimco, you never will. Kilian has cutting-edge furniture and home accessories, as do Ingear, Urban Barn and Joints across the road. Pages Books on Kensington is a fine independent bookstore, The Galleria has loads of artisan crafts and Honey B's has painted vintage furniture and collectibles. Visit Kensington for gourmet goodies, too — The Roasterie is Calgary's original coffee roaster, Janice Beaton Fine Cheese has a retail cheese store and there's a great selection of wines at Kensington Wine Market.

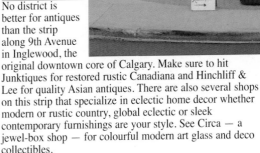

INGLEWOOD

No district is better for antiques than the strip along 9th Avenue in Inglewood, the original downtown core of Calgary. Make sure to hit Junktiques for restored rustic Canadiana and Hinchliff & Lee for quality Asian antiques. There are also several shops on this strip that specialize in eclectic home decor whether modern or rustic country, global eclectic or sleek contemporary furnishings are your style. See Circa — a jewel-box shop — for colourful modern art glass and deco collectibles.

SPECIALTY AND OUT-OF-THE-WAY SHOPS

Calgary is a paradise for outdoor sports, and the requisite outdoor sportswear and equipment. The mother of all outdoor stores is MEC (Mountain Equipment Co-op), with a great selection of everything from tents and sleeping bags to kayaks, clothing and skis. The city also has many good specialty stores for fly fishers, cyclists and skiers. Campers will like Ribtor and Camper's Village. The best selection and deals for rental bikes, tents, kayaks and other gear is the Outdoor Programs department at the University of Calgary.

Down in the southeast part of town, you can visit Lee Valley, the ultimate shop for quality garden gadgets and woodworking tools. Just next door, there's Home Evolution, a source of stylish home furnishings and accessories. Or head to 11th Avenue SW — the new interior design strip — and look for home furniture and accessory shops such as Koolhaus, Soho & Nada, Robert Sweep, Maria Tomas, Chintz and Company and The French Connection for fine French linens and antiques.

While Chinatown has its share of little shops if you're into chinoiserie, a favourite haunt is the Pacific Place mall in the city's northeast. Not only is there a fabulous Asian food market here — T & T Market — but across the way you'll find Utsuwa-No-Yakata, the source for beautiful sushi plates, rice bowls and other Japanese tableware.

Mall rats looking for the biggest selection of chainstores should hit Chinook Centre and Market Mall, while discount shoppers should look for chains such as Winners and its sister home décor store, Home Sense.

27

DINING

CINDA CHAVICH

SALMON AT THE RIVER CAFÉ

While coming to Cowtown inevitably means sampling some world-famous Alberta beef, there's far more to the dining scene in this booming prairie city than cowboy clichés. From fine, fresh sushi bars to Vietnamese noodle houses, Italian trattorias, Irish pubs and French bistros, Calgary has authentic cuisine from every ethnic group imaginable.

The cultural traditions of the first prairie settlers have also influenced the kind of food consumed here. Whether it's a penchant for chili peppers, meat pies, perogies or Swiss fondue, you can likely trace the trend back several generations to early Alberta cowboys, homesteaders or mountain guides.

UPSCALE AND REGIONAL

Top city chefs are now exploring contemporary regional cuisine, inspired by the freshest local ingredients available. From cold-smoked trout and prairie pickerel to wild game such as venison and bison, from morels and chanterelles foraged from the mountain wilderness, to organic meats, heirloom vegetables and berries such as the indigenous saskatoon, these local products add up to meals with a real Western Canadian pedigree. Take a walk to Prince's Island and the rustic elegance of the River Café for the ultimate experience in regional cuisine. The setting is spectacular, offering a view of the Bow River and downtown skyline.

In the city's southern suburbs, The Ranche does a contemporary Alberta-style menu in

an elegantly restored historic ranch house, nestled in the urban wilds of Fish Creek Park. And just south of the Calgary Zoo there's Rouge in another of the city's beautiful historic homes — wonderful continental food with a contemporary twist, featuring the freshest local ingredients.

For fine (albeit expensive) food, the restaurant strip along the downtown Stephen Avenue pedestrian mall (8th Avenue) is another good bet. Catch wins awards for its boisterous oyster bar, extensive selection of fresh seafood and second-level Grill Room, where chefs turn out dishes such as bacon-wrapped monkfish and Digby scallops in foie gras mushroom foam. The Belvedere is compact and New York-stylish, with creative continental cuisine that lives up to the sleek décor. Just a few doors down at Divino, well-chosen wines are paired with an extensive "cheese list" and casual French bistro fare from the wood-fired grill. At Teatro, inspired Mediterranean cuisine is served in a historic bank building, Centini has contemporary Italian cuisine, while at Murrieta's West Coast Bar & Grill, the old sandstone Alberta Hotel Building is the setting for a lively jazz bar and restaurant.

A short cab ride away, you can wander along 4th Street SW and check out other fine dining — Fleur de Sel features authentic French bistro fare in a snug spot, while Wildwood serves eclectic Rocky Mountain cuisine and handcrafted beers from its own brew pub.

TEATRO BAR & RISTORANTE (TOP)

THE STEAK HOUSE EXPERIENCE

Still, Alberta is cattle country and our barley-fed beef is known as a premium product around the world. Whether it's prime rib, T-bone or tenderloin, big portions of AAA beef are de rigueur in Calgary — and if you're up to it, some steak houses will serve you slabs of beef that weigh in at 1.5 pounds and more!

Downtown, the Palliser Hotel's Rimrock dining room is a historic spot for a steak dinner, and both Caesar's Steak House and Hy's Steak House serve up the best beef in a classic, if somewhat dated, steak-house decor. The newly renovated O.N. Bar & Grill at the Westin Hotel features great steak along with dishes featuring local and organic ingredients. Buchanan's offers an eclectic chop-house take on meat meals with a fine selection of wine and single malt scotch, while Saltlik gives the steak-house experience a contemporary twist with a hip décor. Locals still flock to Smuggler's Inn in the city's southwest for the steak-and-salad-bar experience; and for real rodeo cowboys and a two-steppin' dancehall atmosphere, continue farther south to Ranchman's.

EASYGOING AND ETHNIC

If big, beefy meals aren't your style, never fear. Even vegetarians fare well in Calgary and you can eat well without breaking the bank — in a humble haunt in

Chinatown, a funky coffee house or a comfortable pub.

When exploring Chinatown, enjoy dim sum lunch in one of many Chinese restaurants, like the big and busy Silver Dragon, or line up at Thi Thi Vietnamese Submarine for a fresh, spicy satay chicken or grilled vegetable sandwich on a perfectly crisp baguette. Further up Centre Street, Sun Chiu Kee has 350 authentic Asian dishes, from Chinese to Thai.

For Japanese food, Misai offers an authentic Asian experience in slick surroundings while Cafe de Tokyo and Uoza serve fresh sushi and noodles in simpler digs. For a fast, inexpensive bowl of Vietnamese noodles or fresh salad rolls, try Trong Khanh, or head to The Orchid Room or The King

JAMES JOYCE IRISH PUB

& I for more upscale southeast Asian.

Italian food runs the gamut from stylish, expensive spots such as Il Sogno and Da Guido to more casual lunch counters such as Spolumbo's Deli — the place for a gourmet Italian sausage on a bun — or Lina's Italian Market and café for homemade pasta and sandwiches.

Cilantro has creative, California-inspired cuisine and one of the city's most secluded patios for dining on a hot summer night. Nearby, Brava Bistro on 17th Avenue has equally stylish cuisine and wine, or try the hip Living Room for fondue, whole roast chicken or seafood platters designed for sharing. Piato Greek House is the place for a creative (and upscale) take on Greek food, with a busy oyster bar next door, The Big Fish. Or check out Muse in Kensington — creative cuisine in a whimsical, sexy space.

For classic Montreal smoke-meat sandwiches there's the counter at Palace of Eats or the more extensive Jewish deli menu at Grumans Delicatessen, complete with homemade potato knishes and matzo-ball soup. Local casual concepts such as Earl's, Joey Tomato's Kitchen and Joey's Only Seafood (each with several locations) have fun, family fare that's a cut above the usual chains.

Pub-crawlers should start at the Guinness-inspired James Joyce Irish Pub and continue to The Barley Mill, Brewsters brew pub and perhaps join the 20-something crowd at the Ship & Anchor Pub.

Vegetarians flock to Anpurna Curry Pot and Buddha's Veggie Restaurant. Lovers of Indian spices won't want to miss Mango Shiva, an upscale restaurant with a stylish, contemporary take on Indian cuisine, or the more traditional Punjabi food at Clay Oven.

GOOD EARTH CAFÉ

The coolest places to stop for a light bite and a latte for breakfast or lunch? Diner Deluxe uses local, organic ingredients for its big breakfasts, sandwiches and other quality diner-style dishes. The Siding Café downtown has all-day breakfast and cool comfort food, while Good Earth has several locations featuring fair-trade coffee, great baking, sandwiches and soups. Just want a picnic? Head to Janice Beaton Fine Cheese (two locations) for cheese, sandwiches and other gourmet goodies, or Manuel Latruwe Belgian Patisserie for great baguettes, gorgeous cakes and chocolate ice cream.

MUSEUMS

BOB BERGEN

Calgary's museums offer visitors a chance to peel back the historical layers that have made this city what it is. Be advised, the prominence of the military in the cultural history of the West may come as a surprise. A good place to get an overview of the historical journey is right in the heart of downtown Calgary's arts and shopping district at the Glenbow Museum, Western Canada's defining cultural institution.

GLENBOW MUSEUM DISPLAYS: WEST AFRICAN COLLECTION

THE GLENBOW

The Glenbow Museum is a legacy of its founder. In 1966, Calgary millionaire oilman, lawyer, rancher and philanthropist Eric Harvie donated his personal collection of artifacts from North and South America, Europe, Africa and the Orient to Albertans as a gift to commemorate Canada's centennial. The Glenbow is stunning in its multi-disciplinary approach, offering more than 8,640 square metres of exhibition space spread over three floors.

GLENBOW MUSEUM: FIRST NATIONS

The best place to begin an overview tour is on the fourth floor, where the bountiful and beautiful treasures of the mineral world reflect

Harvie's geological background as an oilman. Harvie's wide-ranging travels spawned the adjacent celebration of West African achievement. Stunning art, masks and artifacts are masterfully presented in luscious, dark, red-brown galleries. The next gallery, devoted to warriors through five centuries, reflects Harvie's belief that, over time, the history of man is the history of war, and that citizen soldiers demonstrably reflect their societies, whether they lived in the 14th century or the 20th.

The Glenbow's third floor traces the settlement of the Canadian west, beginning with the First Nations and the fur trade that linked the Canadian frontier with European economies. The major part of the gallery is devoted to the Blackfoot (Siksika) Nation. The fur trade industry is depicted from the trapping of beaver pelts by the North West Company through to more modern hunting with snowmobiles and the emergence of the debate over animal welfare/rights, trapping methods and the industry's future.

The arrival of the North West Mounted Police to stem the whiskey trade is traced as painstakingly as the arrival of Catholic, Methodist and Anglican missionaries. Then come the settlers, who are reflected — whether from the Ukraine, Scotland, Poland or Southern Russia — in their clothing, costumes, tools, artifacts and household items.

FROM THE GLENBOW'S GALLERIES DEVOTED TO NATIVE HISTORY (TOP AND BELOW) AND THE HISTORY OF WAR (ABOVE)

The role of the Canadian Pacific Railway in the settlement of the Canadian West is captured in a recreation of the Brooks rail station and a fascinating miniature of the Stoney Creek bridge, built in 1886. These are placed in the context of such major events as the Confederation of Canada in 1867 and the driving of the last spike at Craigellachie, west of Revelstoke, B.C., which linked Eastern and Western Canada.

The museum's second floor is home to only one permanent exhibit — *Many Faces, Many Paths: the Art of Asia*. It is an oasis of peace and serenity dedicated to the sacred and complex art of Buddhism that reached China in the 2nd Century A.D., and Hinduism, which evolved in India over the past 5,000 years. The balance of the floor is given over to touring art shows and exhibits.

The Glenbow is celebrating Alberta's 2005 centennial with the installation of a new $8.5 million permanent gallery, *Mavericks: An Incorrigible History of Alberta*, based on the book of the same title by well-known Alberta author Aritha van Herk. Scheduled to open in 2007, the gallery celebrates the legendary tales and colourful personalities who shaped and defined Alberta's history.

MUSEUM OF THE REGIMENTS

Altogether, the Glenbow has a 27,000-piece art collection and more than 100,000 books, archives, periodicals, journals, catalogues and reference maps in its reference library. Its archives include more than four kilometres of unpublished archival records, one million photographs, 350 hours of film footage and 1,500 sound recordings. A café offers a place to rest and its gift shop has a wide array of souvenirs and gifts.

THE MUSEUM OF THE REGIMENTS

It is no accident that this historical jewel is the second largest military museum in Canada, behind only the Canadian War Museum in Ottawa. It is a 15- to 20-minute drive from downtown Calgary. The museum has more than 1,800 square metres of display area that spans the arrival of the RCMP and the city's military history from the first militia formation in the late 1870s by Maj. Samuel B. Steele through to Calgary-based soldiers' United Nations service in the former Yugoslavia in the 1990s.

Four spectacular, high-tech, computerized galleries walk visitors through the battles, the heartbreaks and honours won by the Lord Strathcona's Horse (Royal Canadians), the Princess Patricia's Canadian Light Infantry, the King's Own Calgary Regiment and the Calgary Highlanders. Gallery for gallery, the museum is unmatched in its attention to detail, historical scope and imaginative use of computer-activated light, sound and music to not only replicate the battles, but also to situate them in Canadian history.

DISPLAY AT MUSEUM OF THE REGIMENTS

THE NAVAL MUSEUM OF ALBERTA

Visitors are often surprised to learn that the Calgary area has a long-standing relationship with naval warfare, and that 41 Kananaskis Country mountain peaks are named after British Royal Navy ships, actions and admirals. The museum is the second largest naval museum in Canada.

THE NAVAL MUSEUM OF ALBERTA

It has an impressive collection of three painstakingly restored RCN fighter aircraft and a multitude of other naval weapons and armaments, including torpedoes, torpedo throwers, launchers and naval guns. The second-floor picture gallery is dedicated to Canadian warships and the Canadian Pacific ships that carried 810,000 troops, munitions and supplies and essential goods and services during the First World War. With some 4,000 volumes, the naval museum has one of the largest naval libraries in Canada and is currently cataloguing some 20,000 naval photographs. The museum has a gift shop with unique naval books and other items.

THE AERO SPACE MUSEUM

CALGARY AERO
SPACE MUSEUM
(ABOVE AND BELOW)

Calgary is largely remembered as an army garrison town, but those who remember the city from the Second World War remember it more as a sea of air force uniforms. It was a key center for the British Commonwealth Air Training Plan (BCATP) in Canada, which eventually trained 131,355 airmen including observers, navigators and some 50,000 pilots. The Aero Space Museum, at 4629 McCall Way N.E., near the airport, is housed in a former Royal Air Force drill hall of the BCATP. Its collection of 58 aeronautical engines is the second largest such collection in North America, behind the Smithsonian. The museum's photo galleries, plus 12 meticulously restored aircraft indoors and eight outdoors, forge a tangible link to Canada's Western aviation heritage. Highlights include a 1916 Sopwith Triplane, one of only six left in the world, and the Dr. Robert Thirsk Communications Centre, which explores Canadian space history. Six computers allow users of all ages to attempt a simulated docking of the Space Shuttle to the International Space Station. The museum has a well-stocked gift shop.

FESTIVALS

BRIAN BRENNAN

A festival city for all seasons, Calgary always has something on offer for the visitor who enjoys comedy, music, theatre, film or dance.

REVELLERS AT THE CALGARY FOLK MUSIC FESTIVAL

SPRING

The festival season begins in early May with the FunnyFest Calgary Comedy Festival, a two-week celebration of humour featuring 15 comedy themes, 70 stand-up comics and 10,000 punchlines.

One of Canada's top events for young audiences, the Calgary International Children's Festival, brightens Olympic Plaza for five days in late May. The third-largest festival of its kind in North America, it offers music, theatre, dance and puppetry from around the world, plus face-painting, crafts and storytelling.

JENNY ALLEN AT THE CALGARY FOLK MUSIC FESTIVAL

Come the last Sunday in May, folks turn out by the thousands for the Lilac Festival on Fourth Street, a funky afternoon street carnival.

SUMMER

Carifest, in mid-June, is Calgary's premier celebration of Caribbean culture featuring a Carnival-style parade and a daylong presentation of reggae, soca and other island sounds at Prince's Island Park.

Next comes the Canada Trust Jazz Festival Calgary, when for 10 days at the end of June, jazz fans try to soak up enough concerts and club gigs to last them all year. A typical festival program will feature such top artists as David Sanchez, Solomon Burke, Terence Blanchard, David Murray and Queen Mab 3.

If visitors can catch just one festival, it should be the Calgary Folk Music Festival at Prince's Island Park. Long overshadowed by the larger Edmonton and Winnipeg folk fests, this open-air, late-July event has finally found its groove. The main stage features such artists as Steve Earle, Kate and Anna McGarrigle, Bill Frisell, Shelby Lynne and Oscar Lopez.

Calgary lacks a professional Shakespeare series, but each summer the theatre students from Mount Royal College do a credible job of mounting two or three of the Bard's works for free at Shakespeare In The Park.

Early August brings the Calgary Dragon Boat Festival, offering visitors a spectacular three-day display of racing competition and Chinese festive celebration. Come mid-August, you can escape the summer doldrums at Afrikadey! It ranks as Western Canada's largest tribute to African culture, world beat and urban music. It is followed by the Calgary International Reggae Festival, the Calgary Hispanic Festival and Global Fest at the end of the month.

CALGARY INTERNATIONAL CHILDREN'S FESTIVAL (TOP); CEPHAS-WIGGINS AT THE CALGARY FOLK MUSIC FESTIVAL (ABOVE); MICHAEL GREEN IN *HIGH PERFORMANCE RODEO* (BELOW)

FALL

In September, the Calgary International Film Festival presents screenings at the city's three art-house cinemas. Also in September, the Artcity Festival is a celebration of art, architecture and design, featuring a wealth of exhibitions and talks.

In October, there's stargazing for the literary community at WordFest. Staged in Calgary and Banff, this is the third-largest literary event of its kind in Canada.

Calgary is also home to two world-class keyboard competitions, each staged with an accompanying festival. The Calgary International Organ Festival and Competition and the Esther Honens Calgary International Piano Competition and Festival are held every four years. The organ event attracts the planet's best young concert organists, who vie for the largest prize package in the organ world. The Honens is an international contest for emerging pianists — again with a hefty prize purse.

WINTER

Heritage Park puts on its 12 Days of Christmas festival on weekends from mid-November until just before Santa's arrival. Horse-drawn wagon rides, caroling and craft vendors transport visitors to the festive season circa 1910.

Another Christmas tradition for Calgarians is the Enmax Wildlights at the Calgary Zoo. Throughout the holiday season the zoo is festooned with 750,000 twinkling lights.

When January tightens its grip, it's time to retreat indoors for two nationally respected theatre celebrations. Alberta Theatre Projects puts on the Enbridge playRites Festival of New Canadian Plays, the country's only major festival dedicated to new Canadian stage works. The cutting-edge One Yellow Rabbit Performance Theatre produces its High Performance Rodeo, a hip event that could be described as the anti-Stampede.

CALGARY STAMPEDE

BOB BERGEN

Ask ten people who have been to Calgary during the ten days of the Calgary Stampede exactly what the Stampede is and you will get ten different answers. Some might talk about trips to the Calgary Exhibition and Stampede grounds to watch the afternoon rodeo or the night-time chuckwagon races and grandstand show. Others might speak of Canada's biggest outdoor summer party with seemingly endless numbers of free pancake breakfasts, neighborhood parties and company barbecues that take place city-wide.

True aficionados refer to something intangible: a sense of excitement, a sense of energy that can't be quantified. But it's there and you can feel it as the first Friday of the Stampede approaches. Drug store cowboys and cowgirls by the thousands pull on their jeans and cowboy boots and hats and transform the city into a destination holiday magnet that draws visitors from all over the globe.

Calgary tourism officials agree that above all else, the

COWBOY AND BULLS
AT THE STAMPEDE

37

BULL RIDING

three images of Calgary they market world-wide are the city's reputation as being clean, safe and comfortable; its proximity to the Rocky Mountains; and its western heritage, embodied in the Calgary Exhibition and Stampede. Of the three, the Stampede is the drawing card. One of the secrets to its success is simplicity. Almost anyone can look like a cowboy or cowgirl. All it takes is jeans and a relatively inexpensive cowboy hat — at least initially. There is also a lucrative fashion industry built on the image and, in Calgary, the look is always in style.

THE PARADE

The ten days of Stampede usually start officially on parade day, the first Friday of July, but that can vary from time to time, depending on its proximity to the July 1 long weekend, a statutory holiday in Canada. An estimated 250,000 spectators line a four-and-a-half-kilometre route through downtown Calgary for a kick-off parade that begins at 9 a.m. sharp. It is a spectacular two-hour sight-and-sound extravaganza that features more than 4,000 participants, hundreds of horses, horse-drawn and motorized floats, dozens of marching bands from Canada, the United States and overseas, and hundreds of First Nations participants. It is a memorable event in itself.

After the parade, many Calgarians don't go back to work because, to put it simply, the party has begun. Most pubs, bars, restaurants and clubs are jammed with young

NATIVE DANCING

and old alike, dancing and honky-tonking to the near-universal strains of country music that will continue for ten days, particularly in the wildly popular country bars.

CHUCKWAGON RACING

THE RODEO

The Calgary Stampede and Exhibition's grounds are within walking distance of the downtown parade and draw up to one million or more visitors annually. The afternoon rodeo prize money at the exhibition grandstand is among the richest in North America for the saddle bronc riding, wild horse racing, novice bareback riding, women's barrel racing, wild cow milking, novice saddle bronc riding, steer wrestling, bareback riding and bull riding events. As a result, the rodeo is world-class and Canada's largest.

One of the most popular grandstand draws is the electrifying Rangeland Derby of chuckwagon races. The chuckwagons are modern racing versions of the horse-drawn kitchens or chuckwagons of cattle drive lore and are now powered by teams of high-spirited racehorses. The "chucks" begin with a klaxon horn and outriders loading imitation stoves into the back of the wagons, which circle around a barrel or obstacle before thundering around the track. Each evening, nine heats of four wagons and 16 outriders vie to establish the best aggregate time over the course of the first nine days. On the final day of racing, the ninth and sudden death heat establishes the grand winner. The prize? A $50,000 cheque, the largest single purse in the sport of chuckwagon racing.

"THE GREATEST OUTDOOR SHOW ON EARTH"

(If you go, remember the Stampede is billed as the Greatest Outdoor Show on Earth and weather can be a factor in the rodeo and chuckwagon events. July weather in Calgary is normally sunny and warm, with temperatures ranging between 25 and 30 degrees Celsius, but rain and cold can come out of the mountains on short notice.)

THE SHOW

Included in the admission to the chuckwagon races is the Grandstand Show, which features the 175-member Young Canadians song and dance

THE STAMPEDE GROUNDS AT NIGHT

troupe and a host of guest entertainers. The show ends each night with a blaze of fireworks. The Stampede always stresses the family nature of its entertainment and this is reflected in all of its other offerings throughout the park, including headline acts on the free Coca-Cola stage. Also on the grounds, the 2,100 square-metre Nashville North Saloon, holding about 1,550 party animals, rivals any of the large popular country bars in the city with their big-name country music entertainment.

The stated purpose of the Calgary Exhibition and Stampede is to preserve and enhance Alberta's agriculture legacy reflected in more than 45 international stock show events. More than 1,000 agriculture exhibitors attract 39 per cent of the Stampede's visitors. The highlight is a competition between the breeds of cattle, with the Grand Champion of each breed competing for the title of Supreme Champion.

Another popular attraction is a re-creation of the Plains Indian Village, in which families from the various aboriginal nations live for the duration of Stampede demonstrating native dancing, games and tepee-building skills. The exhibition grounds also include midway rides, a casino, the Stampede market and the Western Showcase of arts and crafts, artists salons, floral artistry, kitchen theatre, an international photo exhibit and western art show.

Each day there are numerous free Stampede breakfasts throughout the city, including a number sponsored by major shopping centers that include live top-name entertainment and draw crowds of up to 75,000. A number of major hotels also hold huge saloon-like gatherings inviting patrons to "party flat out," for example.

Hotel and motel accommodation is plentiful and the vast majority of the Stampede's out-of-town visitors are from the United States. But the Stampede also estimates it attracts 150,000 overseas visitors every year.

Many tourism officials elsewhere want to know the formula for Calgary's success, because most cities and towns have exhibitions, festivals or fairs of some kind that

GRANDSTAND SHOW

pale in comparison. That formula is often associated with another intangible known as the "Spirit of Calgary," reflected in the fact that Calgary is a city of volunteers.

It takes an army of 2,500 citizen volunteers to make the not-for-profit Calgary Exhibition and Stampede work. If they had to be paid, the Stampede would go broke. It is spirit that compels all of Calgary to take part in the Stampede and gives it the energy that drives the 10-day celebration.

KANANASKIS

KANANASKIS COUNTRY

DARLENE BARRY QUAIFE

MT. INDEFATIGABLE (ABOVE)

The most diverse outdoor playground in Alberta, set in a landscape that rivals the Alps and is sister to the Andes, Kananaskis Country is located 90 kilometres west of Calgary, running from the Bow River Valley to the Crowsnest Pass. To drive west from the city on the Trans-Canada Highway is to travel a route between the prairies and the Rocky Mountains that has seen human traffic for thousands of years. In 1858, the English explorer John Palliser guided his horse up a mountain pass above lakes and rivers into the heart of what would become Kananaskis Country on October 7, 1977. Captain Palliser, head of a British scientific expedition, named the river and two passes "Kananaskis" after a native who, according to legend, survived an axe blow to the head. The word Kananaskis is thought to mean meeting of the waters.

Kananaskis Country, better known as "K-Country," is part of the Canadian Central Rockies Ecosystem. Bighorn sheep, elk, deer, moose, black and grizzly bears, hawks, bald eagles and osprey range throughout its 4,000 square kilometres. A multiple-use area, K-Country comprises mountain and foothill terrain

BOW VALLEY PROVINCIAL PARK

dedicated to recreation activities that go beyond those experienced next door in Banff National Park. Multi-use means that roughly half of K-Country has been designated as provincial parks and protected sites, while outside of these preservation areas some logging, ranching, natural gas and hydroelectric power production take place.

This diversity allows for a broad range of outdoor sports and the associated facilities, from Olympic-calibre ski complexes to off-road vehicle trails. Barrier Lake Visitor Information Centre provides an impressive directory of professional guides and instructors licensed to operate in Kananaskis Country. Their "real adventure" services include: bicycle and mountain bike trips; bird watching and nature study; canoeing, kayaking and river raft trips; cross-country skiing, downhill skiing, snowboarding, ski touring and winter mountaineering; snowshoeing; dog sledding and skijoring; river, lake and ice fishing; day hikes and overnight trips; mountain climbing, rock climbing and ice climbing; orienteering; natural history tours; horseback riding and pack trips; hay and sleigh rides; photography and painting; sightseeing tours; and hunting trips.

Kananaskis Area

43

OUTDOOR RECREATION

DARLENE BARRY QUAIFE

HIKING ABOVE KANANASKIS LAKES

The recreational opportunities of Kananaskis Country are as vast as this piece of paradise itself on the eastern slopes of the Rocky Mountains. But you can be your own guide whether you're hiking into an alpine valley or going for a walk around Allan Bill Pond. Pick a destination: K-Country can be divided into several distinct get-away zones and still have attractions left over. Just take the Trans-Canada Highway (1) west from Calgary to Kananaskis Trail (40).

THE BOW VALLEY

The Bow River Corridor is your "Gateway to the Rocky Mountains," and a path worth exploring. Stretch your legs

with a hike up Heart Mountain Trail or take to the mountain bike trails of Quaite Valley, Prairie View and Jewell Pass — a circle trip; do a bit of angling in the Bow River or adjacent streams (Alberta angler's license required); canoe or go sailboarding on Lac des Arcs. Modest accommodations and restaurants are available at Deadman's Flat, just off the Trans-Canada Highway. There are a number of campgrounds for tenters and those with trailers and RVs.

Bow Valley Provincial Park, a natural heritage site, is home to rare and endangered plants. It is a naturalist's haven with its open meadows, forests and mountains. There are four interpretive hiking trails, developed to explore the diversity of landscapes, plants, animals and birds. Their names are suggestive of the terrain: Many Springs,

Middle Lake, Montane and Flowing Water trails. Beyond its appeal to birdwatchers and photographers, Bow Valley Park offers hiking, biking and riding trails. Accommodation is available at the Brewster's Kananaskis Guest Ranch, Rafter Six Guest Ranch and campgrounds in seven different areas of the Park. Backcountry camping is allowed with a permit.

KANANASKIS VALLEY

Kananaskis Valley, the heart of K-country, should be considered a home base for any traveller into the Rocky Mountains. Kananaskis Village is a visitor's home away from home. At the centre of the village are the Kananaskis Resort and Delta's Lodge at Kananaskis. Flanking a treed village square that boasts a pond, these two hotels and their dining facilities are geared to a range of needs from honeymooners to families. Rooms range from deluxe to standard, restaurants from fine dining to casual with a choice of lounges, pubs, cafés, and shops in between. The village common provides tennis courts, a fitness circuit, paved trails for walking, in-line skating and biking.

KANANASKIS VILLAGE

Once your creature comforts are secured, Kananaskis Village becomes a base camp from which you can explore the Nakiska ski resort, the world-class Kananaskis Country Golf Course, the Kananaskis River by kayak or canoe, and the delights of fishing in stocked ponds.

Kananaskis Valley has something for everyone. Beyond the self-contained world of Kananaskis Village are the Mt. Kidd RV Park, Kananaskis Wilderness Hostel, Sundance Lodges (tepees, trapper's tents), and Boundary Ranch. Playing in the Kananaskis Valley means mountains, rivers and lakes at every bend in the road, and a country so big that a visitor could cross-country ski, snowshoe, hike, bike or horseback ride a different trail every day for two weeks and have many more to choose from.

WHITEWATER RAFTING ON KANANASKIS RIVER

PETER LOUGHEED PROVINCIAL PARK

Peter Lougheed Provincial Park offers a rare combination of facilities and wilderness adventure. This Kananaskis park boasts the William Watson Lodge, a universal access facility for physically and mentally challenged visitors; an interactive interpretative exhibition and program at the Peter Lougheed Park Visitor Information Centre; and Mt. Engadine Lodge at hand to the Mt. Shark Trailhead. The Mt.

Shark area features an extensive cross-country ski trail system rated for all levels of ability and a helicopter pad for flights into the backcountry, in particular to rustic Assiniboine Lodge at the foot of what has been called the Canadian Matterhorn — Mount Assiniboine.

SKIING ON ROBERTSON GLACIER

Besides numerous hiking trails, over 80 kilometres of mountain bike trails, and two large lakes for boating and fishing, Peter Lougheed Park beckons the adventuresome with glacier skiing in July and backpacking the Continental Divide — the backbone of the Rocky Mountains. A trip into the Robertson Glacier is physically demanding and requires proper gear and some glacier travel experience or a guide. A backpacking trip on Northover Ridge requires some of the same. This 34-kilometre loop gains 1,130 metres of elevation reaching 2,800 metres on the Continental Divide — the view is spectacular. This is wilderness at its best: at this elevation there are meadows full of wildflowers, prime habitat for grizzly bears.

SPRAY LAKES PROVINCIAL PARK

Spray Lakes Provincial Park borders the Peter Lougheed Park and can be reached by driving the Smith-Dorrien Trail through Peter Lougheed Park or off the Trans-Canada Highway at the town of Canmore along the Spray Lakes Road. The Spray Lakes Valley is solitude itself. The legend goes that two minutes off the road and you're "back of beyond and into the wild."

ASSINIBOINE LODGE

Lace up your hiking boots, strap on your snowshoes, your cross-country skis, or hire a dog sled and take the trails less travelled. Content to sit, you can ice fish for trout on Spray Lake. The evening could find you in front of the fireplace at Mt. Engadine Lodge, which offers European hospitality and first-class cuisine in a wilderness setting.

CANMORE NORDIC CENTRE

Canmore Nordic Centre Provincial Park was created for the 1988 Olympic Games. Within walking distance of the town of Canmore along Olympic Way/Spray Lakes Road, the Nordic Centre is host to a variety of winter and summer

activities. Its 70-plus kilometres of scenic world-class cross-country and biathlon ski trails are groomed and tracked for classic and skating techniques. There is night skiing as well. In the summer the Nordic Centre is home to mountain biking, roller skiing, rollerblading, disc-golf and such spectator events as national and international marathons and mountain bike challenges. For those with a competitive spirit there are running events to take part in, from fun runs to half marathons to mountain running. There is a full-facility day lodge at the Nordic Centre that also includes lockers, showers, cafeteria, equipment rentals, lessons and guides.

ELBOW-SHEEP WILDLAND PROVINCIAL PARK

Elbow-Sheep Wildland Provincial Park is 800 square kilometres of wilderness on the east side of the Kananaskis Trail extending from Barrier Lake in the north to the Lineham day use area in the south. Part of Alberta's network of protected areas, the Wildland Park consists of three distinct regions: Sibbald Area (northern), Elbow River Valley (central), Sheep River Valley and Highwood/Cataract Creek Area (southern). These are drive-to destinations with the Sibbald Area being readily accessible from both the Kananaskis Trail and the Trans-Canada Highway. Locally known as Sibbald Flats, this area offers a campground at Sibbald Lake and for those hiking, mountain biking, cross-country skiing and snowmobiling into the backcountry, camping is allowed with a permit. This is a great place for a day outing with maintained picnic sites, easy hiking trails, fly-fishing and a 10-kilometre self-guided auto tour of the Jumpingpound Demonstration Forest. Walk the short interpretive trials along the route and learn about Alberta's forest resources.

MOUNTAIN BIKING AT THE CANMORE NORDIC CENTRE

ELBOW FALLS

The Elbow River Valley is considered the stairway to the mountains. Travel from grasslands, to aspen parkland, to subalpine forest before taking on the mountains.

If you're not interested in staying in the Little Elbow campground, then the hamlet of Bragg Creek is your home base. Accommodation is limited to B&Bs, most offering excellent arrangements. At the heart of this country community are shops, restaurants, art galleries, craft stores and service centres. Downtown Bragg Creek's architecture has a western flair that reflects the ranching heritage of the area.

The eastern sections of the Elbow Valley are multiple-use areas where you will find hiking, cross-country skiing, mountain biking, camping and fishing. Snowmobiling and off-road vehicle trails are found in the McLean Creek Off-Highway Zone. In this multiple-use area,

BIGHORN SHEEP

**BRAGG CREEK
(BOTTOM)**

recreation is intermixed with cattle grazing and gas wells.

The Sheep River Valley is a backcountry wilderness of commanding peaks, pastoral meadows and deep gorges. Although the area is accessible on foot or mountain bike, one of the best ways to see the foothills and valleys that ascend to the mountains is on horseback. There are a number of outfitters and guides for hire working out of local ranches.

For one of the most spectacular mountain vistas in the Rockies, try driving the Highwood Road to Cataract Creek. Follow the Kananaskis Trail (HWY 40) south past Peter Lougheed Provincial Park. In your climb to the Highwood Pass you're bound to see bighorn sheep and if luck holds, moose and black or grizzly bear as you drive through the Highwood Road Corridor Wildlife Sanctuary. This high country area, popular for its creek and mountain lake fishing, is open from June 14 to December 1.

NAKISKA

Nakiska, in the Kananaskis Valley, was computer designed to host the alpine ski events for the '88 Olympic Games. It offers long fall line runs, two competition level half pipes, a terrain park, slow zones for beginner and family skiing and day lodges at mid-mountain and the base. Snowmaking to 85 per cent of the mountain, long cruising runs and remarkable corduroy contribute to exceptional downhill skiing over 325 acres. On-hill services include equipment rentals, lessons, child care, a restaurant, cafeteria and lounge. For those without a vehicle, transportation to Nakiska is available from the hotels at Kananaskis Village. Lifts: two express quads, triple, double chairs, T-bar and magic carpet. Runs: 28 plus glades, half pipe, border-cross course. Snowfall: 250cm (98in). Levels: green 16%, blue 70%, black 14%. Elevation: vertical 735m (2412ft).

Cross-country ski trails map the face of Kananaskis Country. Information on every aspect of these trails from snow conditions to shelters can be obtained from the visitor information centres.

CANMORE

DARLENE BARRY QUAIFE

Canmore is a destination and a jumping off point. This historic town nestled among such giants as Mount Rundle and the Three Sisters cozies up to the Bow River, home of the bull trout. Once a mining town, Canmore now lays claim to exceptional accommodations, restaurants and access to K-Country. Canmore is flanked by the Trans-Canada Highway and the gates to Banff National Park. Located 110 kilometres west of Calgary, transportation can be arranged from the Calgary International Airport to Canmore.

Most visitors settle into a hotel, lodge, inn or bed and breakfast, and then arrange a Kananaskis tour by van, helicopter or dogsled. Transportation is available to the Kananaskis ski resort of Nakiska. Rent a car for a short drive into Spray Lakes and Peter Lougheed provincial parks, then on into the Kananaskis Valley.

Canmore is a place to play hard with a whole host of activities that can be arranged through local adventure and tour companies. Along with skiing and hiking there are guided canyon ice walks, cave tours, river rafting, fishing trips and snowmobile tours to name but a few. Staying around town can put you in touch with the vibrant arts community. There are a variety of galleries and artist studios to visit between cappuccino bars and coffeehouses.

FESTIVALS

Canmore's Winter Festival in February showcases the International Ice Climbing Festival and the International Sled Dog Classic. The Winter Festival is a family affair of ski races, hockey, theatre, music and ice carving — fun and free.

LADY MACDONALD COUNTRY INN

FISHING ON THE BOW RIVER

CANMORE MAIN STREET

The Ice Climbing Festival (Ice Fest), a great spectator event, is open to novice and expert climbers utilizing an indoor climbing wall, an outdoor constructed ice wall and climbing clinics.

The International Sled Dog Classic is not to be missed. A hundred sled-dog teams gather at the Nordic Centre to compete in sled-dog sprint races. Howling dogs and colourful mushers make for an unforgettable winter experience and great photos.

Mountain culture is not short on the arts in Canmore with artSPeak Arts Festival in June, the Canmore Folk Music Festival in July, Mozart on the Mountain in August, the Canmore Highland Games in September and Art on the Mountain in October.

BOW VALLEY AND K-COUNTRY GOLF

The Bow Valley and Kananaskis Country offer golfers 99 holes over six courses, all set in spectacular Rocky Mountain scenery that is as breathtaking as the signature holes and championship designs.

"Where Nature Plays Through" is the motto for SilverTip: a 7,200-yard, 18-hole championship course rising above the Bow Valley on the side of Mount Lady MacDonald.

Across the Bow Valley from SilverTip is Stewart Creek Golf Course. Perched above Canmore, the 18 fairways have been designed to take advantage of the natural contours of this exceptional geography.

Sharing the valley bottom with the Bow River is the Canmore Golf Club. Dating from the 1920s, it is not to be overlooked. Reasonably priced, it provides scenery and player challenges.

SNOWY OWL DOG SLED DOG TOURS

For a relaxed family experience there is the 9-hole Kananaskis Ranch Golf Course near Exshaw with its fine view of Mount Yamnuska.

"The best natural setting I've ever been given to work with," is how legendary architect Robert Trent Jones described Kananaskis Country Golf Course. His contribution to the Kananaskis Valley is two unique 18-hole courses: Mt. Lorette with its many water hazards and Mt. Kidd with its change in elevation.

NATIONAL
PARK

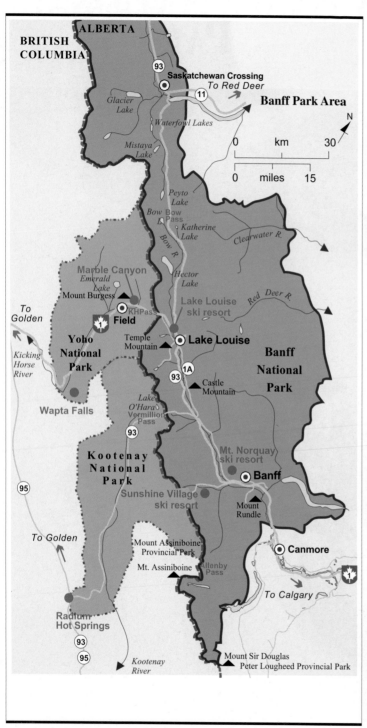

BRITISH
COLUMBIA

ALBERTA

93

Saskatchewan Crossing

To Red Deer

11

Banff Park Area

N

*Glacier
Lake*

Waterfowl Lakes

0   km   30

0   miles   15

*Mistaya
Lake*

*Peyto
Lake*

Bow Bow
Pass

*Katherine
Lake*

Clearwater R.

Bow R.

Marble Canyon

*Emerald
Lake*

Mount Burgess

*Hector
Lake*

Red Deer R.

Lake Louise
ski resort

KHPass

1

Field

Temple
Mountain

Lake Louise

**Banff
National
Park**

**Yoho
National
Park**

*To
Golden*

*Kicking
Horse
River*

93

1A

Castle
Mountain

*Lake
O'Hara*

*Vermillion
Pass*

93

Wapta Falls

**Kootenay
National
Park**

Mt. Norquay
ski resort

Banff

95

Sunshine Village
ski resort

Mount
Rundle

To Golden

Mount Assiniboine
Provincial Park

Mt. Assiniboine

Allenby
Pass

Canmore

To Calgary

Radium
Hot Springs

93

95

*Kootenay
River*

Mount Sir Douglas
Peter Lougheed Provincial Park

EXPLORING BANFF

SUSAN MATE

Glittering snowcapped peaks, unbelievably blue-green lakes, flowered alpine meadows, vast glaciers, hot springs, waterfalls and abundant wildlife make Banff National Park a world treasure. The scenery and vistas of the park are among the most familiar mountain images in the world. Banff and the neighbouring national parks of Jasper, Yoho and Kootenay contain such important and stunning natural features that they have been collectively designated a UNESCO world heritage site. Banff is the most popular destination of the four Rocky Mountain national parks because of its spectacular scenery, ease of access and long tradition of hosting visitors from around the world.

MOLAR PASS

More than four million people come to Banff National Park each year to climb, soak in the hot springs, hike the park's 1,600 kilometres of trails, tour historic sites, participate in outdoor activities, ski at the park's three world-class areas or enjoy drives, interpretive programs and wildlife spotting.

BIGHORN SHEEP NEAR LAKE MINNEWANKA

WILDLIFE

From the tiny pygmy shrew, up to the beaver, which can reach 25 kilograms, the park is home to many small mammals including the Columbia Ground Squirrel, Hoary Marmot, porcupine and pika. Most visitors will see elk, mule or white-tailed deer and,

if they're lucky, moose, Woodland Caribou, bighorn sheep, mountain goats, coyotes, and even wolves, cougars or lynx.

Birders come to see some of the 260 species recorded in the park, among them Clark's Nutcrackers, Pygmy Owls, swallows, finches, warblers and juncos. The most infamous residents of the park are the black and grizzly bears. Keep in mind that it is illegal to feed, entice or disturb any animal in a national park. Parks Canada hands out written material at the park gates advising visitors on the best way to keep safe while enjoying all that the park has to offer. Spend the time to read this material — even tame-looking elk can be dangerous. Observe park highway speed limits, as animals often cross the roads. Be extra cautious in winter when road conditions can be treacherous.

The vegetation in the park ranges from grassland and alpine meadow to towering forests of evergreen with the dominant sub-alpine forest spreading down the valleys. There are 996 species of trees, grasses and flowers, and lots of specialist guidebooks available to help you identify the painter's canvas of summer wildflowers.

ELK ALONG HIGHWAY (TOP); HOVERFLIES ON THISTLE (INSET)

WEATHER

The weather in Banff National Park varies as much as the recreation. The summer sees sunny, warm days perfect for hiking, biking, camping and climbing. Winter's crisp, snowy days mean skating, snowshoeing, dogsledding and skiing. The relative dryness of the air and frequent sunshine in Banff, however, make extreme temperatures more bearable.

Vacationing in such a variable climate means thinking ahead. If you plan to ski, hike or drive in circumstances where the weather could be a danger, get the most up-to-date condition reports from the Visitor Centre in Banff or from the Banff Weather Office.

The national parks collect a daily entrance fee at park gates of $7 for adults, $6 for seniors and $14 for families/groups of up to seven people arriving in the same vehicle. Several campgrounds operate throughout the park and most accommodate recreational vehicles. Campgrounds operate on a first-come, first-serve basis.

A SHORT HISTORY

While Banff's tourism tradition dates back to the 1880s, the history of the area is a 10,000-year story. Parks Canada archaeologists have found 84 campsites in the Bow Valley left by an ancient mountain culture whose origins date back to the end of the last glacial epoch. The digs have uncovered ancient campsites and artefacts, buried hearths, arrowheads, stone tools and piles of splintered, burnt bones. Thousands of years before the bow and arrow, these ancient people hunted bison, deer and mountain sheep in these valleys using stone-tipped spears. They quarried native chert (a flint-like stone) to make hide-scrapers, stone hammers and lance points. One of their quarries was located just a kilometre north of Banff. Stone net-sinkers have been found in the mountain parks, telling us that these people fished to supplement their diet of game.

CASCADE PONDS, NORTH OF TOWNSITE

DAMSELFLY ON WATERLILY

Centuries later, the Kootenay Indians occupied the mountains near Banff for more than two thousand years until they retreated west across the mountains early in the 17th century after disastrous smallpox epidemics. The Kootenay, Stoney, and Blackfoot Indians, and then fur traders, explorers and surveyors all left traces of their existence in the mountains of Banff. Their camps are found anywhere water, food, fuel and a

southern exposure to the low winter sun combine to offer the necessities of life. Archaeologists have found evidence that the Stoney and Blackfoot used Banff's hot springs as a peace ground where the two tribes came to trade for horses and blankets.

THE FUR TRADE

The first Europeans on the scene could not venture into the Banff area because of the hostile Blackfoot. In 1832, the Hudson's Bay Company traders managed to set up a trading post near Bow Valley Gap, but it was boycotted by the Natives and finally abandoned and burned to the ground. Until the railroad surveyors arrived in the 1880s, only nine parties of white travellers are known to have come anywhere near Banff. Most of these merely passed through the area, but the Reverend Robert Rundle left a lasting impression on the Natives and had his name given to one of the world's most photographed mountains, Mount Rundle. The Hudson's Bay Company sponsored Rundle, a missionary, in the 1840s. He taught hymns to the Natives and they shared their food and lodging with him, although not their carefully guarded secret of the sacred hot springs, which lay only a few kilometres from the missionary camp.

In 1857 Captain John Palliser headed west to answer a host of questions posed by England's Royal Geographical Society: What minerals could be mined? Could farms be established on the plains? Was there a route across the Rockies for a road to British Columbia? Dr. James Hector, a Scottish physician and geologist on the Palliser

SAXIFRAGE (BELOW);
THE RAILWAY
(BOTTOM)

expedition, rode into the Bow Valley in August of 1858 and set up camp near Cascade Mountain. Hector reported that in the vicinity he observed "some warm mineral springs which deposited iron and sulphur, and seemed to escape from beds of limestone."

THE HOT SPRINGS

In 1867, Canada was created and the transcontinental railway project begun. Major A. B. Rogers, the man chosen to survey a route up the Bow River for the railway, found a pass through the mountains (Rogers Pass) but missed the springs, as did the men who worked for him. The park was named by William Cornelius Van Horne, general manager of the Canadian Pacific Railway. Not long after he visited the region, Van Horne approved the name "Banff" for the area around Siding 29. The name was suggested at a CPR board meeting by member Sir George Stephen, a native of Banffshire, Scotland. The idea for the park came from Van Horne and from CPR chief engineer Sir

Sandford Fleming, brought out of retirement in England to inspect the proposed route for the railway. A discovery by three CPR workers turned Van Horne and Fleming's notions into a reality.

The three workers, William McCardell, his younger brother Thomas and Franklin McCabe, set out to do some prospecting on November 8, 1883, when work on the railway had shut down for the winter. The trio were intrigued by an unusual-looking mountain (Sulphur Mountain), and rigged up a raft to cross the river. As they slogged through a swamp at the base of the mountain, they discovered that the frigid water was miraculously getting warmer. They carried on until they found a large basin of steaming water.

CAVE AND BASIN NATIONAL HISTORIC SITE

McCardell describes their reaction to the find in his unpublished memoirs: "Our joyousness and the invigorating thrill we experienced in thus locating this strange phenomena and hidden secret of the wilderness knew no bounds." The three men then followed the sulphur smell up the bank and found the opening of a cave. This same opening is still visible today at the Cave and Basin National Historic Site. A few days later, the trio returned and, using a jack pine ladder and a safety rope, lowered themselves down into the cave and saw, "beautiful, glistening stalactites . . . like some fantastic dream of the Arabian Nights."

UPPER HOT SPRINGS

THE PARK

McCabe and McCardell's efforts to exploit the springs by registering a claim ended when the site was set aside as a reserve by a forward-thinking (and money-conscious) Canadian government. Creation of the Hot Springs Reserve in 1885, and the Rocky Mountain Park two years later, would lead to the establishment of Canada's first national park and the world's third. Canada now protects and preserves 39 national parks and 143 national historic sites.

The Cave and Basin National Historic Site tells the story of the founding of Banff National Park at the site of that hot springs discovery. You can see, smell and experience this monumental discovery by touring the cave, dipping a hand in the warm water, exploring exhibits and walking an interpretive trail.

By the late 1800s, the railway station, the Banff Springs Hotel and the Banff Upper Hot Springs were all in place, and Canada's most famous national park was well on its way. Along with sightseers and those who came to bathe in the "curative" springs, mountain climbers and guides began to arrive in numbers. Their story is told at The Whyte Museum of the Canadian Rockies in the town of Banff.

Hiking and Climbing

Susan Mate

Spelunking

Banff offers 1,000 miles of hiking trails, which means that the following suggestions are only highlights. There are excellent hiking books available at the Banff Visitor Information Centre. Before heading out, remember you are in bear country and prepare yourself by reading information given out at the park gates. Be cautious also of other wildlife — as cute as they are, even deer, moose and

Hikers in Johnston Canyon

elk can be dangerous in the wrong situation. Drinking water can be a problem in the park, so use iodine tablets, water filters or bring your own water with you. Don't attempt a hike without taking along storm clothing and proper footwear. Conditions can change quickly in the mountains.

Johnston Canyon and the Ink Pots

Johnston Canyon is a favourite with visitors. So much so that an early or late-season hike is a good option to avoid the crowds. Located 16 miles from Banff on the Bow Valley Parkway, Johnston Creek has eroded a deep cleft in the limestone, which is made accessible by a carefully constructed catwalk. The spectacular Upper Falls is just over a mile from the trailhead. Further along are the Ink Pots, a series of cold-water springs, normally clear blue in colour, but sometimes changing to an

inky black. Count on about four hours round-trip if you go all the way to the Ink Pots, about two hours for Upper Falls.

SILVERTON FALLS

Silverton Falls is a one-hour hike that begins at the parking lot on the north side of the Bow Valley Parkway just east of Castle Junction. The trail marker will say Rockbound Lake Trailhead. To see the lake, bank on a six-hour trip. Other popular lake destinations include Boom Lake, which leaves from the parking lot on Highway 93 South, past Castle Junction en route to Radium; and Arnica and Twin Lakes, also on Highway 93 South. Boom Lake and the Twins are beautiful and the Boom Lake trail is broad and gentle.

CITADEL PASS AND SUNSHINE VILLAGE

To gain vistas with minimal sweat, head for Citadel Pass. To reach the trailhead, take the shuttle bus up to Sunshine Village. If you are driving from Banff, take the Trans-Canada Highway 5.6 miles west from Banff to the Sunshine Village road and drive another 5.6 miles to the parking lot where you can take the shuttle operated by White Mountain Adventures, which also offers guided hikes. The 11.5-mile trek takes you through meadows that straddle the Continental Divide. You can take in views of some of the highest peaks in the park and are sure to spot wildlife, especially mountain goats and even grizzly bear. Fit hikers can head past Howard Douglas Lake and reach Citadel Pass in about two and half hours. For even more

LAKE MINNEWANKA

spectacular views, continue on another 15 minutes to Fatique Pass. If you would like your vistas sprinkled with wildflowers, try the hike to Healy Pass, which also begins at Sunshine Village.

MINNEWANKA, NORQUAY AND BOURGEAU

If you want to spend a day on the trails, Aylmer Pass and Lookout are good possibilities. From the lookout site you can see the winding inland fiord of Lake Minnewanka. From the Minnewanka Interchange on the Trans-Canada Highway, take the Lake Minnewanka Road, following it to the west end of the lake about three miles beyond the Trans-Canada junction.

ABOVE GRASSI LAKES

Another popular destination is Bourgeau Lake. This five-hour round-trip hike leaves from the Trans-Canada Highway, west of the Mount Norquay Interchange. If you've got the energy, continue on the short ascent to Harvey Pass to get a view of distant peaks, including Mount Assiniboine. For even more fun, start early in the day and give yourself time to scramble to the summit of Mount Bourgeau.

OTHER HIKES

Looking for a challenge? Try the six-hour Cory Pass hike, which leaves from the Fireside Picnic Area at the eastern end of the Bow Valley Parkway. This is one of the most strenuous hikes in Banff National Park. Strong hikers who are good route finders can return from Cory Pass by making a loop around Mount Edith and descending the Edith Pass Trail. Check a trail guide for detailed directions.

There are also endless possibilities for multi-day backpacking trips in the park, but those who try this should be very experienced in the outdoors, with good knowledge of navigation and wilderness first aid. You must obtain a wilderness pass from the parks service before you head out.

CLIMBING

Banff National Park's rock climbing season can begin as early as May at the lower elevations along the east side of the park. Alberta's most popular multipitch climbing crag, Yamnuska is actually not in the park, but just 20 kilometres east. There are a number of 8,000-foot peaks near the town of Banff that are popular for their rock routes, but you may have to wade through snow on approach trails that can last until June. The higher alpine peaks come into reasonable summer conditions in late June or early July.

There are several popular moderate scrambling peaks in the park with trails to their summits. These include Cascade Mountain and Mount Rundle. Mounts Edith and

HIKING ON YAMNUSKA

Cory have moderate roped rock climbs and are located close to the road near Banff. Mount Louis is a challenging multipitch limestone rock climb to a spire-like summit. Just west of Banff, Castle Mountain offers a number of steep rock routes. The high summits surrounding Lake Louise and Moraine Lake are among the most popular alpine climbing areas in North America. Extensive trails provide good access and this is a good area to focus a first summer climbing trip to the Rockies. The Columbia Icefields area northwest of Banff is home to many of the highest mountains in the Canadian Rockies. All travel there requires crevasse rescue and whiteout navigation skills. It is recommended that you use a guide when climbing or mountaineering in the park. The quality of rock varies and helmets are a must. Inquire with the park about a permit and to get an idea of what to expect.

Skiing and Other Winter Sports

SUSAN MATE

The downhill ski and snowboarding resorts in Banff National Park — Lake Louise, Sunshine Village and Banff Mount Norquay — are legendary for their endless powder, awesome views, first-rate service and favourable exchange rates. They are also known for their relatively short lift lines, spectacular scenery and challenging skiing conditions. But what international skiers appreciate most is the limitless space. During the week, given that the three resorts offer 7,500 acres of skiable terrain, each visitor gets about an acre.

NORQUAY

Although Banff Mount Norquay is known best for its steep and challenging terrain and well-groomed intermediate slopes, the resort invested $1 million several years ago to become more beginner-friendly. Norquay is the only Rockies destination to offer night skiing and also welcomes snowboarders. If you're staying in the town of Banff, Norquay is literally minutes from your hotel hot tub. Many skiers planning to tour different hills start out at Norquay to get their "ski legs" before moving on to other resorts in the area. The resort is economical as well, with lift prices about 30 per cent cheaper than Sunshine or

SUNSHINE VILLAGE

SUNSHINE VILLAGE

Lake Louise. Known for its intimate feel, short lift lines, lack of crowds, and challenging skiing, Norquay has many fans.

SUNSHINE VILLAGE

Sunshine Village has variety to please everyone, from Delirium Dive and The Wild West for serious experts (pitches approach 50 degrees) to beginner or "green" runs galore, and everything in between. Sunshine is known for its 100 per cent natural snow (33 feet each season), a long ski season (most years right through to the end of May) and 12 lifts (including five high-speed quad chairlifts) that can accommodate up to 20,000 skiers per hour. Recent renovations have included upgrades to the high-speed, eight-passenger gondola that shuttles skiers and boarders (as well as sightseers) from the parking lot to the ski hill base. At day's end, many visitors skip the gondola and zip back to their cars via the nicely groomed ski-out — a trip that takes less than 30 minutes top to bottom. Many visitors spend an entire ski vacation at this hill and never get bored — true diehards can even stay right on the hill at the 84-room Sunshine Inn.

LAKE LOUISE

Lake Louise, Canada's largest ski area, spreads over four mountain faces and is a skiers' paradise, offering more than 100 runs and thousands of acres of wide open bowls. The resort, which is ranked "the most scenic resort in North America" by *SKI* and *Mountain Sports & Living* magazines, guarantees that skiers will be riding one of their three base area lifts in less than 10 minutes. You can find more detail in the section on Lake Louise.

All three resorts offer kids' programs, lessons, tours and snowboarding. It's possible to purchase a three-area lift ticket that includes transfers from hotels in Banff or Lake

LAKE LOUISE

Louise to any of the mountains. Banff Mount Norquay has a snowboard park groomed daily that is lit for night boarding. Sunshine has a half pipe, permanent boardercross and snowboard park. Lake Louise has two half pipes and an expanded terrain park — the Jungle — making it the largest terrain park in North America. The Super Pipe, only the second pipe of this size in western Canada, makes for more speed and big air off the high walls.

NORDIC AND BACKCOUNTRY

Downhill not for you? Cross-country skiers can head off on a trackset trail near Banff or Lake Louise, or else go ski touring in the backcountry. Some of the popular trackset trails near Banff include the Cascade Fire Road, Carrot Creek, Johnson Lake, Cascade, the Banff Springs Golf Course, Spray River, Cave and Basin, and Sundance. Your best bet is to stop in at the Visitor Centre and get a trail guide and advice.

LAKE LOUISE

BACKCOUNTRY IN HEALY PASS

GET TO POWDER BY BACKCOUNTRY TREKKING (ABOVE) OR HELISKIING (BOTTOM)

Backcountry ski touring can be marvellous, but here you should be cautious. Banff holds the record for the highest number of avalanche accidents in Canada. The key is getting enough information to make wise decisions. Phone the park's daily avalanche bulletin. If you would prefer a tamer backcountry experience, you can head to one of the backcountry lodges (Skoki Lodge, Banff Sundance Lodge or Shadow Lake Lodge) and have a warm base for touring with great food.

Telemark skiing can be done at the three downhill areas in the park: Banff Mount Norquay, Sunshine Village and Lake Louise. You can also find steep slopes while on a ski touring trip in the backcountry. And helicopter skiing can take you up where you belong for a price. A helicopter will deposit you at the top of a remote mountain and pick you up at the bottom after a run down untouched powder. Companies offering heli-skiing include Canadian Mountain Holidays, with multi-day programs.

A toastier way to enjoy the Rockies is bundled up in a sled pulled through the forest by a team of huskies – Snowy Owl and Howling Dog, based in nearby Canmore, are two major operators. Or you can go snowshoeing just about anywhere in the park, with the usual avalanche awareness caveat. A good way to explore is to join a tour that includes lots of information about wolves, wolverines and other winter wildlife in the park.

SUMMER RECREATION

SUSAN MATE

MOUNTAIN BIKING

Mountain biking in the park can get you to that matchless scenery much faster than hiking, but is permitted only on these trails: Sundance, Healy Creek, Brewster Creek, Spray River, Goat Creek, Rundle Riverside, Johnson Lake Loop, Lake Minnewanka, Cascade, Redearth, Temple Access Road, Pipestone, Saskatchewan, Alexander. Most of these are fireroad and jeep track trails, with some single track, and mountain bikers share the trails with hikers and horses. Bikes can be rented from a number of shops in Banff and Lake Louise.

One favourite trail starts at the Cave and Basin National Historic Site along a paved pathway to Sundance Canyon. The Healy Creek Trail branches off from the paved trail and meanders through aspen, spruce and pine montane. If you want more, the Brewster Creek Trail (an old fireroad) branches off this trail just before it joins up with the Sunshine Road. There are some stellar views back toward the Bow Valley. If you're in good shape, have

SUNDANCE CANYON

RAVEN

MOUNTAIN BIKING

lots of time and good lung power, head toward Allenby Pass and connect to the Bryant Creek Trail and the Spray River Fire Road to get a 100-kilometre loop to and from the town of Banff. The Lake Minnewanka Trail takes you across a large wooden truss bridge to a narrow side trail that wanders up Stewart Canyon. The main trail swings left and then switchbacks uphill through a forested area before opening up and then goes to the lake. The lake attracts a lot of wildlife, in case you want to bring along a camera. Pick up a trail map from the Visitor Centre and don't forget to wear a helmet and make lots of noise to avoid startling a bear.

WATER SPORTS

CANOEING (BELOW) AND SCUBA DIVING (BOTTOM) IN LAKE MINNEWANKA

Water sports include rafting, canoeing and motor boating. Scenic trips along the Bow River last from one to three hours. A number of companies offer rafting. The canoeing is limited, but you can go paddling on Lake Minnewanka

or take a Voyageur canoe trip down the Bow River. Motor boating is restricted to Lake Minnewanka, where you can rent boats. You can also go for a boat cruise with Lake Minnewanka Tours. Don't even think about swimming in the park's glacier-fed waters. Instead, save your swimsuit for the world-famous hot springs.

GOLF

Golfers usually find that the Banff Springs Golf Course knocks their socks off with both design and scenery (some say it's the most beautiful mountain course in the world). The late Stanley Thompson, one of the world's foremost golf architects, designed the course's original 18 holes, which have benefitted from a $4-million restoration and the addition of nine holes (a course known as Tunnel

**BANFF SPRINGS
GOLF COURSE**

Nine). Walled in by three massive peaks, the course winds its way through a stunning river valley. The course offers wide driving areas, but also a preferred angle of attack for every hole. Greens range from large and undulating to small and flat. Many are raised and multi-tiered, and rookies usually find the course a tough test. High-season rates will run you $180 for a round of 18, though guests at the Banff Springs Hotel get a preferred rate.

HORSEBACK RIDING

Another way to explore the park is on horseback — available by the hour, the day and the week. Check out the Brewster Lake Louise Stables, next to the Chateau Lake Louise, which specializes in guided half-day trail rides around the lake and up to the Plain of Six Glaciers, or all day trips farther afield. Local trail rides from the Banff area start at the Banff Springs Corral or Martin's Stables on Birch Avenue. A good ride for children is the 10-mile route along the Bow River to Sundance Lodge on Brewster Creek for a two-day stay.

FISHING AND HELITOURING

Fishing for Rocky Mountain whitefish and seven species of trout is a favourite summer pastime. Local outfitters in Banff or Lake Louise can get you equipped or guide you. Their fees can include licenses, all fishing gear, tackle and bait and transportation to and from your hotel. Helicopter tours are available to take you into the backcountry for a walk in the wilderness, a picnic or even a week-long trip. Sightseeing from the air is a great way to take in the grandeur of the Rockies and snap some unbelievable photos. Alternatively, you can get into the backcountry painlessly on a Hummer tour in rugged luxury.

HORSEBACK RIDING

EXPLORING THE TOWN OF BANFF

SUSAN MATE

A CARRIAGE RIDE THROUGH TOWN

Some view the town of Banff as a mountain resort offering plenty of action, great places to eat, international shopping and a wonderful mountain flavour; others see it as an overcrowded hive characterized by shoulder-to-shoulder jostling along its main drag, Banff Avenue, and motor coaches disgorging camera-toting tourists. Parks Canada has worked hard to keep Banff from becoming a Niagara Falls of the mountains, introducing strict limits to growth and a residency requirement while focusing on preserving history. But growing numbers of visitors and pressure from the local business community sometimes win out. If you've come to Banff National Park for the mountains, the wildlife and a sense of renewal, get out of town quickly. If you enjoy the buzz of a fun, bustling base for your trip — in fact, the largest and busiest urban focus of any national park anywhere in the world — then read on.

Banff is home to 7,600 residents, about 30 per cent of whom are seasonal residents such as ski lift operators who live elsewhere in the off-season. Most residents depend on tourism for their livelihood. Along Banff's bustling main avenue, you will hear virtually every language from German and Swedish to French, Spanish and Mandarin Chinese, and you'll spot a great many signs in Japanese, unofficially Banff's third language. Elk walk the snow-covered back streets as casually as skiers and snowboarders. From a sleepy summer resort town that used to close its doors in the winter months, Banff has grown into a year-round attraction that plays host to more than

DAHLIA IN A GARDEN

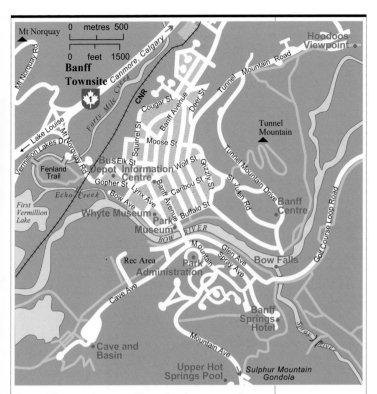

Banff Townsite map with scale: 0–500 metres / 0–1500 feet. Labels include Mt Norquay, Mt Norquay Rd, Lake Louise, Vermillion Lakes Dr, Fenland Trail, First Vermillion Lake, Echo Creek, Forty Mile Creek, Canmore, Calgary, CNR, Cougar St, Banff Avenue, Deer St, Moose St, Squirrel St, Bus Depot, Information Centre, Elk St, Gopher St, Lynx Ave, Wolf St, Grizzly St, Caribou St, Bow Ave, Buffalo St, Whyte Museum, Park Museum, BOW RIVER, Rec Area, Park Administration, Cave Ave, Mountain Ave, Glen Ave, Spray Ave, Bow Falls, Cave and Basin, Upper Hot Springs Pool, Sulphur Mountain Gondola, Tunnel Mountain Road, Tunnel Mountain Drive, Tunnel Mountain, St Julien Rd, Banff Centre, Golf Course Loop Road, Spray River, Banff Springs Hotel, Hoodoos Viewpoint.

three million people a year. Yet, only minutes away from the downtown action, visitors can still find a quiet place to walk and admire the scenery along the banks of the glacier-fed Bow River.

Most visitors travel to Banff by car. The townsite is 130 kilometres west of Calgary, a pleasant, 90-minute drive along the Trans-Canada Highway. The highway runs past Canmore and Banff to Lake Louise and continues west through the Rockies towards Vancouver.

CONVENTION CENTRE, BANFF SPRINGS HOTEL

THE FAIRMONT BANFF SPRINGS HOTEL

With its spectacular mountain setting and its majestic presence, the Fairmont Banff Springs Hotel is frequently called Canada's Castle in the Rockies. Those lucky enough to be guests at this grand hotel (with its kingly room rates) can easily imagine themselves to be visiting royalty. Quite apart from the views and the stylings — Scottish baronial with a hint of French chateau — the Banff Springs has history, class, luxury, comfort (in the form of a world-class spa) and even boasts a couple of ghosts.

This landmark of the Canadian Rockies is the product of one man's

FAIRMONT BANFF SPRINGS HOTEL

VAN HORNE STATUE

vision. William Cornelius Van Horne, the general manager of the Canadian Pacific Railway, recognized the tourist potential of the hot springs near the railway station of Banff and set out to build a hotel that would cater to every need of a traveller. "Since we can't export the scenery, we will have to import the tourists," was Van Horne's philosophy. He chose the confluence of the Bow and Spray Rivers for the project, and construction began in 1887.

The hotel's original four-storey wooden structure was built for a quarter of a million dollars and featured room rates of $3.50 per night. Many additions and renovations later, the Banff Springs Hotel was finished to its current dimensions in 1928. Since that time, all of the rooms have been remodelled; a $23-million, state-of-the-art Conference Centre was added in 1991, and a $12-million spa in 1995.

Today the Banff Springs Hotel can accommodate 1700 guests in 770 rooms. It offers tennis courts, conference facilities, a 27-hole championship golf course, a bowling centre, a games area, 15 shops and boutiques, a grocery store, 12 food and beverage areas, and Willows Stream, a world-class European-style spa that was renovated in late 2003 at a cost of $2.3 million. The spa is also available to those not staying at the hotel, and anyone seeking to be spoiled will find it well worth an hour or even a half-day, although you'll pay a premium — access is $49, although the fee is waived when treatments are booked (some restrictions apply). With cascading waterfalls, mineral whirlpools and indoor and outdoor saltwater pools, Willow Stream is a retreat within a retreat. There are many ways in which guests can choose to melt away stress with about 15 treatment rooms, private solariums, lounges with fireplaces, steam rooms and saunas. Treatments range from soothing to invigorating and include various types of body treatments, wraps, mineral/herb baths, facial treatments and massages. Prices start at about $50 and range to more than $400 for complete pampering.

About those ghosts . . . one is a loyal employee, a bellman named Sam who can't seem to retire. The other is a young bride who stumbled and fell to her death down a marble hotel staircase. Not to worry, though — both ghosts are harmless. Guests have told stories of being helped by a friendly and polite bellman who vanishes before you can tip him, and of seeing fleeting visions of a beautiful girl in a long flowing white dress dancing in the ballroom or gliding down that fateful staircase.

PARLOUR OF THE VICE-REGAL SUITE

If you are visiting in the fall or spring, investigate the hotel's off-season rates. Rooms range from standard to spacious suites. If high-season prices scare you off, be sure to drop by the hotel for a stroll, afternoon tea, or a cocktail in one of the elegant bars, or the world-famous Sunday brunch — an incredibly lavish feast that costs $38 ($35 seniors; $12.95 children; kids five and under are free). To get there, head east along the town's main street, Banff Avenue, until the road splits just beyond the bridge that crosses the Bow River. Hang a left and drive until you see the "castle." It's a pleasant stroll from downtown Banff if you don't mind walking uphill.

ROCKY MOUNTAIN GAME PLATTER, BUFFALO MOUNTAIN LODGE

PLACES TO EAT

Banff has more restaurants per capita than anywhere else in Canada. With more than 100

eateries to choose from, the variety is endless, and includes everything from fast food outlets to sophisticated ethnic cuisine. Many Banff chefs offer new regional fare christened Rocky Mountain cuisine, which tempts diners with ingredients originally from the wilderness. Once you have given your hotel's restaurant a whirl, venture out to choose your lunch or dinner spot by browsing posted menus and smelling the cooking aromas wafting out into the street.

If you are looking for a great steak, visit Melissa's — probably Banff's most popular daytime destination. It features hearty all-day breakfasts, steaks and burgers, and features a summer patio — a great place to kick back and relax. (Melissa's is also known for organizing a 10-kilometre and half-marathon race that draws huge crowds to Banff every fall.) Bumpers is another local favourite with its open-beam construction, loft lounge and salad bar. Alberta beef is the choice here, with everything on offer from steaks and ribs to burgers. Barbary Coast is a local hangout, and why not when you can walk in and find your picture on the wall? It offers a California-style menu, live blues most nights and pool tables to keep you busy. Beef steals the show also at the upscale steakhouse called Saltlik, while the Keg offers a more casual experience that is popular with families.

Cilantro Mountain Café at the Buffalo Mountain Lodge

offers excellent Rocky Mountain cuisine, including local meats, herbs and berries, and also has a nice outside terrace in summer. The restaurant is housed in a quaint cabin and you can watch the chefs prepare innovative light fare. If you are looking for Greek, the Balkan Village is known for its generous portions and belly dancing on Tuesdays. El Toro offers authentic Mediterranean dishes in a casual atmosphere. Caramba! has a warm, inviting atmosphere featuring an open kitchen with a forno pizza oven, rotisserie and flaming grill. This restaurant is Mediterranean-inspired but also features fresh British Columbia seafood and Alberta beef.

Feeling nostalgic? Try Joe Btfsplk's Diner where you can head back into the

1950s. Speedy, friendly service coupled with big portions and low prices give you that old-fashioned diner experience. Try the "blue plate special," which is always good. Despite being part of a chain, Earl's is a perennial Alberta favourite for consistently well-prepared, reasonably priced pastas, pizzas and appetizers.

For a fancy night out, Le Beaujolais offers award-winning French cuisine, a sophisticated menu and elegant décor. Five-star service and excellent cuisine

BOW VALLEY GRILL

make this restaurant worthy of its many accolades. If you want views with your champagne, The Primrose at the Rimrock Resort Hotel features Canadian and international dining with an unbeatable mountain vista; the hotel's Eden restaurant (formerly Classico) has won several awards for its upscale dining and extensive wine list. There are a number of possibilities at the Banff Springs for elegant dining, as well, including the very traditional Banffshire Club and Waldhaus. You could also try the Buffalo Mountain Lodge with its open-beam construction and tasteful décor. Here you get innovative, tantalizing choices with great presentation and a comfy atmosphere where single travellers can feel right at home.

For Italian food, you have options: Tony Roma's, Aurora Restaurant (a restaurant and expansive nightclub that appeals to the over-30 set), Giorgio's Trattoria (eat here before 6 or after 9 p.m. to avoid the inevitable line-up), or Guido's, which has been a Banff fixture for more than 20 years.

Coyotes is my lunch recommendation. The award-winning menu offers southwestern cuisine with a dash of Asia and the Pacific-Northwest. Try the "perfect lunch" which is a half sandwich and

ROSE AND CROWN PUB

homemade soup or salad. Barpa Bill's dishes out great fast-food Greek fare including killer souvlaki sandwiches for travellers on a budget.

Good pub food can be found at the Rose and Crown, where you can enjoy traditional English fare in the dining room, pub or patio. It's known for its fish and chips and

WILD BILL'S

THE PRIMROSE

shepherd's pie, and offers live entertainment most nights. If you're just looking for a pint, St. James Gate Irish Pub is the place to go. Tommy's Neighborhood Pub is a fun spot to hang with the locals and get some good eats while you're at it. Wild Bill's is known as the grill capital of Banff.

Chicken and rib combos are the order of the day and you won't push away from the table hungry.

Ticino Swiss-Italian Restaurant has been offering fine European cuisine in Banff for 25 years. The fare is gold-medal-winning superb and the selection impressive. The long-serving Grizzly House does great fondues including oil, hot-rock, cheese and chocolate, along with tempting desserts.

The Japanese influence on Banff makes for great Asian dining — Sushi House Banff is loved by locals, as are the combo plates at Miki and the sushi at upscale Suginoya. Typhoon, meanwhile, serves intensely flavoured cuisine from Thailand, India and other parts of Asia, along with exotics beer and martinis. Cafe Soleil and Caramba! are loved by locals and visitors alike for their unique Mediterranean dishes

Locals regard the Baker Creek Bistro at the Baker Creek Chalets on the pretty Bow Valley Parkway as the park's best bistro. Charming is the word to describe the décor. The bistro provides just the right touches to make for a special evening. It's a great place for casual lunches on the patio on a sunny day, as well.

Just looking for java and goodies? Best bets include Evelyn's Coffee Bar, the Cake Company, Jump Start, The Rundle Lounge at the Banff Springs Hotel, the Upper Hot Springs Café or the Kiln, which is a European-style café, cappuccino bar and gift shop on the Banff Centre campus.

NIGHTLIFE

Most of Banff's larger hotels and restaurants offer nightly entertainment. If you want to go where the real action is, head along the main drag: Banff Avenue. Go early, though, as demand exceeds supply, resulting in frequent line-ups. Most popular with the locals is Wild Bill's Legendary Saloon, where you can try line dancing or just sit back and watch the

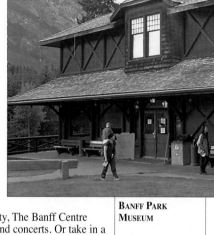

action. This country-themed bar hosts live bands Wednesday to Sunday. The Barbary Coast also features live music. Bumper's Lounge is a good spot for a before or after dinner drink. The Rose and Crown Pub brings in live entertainers all week to go with an English-style pub meal. Newer hotspots for young club-goers include the Hard Rock Café, Hoodoo Lounge and Nightclub and Outabounds dance club. King Eddy Billiards in the King Edward Hotel is the hippest place to shoot pool, and if you're looking for a pint, the St. James Gate Irish Pub is the place to go for an excellent array of fine whisky and beer.

BANFF PARK MUSEUM

For an alcohol-free evening activity, The Banff Centre often features live performances and concerts. Or take in a movie at the Luxe Cinema, do some bowling at the Banff Springs Hotel Conference Centre, go for coffee and dessert and head to your hotel's hot tub for a well-deserved soak.

SHOPPING

There are no secrets to shopping in Banff. Just stroll along Banff Avenue and you'll find everything you need and plenty you don't. As in any mountain mecca, you'll find a wide variety of excellent outdoor gear and sporting goods stores. T-shirt and souvenir shops are also easy to find. Boutiques devoted to Paris and New York designers, upscale jewellery stores and high-end galleries are fun for window-shopping, browsing or even buying if your budget permits. Children might enjoy a stop at the candy, fudge and chocolate shops along the way — Welch's is a personal favourite, an old-fashioned candy store with a vast array of bonbons, chocolates and homemade confections. If you shop at the Cascade Plaza you'll get an unexpected bonus: it's home to the Canadian Ski Museum West, and the story of skiing in the Canadian

UPPER HOT SPRINGS

Rockies unfolds through displays, artifacts and historic and modern video.

THINGS TO DO

Visitors can soak in some history at the Upper Hot Springs Pool and Spa on Mountain Avenue, a visitor attraction since the turn of the century. Once considered therapeutic, the waters are now appreciated for their relaxing effect. The temperature is about 40°C (104°F). The springs are a great place to enjoy the view after a day on the slopes or on the hiking trails. For something even more relaxing, try out the onsite spa where you can sit in the steam room or indulge in aromatherapy.

WEATHER STATION ATOP SULPHUR MOUNTAIN

Your hot-springs history lesson can continue at the Cave and Basin National Historic Site, which commemorates the birthplace of Canada's National Park system, begun here in 1885. It celebrates the growth and development of Canada's national parks with interactive displays and exhibits. You can watch the "Steam, Schemes and National Dreams" video in the Bathhouse Theatre. Naturally occurring warm mineral springs can be found inside the cave, which you can walk through, and also outside, in an emerald-coloured basin. Located at the west end of Cave Avenue, the site offers educational and interpretive programs and trails in the area where visitors can see warm water fish, garter snakes, warm mineral pools and unique plants — even in winter. It's a good spot to bird watch, ride your bike or hike to Sundance Canyon.

WHYTE MUSEUM

The Banff Park Museum is Western Canada's oldest

natural history museum. Housing more than 5,000 wildlife specimens dating back to the 1860s, it shows how animals were studied in the Victorian Era. Relax in the reading room or watch wildlife videos in the hands-on discovery room. It takes about 45 minutes to tour this small museum noted for its early park architecture as well as its specimen collection and story of the museum's first curator, Norman Sanson. You can join a regularly scheduled tour in the summer to get the most from your visit. Admission is cheap and the museum is open from 10 a.m. to 6 p.m. from mid-May to August and from 1 p.m. to 5 p.m. from September to May. The

museum is a town landmark and is easily found on Banff Avenue, next to the Bow River Bridge. Admission is $4 for adults, $3.50 seniors, $3 for youth and $10 for families.

Visiting Banff's third National Historic Site, the Cosmic Ray Station, requires a trip up Sulphur Mountain. You can take the Sulphur Mountain Gondola (mentioned below) or, in summer, hike a rugged, well-maintained trail 5.3 kilometres as it climbs from the Upper Hot Springs parking lot. Also on the Mountain is a weather observatory that allows visitors a glimpse into the life of Norman Sanson, who was the town's meteorologist.

The Whyte Museum of the Canadian Rockies offers art and cultural heritage exhibitions. The eclectic museum is home to three art galleries, a cultural history collection and a renowned research archives, as well as a museum shop. Contemporary and historic art exhibitions change monthly, with works by local, regional and national artists. Ongoing exhibits include "High Country Heritage," where you can enjoy walking back through time to explore the development of Banff and the colourful characters for which the town is famous. This exhibition traces the evolution of Banff National Park into one of the world's most popular tourist destinations. "Artists of the Rockies" lets you experience the history of the region through the work of a diverse collection of artists. The exhibition illustrates the transition from the European style used by early artists to the more modern approach embraced by Canadian landscape artists.

SULPHUR MOUNTAIN

The museum's mandate is to help in educational, cultural and aesthetic pursuits connected with the Canadian Rockies and to examine the relationship between culture and mountains. Open daily from 10 a.m. to 5 p.m. (closed Christmas and New Year's Day), the museum is well worth a visit. The entrance fee is just $6 ($3.50 seniors and students and $15 for families). For an even better deal, buy a Banff Heritage Passport for admission to the Whyte Museum, Banff Park Museum and the Cave and Basin.

The heritage of the natives of the Northern Plains and Canadian Rockies is explored at the Buffalo Nations Luxton

Museum on Birch Avenue. Here you can relive the period when people followed great buffalo herds, hauling their tepees and equipment by travois. The museum takes you to a time when preparing food and shelter meant pounding berries and meat for pemmican and scraping hides for tepees. Learn about the time when Europeans discovered a native culture rich in elaborate ceremonies, dances, songs and legends associated with nature and the spirit world. Displays include costumes, hunting equipment and dioramas of native and pioneer life, and highlight hunter/warrior, daily life, spiritual life and history. The building that houses the museum is an old fort-like structure overlooking the Bow River.

A WATERLILY (TOP); A CARRIAGE RIDE (ABOVE)

Canada Place and Cascadia Gardens at the Banff National Park Administration Building (at the end of Banff Avenue, just across the Bow River Bridge) is open from 10 a.m. to 6 p.m. daily in the summer, with reduced hours during low season. Visitors can discover interactive displays exploring Canada's natural and historical heritage, as well as the events and people who shaped them. Admission is free.

You can take a self-guided historical walking tour of Banff, which introduces visitors to Banff's history as a mountain resort, as well as its many heritage buildings and homes. There are more than 40 historic buildings and sites to visit, including the Park superintendent's residence, the Cascade Dance Hall and the Canadian Pacific Railway Station. Heritage plaques have been located throughout the tour. Pick up a tour guide at the Whyte Museum.

The cultural heart of Banff and the Canadian Rockies is the Banff Centre, which presents year-round performances and exhibitions, concerts and events in the visual, literary and performing arts. The Banff Centre for the Arts has

KAYAKING ON THE BOW RIVER

been a major training centre for musicians, artists and writers for more than 60 years.

The Sulphur Mountain Gondola offers an unparalleled 360-degree view of some of the world's most spectacular and fascinating geological formations. Enjoy an eight-minute ride in a glass-enclosed gondola to the top of Sulphur Mountain. The gondola varies its hours of operation throughout the year, and is closed from the end of November to Christmas.

If you are looking to get active, ice skating (and skate rental) is available at the Banff Recreation Centre. The Bow River is the place to be for a glide when the ice permits. You can also rent skates at Performance Ski and Sports and Abominable Ski & Sportswear. Or how about going for a climb? Mountain Magic Equipment has a 30-foot in-store climbing wall and a 15-foot boulder wall. Beginners can rent equipment and take a class. It's possible to participate in any number of active tours leaving from Banff that will take you into the backcountry in a Hummer, cross-country skiing, on a canyon ice walk, snowshoeing, snowmobiling, ice fishing, downhill skiing, mountaineering, helicopter sightseeing or skiing, river rafting, off-road touring or dog-sledding, to mention a few. Most trips require little advance booking — a day in advance is usually enough. You can also take a tour around Banff in a horse-drawn carriage that leaves from The Trail Rider Store on Banff Avenue.

CANOES ALONG THE BOW (TOP); A MALLARD DUCK (ABOVE)

BOW FALLS

HIKING

Many visitors prefer to walk or hike around town, snapping photos, watching wildlife or enjoying picnics. Sundance is a pleasant scenic trail that starts behind the Cave and Basin Centennial Centre. Formerly a road, its asphalt surface makes for comfortable walking or cycling. The trail runs for 3.7 kilometres beside the Bow River, past swamps made by beavers and wetlands that are home to variety of birds and animals. It ends at a picnic shelter at Sundance Canyon. A short interpretive trail leads up the canyon and then loops back through the forest to its starting point.

The Marsh Loop is the place to spot beaver dams and lodges and see a variety of birds from this wide trail around the marshes below the Cave and Basin. This loop trail turns off the Sundance trail where it first meets the Bow River and then runs downstream between the river and the marshes.

A 4.8-kilometre trail, the Bow River and Hoodoos will take you away from the town's hustle and bustle. From the Bow Falls overlook on Tunnel Mountain Drive, this trail takes you under sheer cliffs on Tunnel Mountain (watch for climbers), through meadows and forests beside the Bow River and up a hillside to Tunnel Mountain Road. From there a trail beside the road leads on to the Hoodoos, weird and wonderful rock formations.

Near the end of the road to Lake Minnewanka, the Johnson Lake trail takes you past natural marvels, historic sites and great places to watch small wildlife and birds. Starting at the parking lot picnic area, the trail encircles Johnson Lake in 3.5 kilometres, never far from its shores. The Anthracite trail starts at the footbridge over the lake outlet and takes you for a look at the site of coalmines and later the Sun Chinese greenhouses. After crossing a footbridge, you will travel underneath towering hoodoos before doubling back on the cliffs above them, with panoramic mountain views, to finish where it started. This trail is 4.4 kilometres.

MOUNT NORQUAY

The 3.9-kilometre C-level Cirque trail starts in the Upper Bankhead parking lot off the Lake Minnewanka Road and takes you to the concrete walls, fenced-off vent shafts and a tailing pile that are all that remains of the coal mine at level "C." At the top, a jumble of rock at the base of a dished-in slope, the cirque, is what is left of a glacier.

You can walk to the Upper Hot Springs on a trail that is shorter than the road and avoids a lot of traffic. The trail starts on a horse path located between the Banff Springs Hotel parkade and the Spray trailhead kiosk. There are straightforward and scenic ways of getting to this point, two kilometres from downtown Banff, depending on whether you decide to walk up Spray Avenue or make your way by a series of trails along the Bow River, past Bow Falls and around the top of the golf course driving range. Once there, turn onto the horse trail and turn left and you are only 1.8 kilometres from the Hot Springs.

If you are looking for a bit of a workout and some stellar views, try the Tunnel Mountain trail. From the hiking sign on St. Julien Road, this trail climbs steadily, crosses Tunnel Mountain Drive, with a switchback to the summit in 2.3 kilometres. You have unobstructed views of the entire town, golf course, Vermilion Lakes and the surrounding peaks including Mount

CASCADE PONDS

81

Rundle. Keep an eye out for deer.

The trail to the summit of Stoney Squaw, Tunnel Mountain's twin, starts near the entrance to the main Norquay ski area parking lot. It is a narrow, 2.3-kilometre trail through thick forest, but the view from the top is worth every step: you can see Cascade Mountain, Lake Minnewanka, the buffalo paddock and the Bow Valley. Bring your binoculars.

PICNICS

Cascade Ponds is a great place to picnic. To get there, turn off the Lake Minnewanka Road onto the first gravel road north of the Trans-Canada overpass. Picnic tables, fireboxes and shelters are located here and a short trail encircles the pond. A 2.5-kilometre trail runs north to join the Bankhead Interpretive Trail.

A self-guiding interpretive trail can teach you about the park's colourful human and natural history. The Fenland trail takes you through an area that is slowly changing from marsh to forest, where beaver, muskrat and other animals are often seen. A flat trail, Fenland makes for a pleasant stroll and is a good one to take children on. From the west side of Mount Norquay Drive you can get onto the trail at two points: one just beside the railway tracks and the other at the bridge in the picnic area. The trail is popular with runners, cyclists and as a route between town and the Vermilion Lakes.

CRUISING

Visitors can also take a cruise on Lake Minnewanka, 24 kilometres northeast of the town of Banff, off the Trans-Canada Highway. The cruise aboard glass-enclosed boats travels through the Minnewanka Valley Devil's Gap. The largest lake in the park, Minnewanka, is the only one where powerboats are permitted. Sixteen-foot boats with outboards can be rented from mid-May to Labour Day.

DEVIL'S PASSAGE, LAKE MINNEWANKA

CYCLING

Cycling is another great way to get around, although you should be prepared for some uphill climbs. Bicycles are allowed on public roads and highways and on a few trails. If you are looking for a longer jaunt, head to the Banff Springs Hotel and take a relatively easy mountain bike trail up an old fire road to a trailhead a few kilometres above Canmore. You can return the same way or ride down to the Canmore Nordic Centre and into town. Bike rentals are available at a number of Banff shops.

LAKE LOUISE

MONTE STEWART

Nestled in the Rocky Mountains, Lake Louise encompasses a much-photographed mountain lake, a village of 1,600 and a world-class ski hill. To get to Louise, as locals calls it, fly to Calgary, rent a car at the airport and drive west along Highway 1. Since Lake Louise is in Banff National Park, you'll need to stop at the park gate (you can't miss it) to pick up a park pass.

CHATEAU LAKE LOUISE

Originally, Native peoples called Lake Louise the "Lake of Little Fishes." In 1882, Tom Wilson, the first white man to explore the area, named it Emerald Lake because of its aquamarine waters. But a year later the Geographical Society of Canada changed it to Lake Louise to honour the wife of the Marquis of Lorne, the governor General of Canada. (The Emerald Lake name did survive, though, when Wilson gave it to another scenic gem in the Rockies, near today's Field, British Columbia.) In modern times, Lake Louise has attracted princesses, kings and queens, as well as movie stars and jet setters, often participating in charity ski events. But the greatest attraction of Lake Louise is that you don't have to be

royal, rich or famous to enjoy its scenery and natural treasures.

Start with the lake itself, one of the most beautiful in the Rockies. You can rent a canoe here, but don't even think about swimming unless you like suffering from hypothermia. Thanks to glacial silt, the water remains ice-cold and life threatening all year round. (If you are bent on swimming, travel to Herbert Lake, a 10-minute drive up Highway 93 North. It's not fed by a glacier and even has a diving board.)

FAIRMONT CHATEAU LAKE LOUISE (TOP), AND THE CHANDELIER IN ITS GRAND LOBBY (RIGHT)

CHATEAU LAKE LOUISE

Overlooking the lake is the Fairmont Chateau Lake Louise, a 487-room palace that includes a shopping mall and nightclub. Room packages range up to $2,547 for five nights with a view of the lake. Chateau Lake Louise is more than 100 years old. In 1888, John Enselwood, a Canadian Pacific Railway employee, built a lean-to shack here as a shelter for fishermen. A year later, entrepreneur Willoughby Astley of Banff recruited CPR carpenters to build a chalet with two bedrooms, an attic and a veranda. In 1891, a fire destroyed that chalet and, two years later, Astley built a Swiss-style rustic chalet on the current site. In 1913, a new wing was added, but yet another fire struck in 1925, destroying everything but the new wing, which remains part of today's structure.

HIKING AND TRAILS

From the front of the Chateau, you can take one the most popular hikes in the Rockies: just follow the three-kilometre Lakeshore Trail, a wide, level and well-groomed path along one side of the lake. During the day, the trees, leaves and mountains combine to produce a kaleidoscope of colours. At night, the moonlight guides you on a leisurely stroll. Don't be surprised if you see mountain goats grazing on the slopes of Fairview Mountain. The trail passes under the cliffs, where rock-climbers gather, at the end of the lake. You can turn back here or continue on to the Plain of Six Glaciers. You can also wander along several other pedestrian loops that start and finish near the chateau.

The Bow River Loop interpretive trail has informative signs about the animals that make the river waters their home. This walk is particularly appealing in the early morning or early evening, when sunlight glistens on the water. If you take the Louise Creek trail, you'll discover a mountain stream. To start along this 2.7-kilometre path, walk across the Bow River highway bridge on Lake Louise Drive. The trail begins on the downstream side of the bridge and follows Louise Creek up a hill. Near the halfway mark, you can veer off to the Tramline or, by crossing the bridge, stay on the Louise Creek Trail until you come to a parking lot that crosses the lake. This route was often used by CPR surveyor Tom Wilson and a Stoney guide he named "Gold Seeker."

If you decide to take the Tramline turnoff, you'll follow the route of a narrow-gauge railway that operated here between 1913 and 1930. Starting behind the train station, on a footbridge that crosses the Bow River, the Tramline also goes uphill, on a 4 per cent gradient, and ends at the Louise Creek Trail parking lot. This route appears easy to navigate, but be sure to cross the bridge where the Louise and Tramline trails intersect. If you want, you can combine these two short loops into a 7.2-kilometre trek.

The Fairview Lookout Trail starts from the viewpoint at Lake Louise and climbs through a spruce forest to a lookout 100 metres above the lake. Just 0.3 kilometres from the start, the trail branches right off the Saddle Back Trail and wends uphill for another 0.7 kilometres to a wooden observation platform. Here, you can gaze across the lake back towards the hotel, with Fairview Mountain providing a picturesque background. You can return the way you came or take a somewhat rough

SUMMIT OF FAIRVIEW MOUNTAIN

CANOEING ON LAKE LOUISE

MORAINE LAKE, VALLEY OF TEN PEAKS

and steep 1.3-kilometre trail through some wet spots to the Lake Louise boathouse.

A short drive will take you to Moraine Lake, which rivals Lake Louise in beauty. Moraine Lake is the site of the first aquatic restoration project within Banff National Park. Biologists here are trying to re-introduce the endangered bull trout to these waters. From here, you can walk along the Moraine Lakeshore Trail, which offers views of the magnificent Ten Peaks, or go to the Consolation Lakes, where you can enjoy views of both Mount Temple and the Ten Peaks.

If you prefer to go on day hikes instead of short walks, you have a wide range of trail options, starting from Lake Louise or from a few kilometres away. The Plain of Six Glaciers Trail, widely regarded as one of the best moderate hikes in the Rockies, is actually the long version of the Lakeshore Trail, which takes you to the far end of Lake Louise. If you continue up the valley, you'll see a rocky creek, moraines (the remains of receding glaciers), gravel fields and, last but not least, Victoria Glacier. You might also spot mountain goats. Farther along this route, you can join up with the Highline Trail, visit a teahouse that serves refreshments and lunch during summer, and explore Abbot Pass and the Death Trap, an ice-laden gorge between Mount Victoria and Mount Lefroy.

Other, more strenuous, day hike trails within walking distance of Chateau Lake Louise are the Beehive paths near Lake Agnes and the steep Saddleback Trail over the slopes of Mount Fairview and down into picturesque Paradise Valley. Near Moraine Lake, Larch Valley, Eiffel Lake and Boulder Pass also offer majestic views. For directions and detailed maps, check the information centres. In July and August, Banff National Park staff provide free guided strolls along the lakeshore and hikes to the Plain of Six Glaciers.

After checking out the trails, you might want to visit the top of the Lake Louise ski hill, otherwise known as

Mount Whitehorn. From May to September, you can get there via an enclosed or open-air gondola. On the way up, you'll see wildflowers, streams and probably some mountain goats or bighorn sheep. Once you're at the top, 2,057 metres above sea level, you can enjoy a panoramic view of Lake Louise and its majestic mountain backdrop, including Victoria Glacier and the peaks of the Continental Divide.

SKIING

In winter, hotels in Lake Louise provide a free shuttle to the ski hill, while you can also catch a bus at most major Banff hotels. In Calgary, Laidlaw Transit runs a bus to the Louise ski hill provided that at least four people book. That's not usually a problem, because the hill attracts skiers and snowboarders from around the world.

HIKERS ON FAIRVIEW MOUNTAIN

Veteran skiers say the ski hill, with runs spread over four mountain faces, compares favorably with the Alps. Look down from the top and you'll feel like you've been cut and pasted into a picture postcard. This magnificent scenery — picture Zermatt, Switzerland, without the Matterhorn — is not the only attraction for skiers. Runs like Paradise, Top of the World and Olympic live up to their names. The ski hill's operators contend that, with more than 17 kilometres of runs connected by a lift and trail system, Louise has more skiable terrain than any other single resort in Canada, although there is one area that is off limits due to avalanche risk. The resort boasts 50 runs that range from novice (25 per cent) to intermediate (45 per cent) to expert (30 per cent). They include moguls, glades, open bowls, groomed slopes, plenty of powder and no shortage of interesting twists and turns. The expert routes are challenging enough that both the men's and women's World Cup circuits hold annual downhill races here each November and December.

The longest run is eight kilometres. The average annual snowfall is 256 centimetres at mid-mountain and 508 centimetres in the back bowls. Facilities include five quad chairs, two triples, one double, one

BACKCOUNTRY SKIERS

expert platter, and a beginner T-bar. Ski Louise operates ski schools for beginners to experts and offers a day care service. For those who tire early, or require liquid refreshment, three-day lodges are scattered around the hill. When heading out to Louise, remember to bring your sunscreen because you'll probably need it to cope with the incredibly bright days.

There are several other major ski hills nearby, including Sunshine, Mount Norquay and Panorama, so some visitors turn their winter holiday into a Rocky Mountain ski tour. If you're into cross-country, you can also check out Moraine Lake or the trails in Peter Lougheed Provincial Park or the Canmore Nordic Centre. There is plenty of powder in the backcountry, but avalanches happen every year, so skiers should explore with at least one other person and bring a locator device.

If you're looking for a place to stay in Lake Louise, the Chateau is the best hotel — but also the most expensive. Visitors can also find excellent accommodation at the nearby Post Hotel, in a seniors' hostel (for those over 55) and in Banff and Canmore. If you choose to rough it, Lake Louise Campground, located about two kilometres from

LAKE LOUISE SKI RESORT

the village, has 220 tenting sites and 189 trailer sites. One word of caution: the lovers who linger here are not always human, as Lake Louise is one of three known grizzly-bear mating areas. At any given time, as many as a dozen grizzlies inhabit the area. Watchful wardens have been known to close the tenting sites when risk is considered high, but you'll be okay sleeping in an RV. The trick to exploring is to do it with a group. The natural noise keeps bears away. Most attacks have occurred when quiet hikers have surprised mother bears watching their cubs.

The Louise campground provides flush toilets, firewood and interpretive programs. You'll also find high-quality camping facilities at Tunnel Mountain, Two Jack Main Campground, Two Jack Lakeside Campground, Johnston's Canyon Campground, Castle Mountain Group Campground, Protection Mountain Campground, Mosquito Lake Campground, Waterfowl Lake Campground and Rampart Creek. Most, if not all, have flush toilets but no

showers. Lake Louise and Tunnel Mountain are the only campgrounds in the park that are open year round. The others are open from May or June to September.

Besides hiking, other recreational options include fishing, whitewater rafting, horseback riding and, of course, mountain climbing. If you visit in November, the Lake Louise Visitor Centre hosts a free speaker series that runs Wednesday nights starting at 8 p.m. Local historians give presentations on the nature and history of Lake Louise and Banff National Park. The mountain scenery is also conducive to painting, drawing and photography.

If you want to kick up your heels after a hard day's hike or other activities, there are at least a dozen watering holes and dance floors to choose from in or near Louise. Brewster Cowboy's BBQ and Dance Barn hosts a shindig with live western music every Saturday night, and sleigh rides are conducted from Chateau Lake Louise between mid-December and mid-April. The Chateau's Glacier Saloon offers entertainment and dancing, and you can get fondue at Walliser Stube or just enjoy the view from the Lobby Bar. You can listen to piano music in the Post Hotel. Most pubs feature rustic fireplaces, giving you a chance to warm up after a cold day on the ski slopes.

GLACIER SALOON (ABOVE)

KOOTENAY, YOHO AND MORE

MONTE STEWART

KICKING HORSE PASS

Kicking Horse Pass earned its unique name in 1858 when the explorer who discovered it, James Hector, was kicked by his horse and knocked unconscious. His native companions took him for dead, and his miraculous recovery was commemorated in a pass and a river. Today's explorers will be knocked out by Kicking Horse's rapturous river, magnificent mountains and natural and man-made wonders. Located high in the Rockies, on the Trans-Canada Highway between Lake Louise, Alberta, and Field, B.C., Kicking Horse Pass — a national historic site — spans the Alberta-British Columbia border, the Banff-Yoho National Parks boundary and the edge of the Great Divide. At 1,627 metres, (5,338 feet), the pass is the highest point on the Canadian Pacific Railway and a wonderful stop en route from Calgary to the Kootenays, the Okanagan Valley or the interior of B.C.

KICKING HORSE RIVER

BIGHORN SHEEP

Don't be surprised if you encounter mountain goats and other wildlife, or an old lamp or other remnants left over from the many train crashes that were common in the late 1800s and early 1900s as engineers struggled to navigate the steep terrain. If you don't have much time, just stop and stretch your legs at the Spiral Tunnels

viewpoint. Built in 1911, the tunnels enable trains to wind through Mount Ogden and Cathedral Crags rather than make a dangerous climb or descent on what's known as the Big Hill. (With long trains, you can watch the front engine come out of a tunnel while the caboose enters it.) If time is no problem, bring your binoculars and check out the glorious vistas. From here, you might also visit Takakkaw Falls, Emerald Lake and the Natural Bridge,

SPIRAL TUNNEL LOOKOUT

which are well marked. (For further directions and maps, stop at the Visitors Centre at Field, B.C.) Depending on when you travel, you can enjoy camping, hiking, cycling, mountain climbing, cross-country skiing, ice climbing and canoeing in this vicinity. Make sure you dress in layers, because as James Hector also discovered, the weather here changes as suddenly as a horse's mood.

KOOTENAY NATIONAL PARK

If you don't care to rough it in the Rockies, Kootenay National Park is for you. Thanks to its close proximity to Radium Hot Springs and other southeastern B.C. locales such as Invermere, Windermere, Fairmont Hot Springs,

EMERALD LAKE

Cranbrook and Kimberley, Kootenay is the rare Rocky-Mountain park that lets you go hiking in backcountry and still get a good night's sleep in a relatively cheap hotel. To reach the park from Calgary, head west on Highway 1, turn off at Castle Junction (located between Banff and Lake Louise) and head south down the Kootenay Parkway, also known as Highway 93, towards Radium. Alternatively, if you're looking for a more leisurely drive, you can travel south from Calgary on either Highway 2 or 22, go west on Highway 3 and then follow the signs. This route takes considerably more time. If you're coming from the west, when you get to Golden, take the Highway 95 turnoff. From the south, take Highway 93/95.

RADIUM AREA AND HOT SPRINGS

As you approach the village of Radium (most locals and regular visitors drop "Hot Springs" from the name) you might not realize that you're in Kootenay National Park until you reach the gate where you buy your park pass. Fees vary according to your group size and age, but it's cheaper to visit Kootenay for a day than to sit in a movie theatre for a couple of hours. To avoid delays, you can also pick up a pass at various businesses in Radium, located on Kootenay's eastern edge.

The hot springs, discovered by James Sinclair in 1841, draw large crowds, especially in summer. At the Radium Hot Springs Pools, built in the 1920s and since redeveloped, you can soak in soothing, odourless mineral water that reaches a maximum temperature of 45.5 degrees Celsius. On any given day, regardless of the time of year, you might find yourself chatting with other bathers from Japan, Europe, the United States, eastern Canada or elsewhere. While relaxing in the pools, you can often spot Rocky Mountain bighorn sheep and mountain goats grazing on the nearby mountainside.

MARBLE CANYON

If you do decide to rough it, at least for a while, campsites (open to RVs and tenters alike) abound inside or near the edge of the park, a short drive in any direction from Radium. The friendly Parks Canada staff at the Hot Springs Pools can give you maps and directions. Don't forget that grizzly bears and black bears, cougars and wolves also inhabit the area, so make sure that all garbage is stored safely in the sealed green containers provided at all sites. Most campgrounds have modern amenities like showers, flush toilets, electrical power, hot and cold water, and pay telephones that spare you the agony of bad cell phone reception.

Redstreak Campground, located on a plateau 2.5 kilometres above Radium, and usually open from May to September, is connected by trail to the village's restaurants. It fills up first. McLeod Meadows Campground, located 27 kilometres north of Radium along the Kootenay River, is

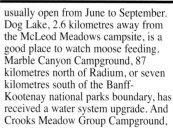

McLeod Meadows Campground

usually open from June to September. Dog Lake, 2.6 kilometres away from the McLeod Meadows campsite, is a good place to watch moose feeding. Marble Canyon Campground, 87 kilometres north of Radium, or seven kilometres south of the Banff-Kootenay national parks boundary, has received a water system upgrade. And Crooks Meadow Group Campground, open from early spring until snowfall, is located 34 kilometres north of Radium on one of the oldest homesteads in Kootenay. Reservations are required. Numerous other campgrounds, like Spur Valley, are located just outside the park, easily accessible from Highways 93 and 95.

Kootenay's numerous hiking trails range from easy to difficult and can accommodate those hiking for a few hours or several days. Try not to miss Marble Creek Trail, a narrow gorge carved by Tokumm Creek, or the Paint Pots, colourful natural mineral pools. Rock Wall Trail, from Loe Lake to Helmet Falls, will take a few days to complete. As you explore the area, you'll encounter majestic mountain peaks, wide-open valleys, frigid glacial waters, tight canyons, lush green alpine meadows and dry grasslands. Inside the park, other recreational opportunities range from whitewater canoeing and rafting to mountain biking and mountaineering. Fishing is also permitted, but a licence is required.

Beyond the gates, you can take your pick of several outstanding golf courses, including the Springs at Radium and Riverside at Fairmont Hot Springs. (Club and cart rentals are offered at virtually all courses.) Wherever you play, you won't be disappointed. However, because these are resort courses, you should expect a five-hour round with plenty of scenery. If you don't have much time, or just want to work on your short game, Spur Valley Greens is a

Paint Pots

nifty nine-hole executive course located on a mountainside. More outstanding golf beckons in Windermere, Invermere, Fernie, Cranbrook and Golden. But the B.C. Rockies golf season is notoriously short, so it's best to hit the links in late April, May, June, July or August.

In winter months there's excellent downhill skiing, featuring plenty of powder snow conditions at Panorama, Fairmont, Kimberley and Fernie, not to mention nearby Alberta ski hills. Excellent hotels and restaurants, ranging from Chinese to classic European, can be found right in Radium.

Three of the most recommended restaurants in Radium are the Old Salzburg, which serves German food, Back Country Jack's (beer and burgers) and the Alta Liebe, which dishes out international fare, including Japanese. You can also find several diverse eateries in nearby Invermere, and Windermere, or further south, in Kimberley, Fernie and vicinity.

North of Radium, the Kootenay Lodge, located at Vermilion Crossing, about 40 kilometres south of Highway 1, is another good place to stay — or stop. The lodge's rustic cabins are open between mid-May and late September. The facility also has a dining room which offers reasonably priced "mountain home style" meals (open until late September) and a visitors' centre (open until mid-October).

YOHO NATIONAL PARK

Yoho National Park takes its name from the Cree word "yoho," which means awe or wonder. Founded in 1886, Yoho is one of the oldest parks in the Canadian park system. Thanks to its mountainous landscape, which contains fossils and other prehistoric rock forms, and its diverse wildlife, which ranges from grizzly bears to mountain goats, Yoho is classed as a World Heritage Site. To get here from Calgary, travel west for about two hours (211 kilometres) on Highway 1, passing through Banff National Park to the British Columbia border. Bordering Banff and Kootenay national parks on the western slopes of the Rocky Mountains and straddling the edge of the Continental Divide, Yoho was originally 26 square kilometres in area, but now encompasses 1,313 square kilometres.

The park appeals to geologists, hikers, campers, sightseers, mountaineers, wildlife and nature photographers, cyclists, mountain bikers, horseback riders, swimmers, canoeists—you get the idea. Whether you want to make a pit stop or stay a while, you'll never lack for things to do or places to see. Here you'll find glaciers, ice fields, steep mountains, and wide U-shaped valleys sculpted by the glacial ice that once covered, and then receded, from the area.

In 1909, American geologist Charles D. Walcott discovered the Burgess Shale fossils, which date back to the Cambrian Epoch 512–520 million years ago. These well-preserved rock forms contain imprints of ancient sea creatures which, geologists believe, were trapped in a huge underwater mudslide. According to

CAMPING NEAR TAKAKKAW FALLS

CATHEDRAL CRAGS

EMERALD LAKE

A TRILOBITE FOSSIL (INSET) FROM THE BURGESS SHALE (BELOW)

scientists, these fossils are proof that the stone in the Rockies once lay on the bottom of an ocean, and the earth's crust was an active, constantly-moving land mass.

It's now illegal to collect fossils in the park, but you can take an interpretive walk through the fossil beds as part of a nine-kilometre hike. As you follow the meandering Yoho River north from the turnoff east of Field, you'll come across Takakkaw Falls, one of the highest waterfalls in Canada. You'll also pass Laughing Falls, Point Lace Falls, Angel's Staircase and Twin Falls.

The Takakkaw Falls campground and parking lot at the end of Yoho Valley Road serves as the starting point for most trails in the Yoho Valley. Many trails connect, allowing you to adjust your hike according to your time limits, stamina and interests. Whichever way you go, pristine Emerald Lake will probably be on or near your route, and it's definitely worth a visit. As you make your way here, stop at the Natural Bridge where the Kicking Horse River has constructed a natural lookout. The lake area is a popular haven for kayakers and horseback riders.

Hikes in Yoho can last one to five days, depending on how near you want to get to some of

the wildlife in the park's backcountry. For longer journeys, Lake O'Hara on the south side of Highway 1 is probably the best place to start, because the region around it divides into five zones. Aficionados contend that these should be experienced one day at a time. However, before you go, you would be wise to e-mail wardens for current information. Lake O'Hara is also an important grizzly bear habitat and trail closures do occur unexpectedly.

The McArthur Valley–Cataract Brook wildlife corridor also passes through the Lake O'Hara area, so be prepared for possible closures there. The best time to travel the McArthur Valley region is probably after August 15.

If you want to venture along the Odaray-Highline Trail, you'll need a permit, which is available at the Field Visitors' Centre. Park wardens request that you do not travel this area between August 15–September 15.

TAKAKKAW FALLS

Whenever you trek along this route, to ensure that no more than four groups per day travel here, check the log-book (which should be available at the head of the trail) and sign it; you might also join another hiking group to reduce what wardens refer to as "disturbances" and use the trail only between 9:30 a.m. and 4:30 p.m. Wardens ask that you keep your group together, and that you don't bring pets or stop to eat.

Also worth the price of admission are hikes to Lake Oesa, and the Opabin Plateau from Lake O'Hara, the Whaleback and the Icefield, accessible from Lake Takakkaw. Unless you're a climber or the weather is perfect, you'll probably want to avoid the difficult Alpine Circuit, an 11.8-kilometre route that includes Oesa, Opabin and Schaffer lakes.

If you want only to take a short walk, five routes can be accessed off the Trans-Canada Highway as you travel west:

SAXIFRAGE

Ross Lake (accessible one kilometre south of the Great Divide picnic area); Sherbrooke Lake (a serene sub-alpine lake accessible from the Wapta Lake picnic area, five kilometres west of the Great Divide); Mt. Stephen Fossil Beds (accessible via 1st St. East in Field); Hoodoo Creek (located on the western edge of the park, 22 kilometres west of Field), where you can visit the hoodoos (pillars of glacial debris topped by stones) and an excellent campground; and Wapta

HIKING IN YOHO

Falls (accessed via a 1.6-kilometre dirt road 25 kilometres west of Field).

No matter how far you're travelling or how long you're staying in Yoho, you'll probably want to camp at one of the many front-country or backcountry campgrounds, most of which contain modern amenities and firewood. Front-country campgrounds are: Chancellor Peak (24 kilometres west of Field), located on an island in the Kicking Horse River; the aforementioned Hoodoo Creek (22 kilometres west of Field), which features several hiking trails; Kicking Horse (three kilometres west of Field), which has a wheelchair accessible washroom and is near wheelchair-accessible trails; Monarch, located in the middle of a meadow; and the previously-mentioned Takakkaw Falls (17 kilometres east of Field) at the top of Takakkaw Falls Road.

There are six backcountry campgrounds, four in the Yoho Valley and two in Ottertail Valley. A wilderness pass (approximately $6 per night to a maximum of $30 per trip) is required for a stay at any backcountry campground. There is no charge for children under the age of 16. The friendly folks at the Field Visitors Centre can provide you with passes, maps and other information that will lead to awesome and wonderful adventures — wherever you go in Yoho National Park.

Blue Moose Tours offer guided camping trips led by Association of Canadian Mountain Guides-certified personnel, between Calgary and Yoho. In this era of eco-tourism, other emerging companies may also offer similar services. Check for info on the Internet, the Yellow Pages or with tourism associations in B.C. and Alberta.

COLUMBIA
ICEFIELD

THE ICEFIELDS PARKWAY

FERN BROOKS

TANGLE CREEK FALLS

Awesome. Spectacular. Majestic. These words won't prepare visitors for the mountain and wilderness views to be seen along the Icefields Parkway, the 230-kilometre drive along Highway 93 between Lake Louise and Jasper. First opened as a gravel road in 1940, the Parkway made the Columbia Icefields accessible to modern tourists in private vehicles. Open year round with temporary snow closures of up to three days in winter, it runs along a chain of massive icefields straddling the Continental Divide. Travellers can see more glaciers from the Parkway than from any other road in North America.

In summer, this stretch of highway linking Banff and Jasper national parks is one of the most heavily travelled corridors in the Canadian Rockies. Allow at least half a day to travel the whole distance, which will give you time to stop and admire the scenery or enjoy a pleasant picnic. There's no toll for travelling the Icefields Parkway, but drivers must pay the national park entrance fee regardless of whether or not they plan to stop inside the park. Ask for the Icefields Parkway brochure at the park gates.

You'll want to stop frequently to take advantage of the many photo ops along the Parkway, from towering, in-your-face mountain cliffs with their snow-streaked peaks to the elk, moose, bighorn sheep and mountain goats that live here. Don't be tempted to stop on the shoulders of the two-

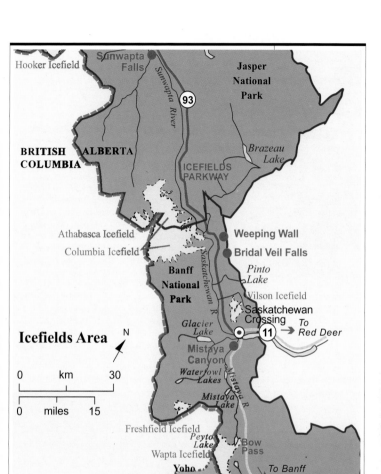

Icefields Area

Hooker Icefield
Sunwapta Falls
Sunwapta River
93
Jasper National Park
BRITISH COLUMBIA
ALBERTA
Brazeau Lake
ICEFIELDS PARKWAY
Athabasca Icefield
Columbia Icefield
Weeping Wall
Bridal Veil Falls
Banff National Park
Pinto Lake
Wilson Icefield
Saskatchewan R.
Saskatchewan Crossing
11
To Red Deer
Glacier Lake
Mistaya Canyon
Mistaya R.
Waterfowl Lakes
Mistaya Lake
Freshfield Icefield
Peyto Lake
Bow Pass
Wapta Icefield
Yoho National Park
To Banff & Calgary

N

| 0 | km | 30 |
| 0 | miles | 15 |

lane roadway, but instead pull into one of the many turnouts that dot the Parkway. And keep your binoculars handy. Besides the Columbia Icefield (see next chapter), notable sights include Peyto Lake with its brilliant turquoise waters; Mistaya Canyon (10 minutes by trail from the highway); Weeping Wall Viewpoint; Sunwapta Falls; and Athabasca Falls, with its many walkways overlooking a canyon.

Want an up-close-and-personal look at the area beyond the views at turnouts? The Parkway is criss-crossed with hiking trails long and short, moderate and steep. Visitor information centres can provide maps and current trail, weather, bear and avalanche reports. Trailheads are generally marked by roadside signs. If you venture out, hike

ATHABASCA FALLS

ALONG THE
ICEFIELDS PARKWAY

with companions. Tell someone where you are going and when you plan to return. Where possible, register at trailheads.

HIKING AND CAMPING

Hiking uphill can quickly dehydrate you. Carry enough water on your hike. Do not drink from mountain streams, however clear the water may look. Most of the trails are snow-covered early and late in the season, so bring adequate footwear. In mountain areas, the weather can change quickly. Dress in layers that you can peel off when it warms up, and add on later in the day. Always remember that this is bear country. Bears usually avoid people, but they don't like to be surprised. Make plenty of noise, especially in heavily wooded areas. A bell works well.

Staying overnight in the back country requires the purchase of a Wilderness Pass, which is available along with detailed trail information from Parks Canada. If you want to stay overnight along the Parkway, there are a number of campgrounds and a few hostels, as well as limited motel-type accommodation, including the 32-room Columbia Icefield Chalet on the top floor of the Icefield

Centre. The Chalet is open from May 1 to October 1. Because accommodations are at a premium between June 15 and September 15, it is advisable to book in advance. Visitors who come looking for a place to stay will likely have to settle farther afield in Banff, Canmore or Jasper.

Parkway campsites are available on a first-come, first-served basis only. For a complete list of campgrounds and their open dates, fees and amenities, ask for a free copy of Parks Canada's "Mountain Guide" at Banff and Jasper park gates. It should be noted that campsites and off-highway roads may be closed in times of high fire hazard.

BOW LAKE, NEAR WAPTA ICEFIELD (TOP); BIKING ALONG A MORAINE (ABOVE); TREACHEROUS WEATHER ALONG PARKWAY (BOTTOM)

ROAD CONDITIONS
The Parkway passes through rugged, remote, high-altitude terrain. Weather and road conditions can be unpredictable and closures are not uncommon, particularly in the off-

COLUMBIA ICEFIELD

season. Check locally for conditions before proceeding. The Parkway roadbed is in generally good repair. However, there are some rough patches which, combined with the turns, road grades and altitude, may trigger motion sickness in sensitive travellers. Motorists should fill their gas tanks before they enter the Parkway, as there is only one station that sells fuel (at Saskatchewan River Crossing, at the junction of Highways 93 and 11; the Crossing Resort also has a cafeteria, dining room, pub and 66-unit motel). This rest station is closed November to March, as are all other services along the route.

TOURS

Want to let someone else do the driving so you can spend your whole time soaking up the scenery? A number of tour companies operate out of Banff and Jasper, the biggest of which is Brewster Transportation Company. Tour drivers provide interpretive commentary, and the tour buses stop along the route for photo ops and short nature walks. Brewster's round trips to the Columbia Icefield from Banff average 9.5 hours; buses depart daily. Check with tour companies for other trips, times and fees.

GLACIER TOUR

THE COLUMBIA ICEFIELD

FERN BROOKS

The Columbia Icefield covers almost 325 square kilometres on the boundary of Banff and Jasper national parks, making it the largest body of ice in the Rocky Mountains. The Icefield, 103 kilometres south of Jasper, and 189 km north of Banff, is a massive sheet of glacial ice that is trapped by higher surrounding land and feeds eight large glaciers. The Icefield is ringed by 13 of the 30 highest mountains in the Rockies. Its maximum thickness is estimated to be 365 metres.

Meltwater from the Icefield pours into streams and rivers that flow into three oceans: the Pacific, the Arctic and the Atlantic. (Siberia has the only other tri-oceanic apex in the world.) These rivers are the freshwater source for millions of western Canadians, as well as their agricultural and industrial sectors.

An icefield forms when snow falling on high mountains builds up year after year with little summer melt. When the snow becomes about 30 metres thick, the bottom layers are compressed into ice. As more snow falls and the depth of ice increases, it eventually overflows into neighbouring valleys and starts flowing downhill, creating a glacier or river of ice.

Ice layers at the bottom of a glacier are under intense pressure and become almost "plastic," able to flow over bedrock without cracking. Ice at the surface flows faster than ice at the base because it is under less pressure. The

COLUMBIA ICEFIELD AT NIGHT

upper layers are more brittle, cracking open into crevasses or fissures on the surface. Meltwater creates channels on the surface of glacial ice and can enlarge the crevasses. Circular holes called millwells are formed, connecting to drainage systems within the glacier, which discharge near the "toe."

A glacier has tremendous erosive power because of its weight. The bottom ice grinds underlying bedrock, while the side ice shears away rock from surrounding mountainside. The ground rubble is known as till. Glaciers create landforms from till called moraines. Lateral moraines are the rocky ridges pushed up against the side of a glacier as it flows downhill. The till left at the toe of a glacier as it retreats is called a terminal moraine.

AVOIDING THE CREVASSES

The glaciers spawned by the Columbia Icefield continue to shrink, as the summer melt has been consistently greater than the winter snow accumulation. (A glacier will advance if the snow accumulation is greater than the summer's melt.) This advance and retreat is a natural process. However, the Icefield has also been losing volume, while its glaciers have retreated at an accelerating rate in the last century. Many scientists blame this on climate change.

THE ATHABASCA GLACIER

The Athabasca Glacier, the focus of most visits to the area, has retreated an annual average of one to three metres in recent years. The glacier is currently six square kilometres in size, with a length of six kilometres and a depth from 90–300 metres. Visitors to the glacier may want to stop first at the Icefield Information Centre across the Icefield Parkway (Highway 93) from the Athabasca Glacier. The centre, open from May 1 to mid-October, is reached by a series of shallow stairways. Let the youngsters run up and down them a few minutes to vent any pent-up energy, then turn them loose in the Glacier Gallery in the centre's lower level. The centre also has wheelchair-friendly ramps and automatic doors for less mobile visitors.

PARKS CANADA GLACIER GALLERY

The Parks Canada Glacier Gallery, open from early May to mid-October, features interactive displays and exhibits that will appeal to young and old alike. Learn about the area's glaciers and alpine environment from videos and information panels dotted around the expansive gallery. Press a button to hear what wailing coyotes or bugling elk sound like. Let the youngsters crawl through a mock ice cave. Learn about aboriginal visitors and the alpine quarries they mined for the chert and other stone used to shape spear and arrow points. Read about the later visitors who explored and mapped the area. And finally, find out if there really are "iceworms" that eat "watermelon snow."

THE COLUMBIA ICEFIELD CENTRE

On the main floor of the centre are restrooms and telephones; an eclectic gift shop where you can buy items from kitchen mitts and Christmas decorations to film and souvenirs; a Parks Canada information booth with maps, brochures and current field reports; and the hotel front desk at the south end where you can purchase tickets for the Brewster Ice Explorer tour of the Athabasca Glacier.

TOURS

More than 600,000 visitors take the daily motorized tour onto the icy slopes of the Athabasca Glacier every summer.

ATHABASCA GLACIER TOUR

Reservations for individuals are not required for the 5-kilometre round-trip journey aboard the Ice Explorer. Visitors should note that traffic is heaviest between 10:30 a.m. and 3 p.m. The guided Ice Explorer tours roll between April and October. However, mountain weather is unpredictable: snow can hit any day of the year on the Icefield and new crevasses can open. Avoid disappointment and call a day before your visit to find out if the glacier tours are running normally.

You can also purchase tickets at the Icefield Centre

SUNWAPTA FALLS
ALONG THE
ICEFIELDS PARKWAY

A PTARMIGAN

for interpretive walks with a trained guide on the Athabasca Glacier. Space on the walks is limited: advance bookings are recommended. Warm clothes, sunglasses and sunscreen are needed. Be aware the walks may be shortened or cancelled due to weather conditions. If you're looking for refreshments, a snack bar and spacious cafeteria can be found on the second floor of the Icefield Centre. The two are open between 9:30 a.m. and 5 p.m. and provide a good selection of hot and cold food at reasonable prices. You can view the Athabasca Glacier while you eat inside, or you can sit out on the balcony. Keep your binoculars handy; you may be able to catch mountain climbers on nearby peaks in your sights.

SHORT HIKES

Want to make just a quick trip up to the glacier? Opposite the Icefield Centre is a small parking lot with two roads. The right-hand road is the public access, leading to a second parking lot beside Sunwapta Lake. A 600-metre trail leaves from here to the toe of the glacier. You can also park in the first lot and walk the Forefield Trail to where it connects with the path from the second parking lot. Observe warning signs, and do *not* walk on the glacier. (Glacial ice is slippery, and it is easy to lose your footing and injure yourself. If you fall into a crevasse, you will be unable to climb out. Visitors have died of hypothermia before they could be rescued.) Visitors should also note that there are no gasoline pumps at the Icefield Centre.

There are a number of other short hikes in the Icefield vicinity. Parks Canada calls the Parker Ridge Trail (5.2 km, two hours) "perhaps the finest short walk in the Canadian Rockies," adding that, if you do only one hike in the Rockies, this should be it. The trail slopes sharply as it

passes through alpine meadows to a ride which offers fabulous views of the Saskatchewan Glacier and the headwaters of the North Saskatchewan River. Ask at the Icefield Centre's Parks Canada booth for information on hiking, hostels and camping in the Icefield vicinity. You can also get the details from the information boards in the parking lot at the foot of the centre's stairways.

JASPER
ONAL PARK

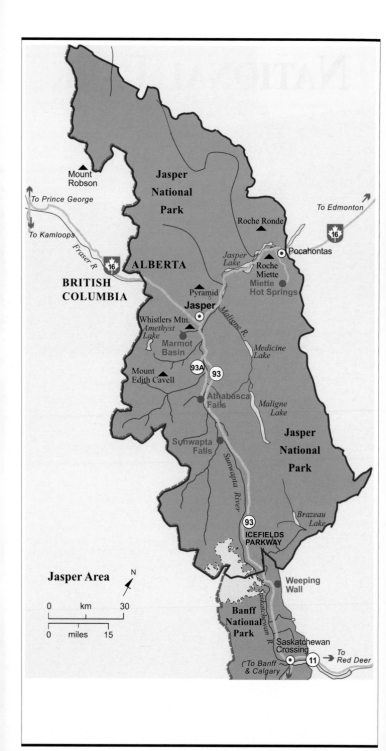

A SHORT HISTORY

RANDY WILLIAMS

Established as a forest reserve in 1907, Jasper National Park is the largest national park and wildlife sanctuary in the Canadian Rockies, encompassing 10,878 square kilometres of breathtaking wilderness. Jasper is also the mountain park with the least commercial development — don't expect to find a Benetton store here. Jasper is a three-hour drive north of the glittery tourist town of Banff and three hours west of the nearest major airport (Edmonton International), so visitors don't tend to wander here on a whim. They come for the unspoiled scenery, the peacefulness of the remote locale, and the unique experience of spotting some of North America's rarest animals, including bighorn sheep, bears, moose, elk, caribou, mountain goats and wolves.

ADMINISTRATION BUILDING, 1914 (TOP); A PARK SIGN (ABOVE)

Because the park is just marking its centennial and the town of Jasper itself only sprang up with the arrival of the railway in 1911, it may seem that the area's history is quite brief. But archaeological findings tell us that aboriginal peoples lived in the mountain valleys of what is now Jasper National Park for more than 8,000 years. The earliest of these were most likely nomadic hunters of bighorn sheep, although there is evidence of more permanent settlements of Sarcee in the 1700s.

AN EARLY TENT CITY

FUR TRADING

By 1800, fur trappers and other Europeans were making their way toward the area. Members of eastern tribes

111

THE TOWN IN 1910 (TOP), AND IN 1914 (BOTTOM)

such as the Iroquois arrived ahead of the Europeans to hawk their services as guides and trappers. When Canada's great fur trade-era explorer and cartographer David Thompson arrived in 1810, it was an Iroquois named Thomas who led his party over the Athabasca Pass. The pass would become famous as part of the main fur trade route between Canada and Oregon, and it was used extensively by the North West Company and Hudson's Bay Company for almost 50 years. These days, the Athabasca Pass is little more than a strenuous backpacking trail in the southwest corner of the park, marked by a historical cairn. The pass is as windswept and wild as it was when Thompson's party first set eyes on it; automobile and rail traffic now cross into British Columbia via the Yellowhead Pass.

Thompson saw to it that Jasper's first permanent structure was built in 1811. One of his men, William Henry, was left behind while Thompson and the others explored the pass. While he awaited Thompson's return, the man built a rudimentary fur trading post at the head of the Athabasca River. The building was known as Henry House, and it became a way station for Pacific-bound voyageurs making the transition from water to land travel before crossing the mountains. Henry House was closed in the 1830s; a monument to the post still stands near Lac Beauvert, but nothing is left of the building itself.

JASPER HOUSE

In 1813, the North West Company built a provision depot on Brulé Lake for traders crossing the Athabasca Pass. The

post was originally known as Rocky Mountain House, but when Jasper Hawes took command of it in 1817, the name was changed to "Jasper's House" to avoid confusion with the better-known Rocky Mountain House on the Saskatchewan River. The Hudson's Bay Company, which had absorbed the North West Company in 1821, moved the post upriver to the eastern end of Jasper Lake

in 1829. By the middle of the century, a sharp decrease in traffic over the pass sent the post into decline. After several temporary closures, Jasper House, as the post had come to be known, was finally abandoned in 1884. Today a pile of chimney stones is all that's left of the building, but Jasper's name settled over the entire district.

JASPER ROOMS — EARLY ACCOMMODATIONS

Fur trading declined after 1850, and there would be few travellers in the area until the railway arrived 60 years later. But a small number of adventurers and mountaineers made their way through. Painter Paul Kane visited Jasper in the company of a small fur brigade and produced a series of illustrations that were published in 1859, providing historians with valuable first-hand observations of life in the fur trade. Members of the Palliser Expedition and the Overlanders visited Jasper; geologist A.P. Coleman and climber Walter Wilcox explored the area in the 1880s and '90s; and British mountaineers Herman Woolley and Norman Collie trekked though to discover the Columbia Icefield in 1898.

MALIGNE CANYON

Even so, much of the area was still unexplored wilderness in 1907, when it became apparent that two transcontinental railways, the Grand Trunk Pacific and Canadian Northern, would soon pass through the Athabasca Valley. The Dominion Government quickly moved to assert its authority over the surrounding land and its precious water supply, creating Jasper Forest Reserve in Parliament on September 14. Acting to protect the water supply marked a change from the standard policy of establishing national parks as a means of attracting wealthy visitors. Jasper was to be a vast conservation area rather than a zone set aside for focused development of tourism; resources would be protected from undue exploitation. To this day, Jasper remains a more rugged and unspoiled northern cousin to the highly commercialized Banff National Park.

COAL AND RAILWAYS

That's not to say that commerce and tourism have ever really been shut out of Jasper. Coal claims were staked in 1908, leading to the formation of Jasper Park Collieries and the little mining town of Pocahontas. When

JASPER RAILWAY STATION, 1930s

Ottawa learned of the Miette Hot Springs in 1909, federal officials immediately began planning for development within the reserve. That same year, Donald "Curly" Phillips became one of the park's first outfitters and guides, hiring out his services to climbing and hunting expeditions. In 1911, railway workers began creating railbed and laying track, leases for commercial and residential establishments began to be surveyed, and a system of streets had been laid out. But it would be quite some time before the area began to look truly settled. The Grand Trunk Pacific officially opened a line from Edmonton to Jasper in 1912, but when World War I began in 1914, Jasper still had no paved streets, no electricity or running water, no garbage collection and no means of treating or disposing of sewage. The Canadian Northern finally opened its line in 1915, but just one year later some of the park's rails were ripped up and sent to France to help with the war effort.

In 1921, both the Canadian Northern and Grand Trunk Pacific railways went belly-up and were absorbed by the crown-owned Canadian National Railways. The park began to issue automobile permits that same year, and bus tours began making their way through the park almost overnight. A road from Edmonton to Jasper was completed in 1928, dramatically increasing auto traffic in the park. The National Parks Act was passed in 1930, establishing a mandate to protect wildlife, restrict logging and prohibit any further mining in the area.

The Jasper-Banff Highway was begun in 1931 and completed in 1939. The road was opened up for tourist traffic in 1940 but didn't become widely used until gas rationing was lifted at the end of World War II. Nonetheless, tourists found their way into Jasper to enjoy the unparalleled scenery and the growing number of world-class amenities such as the golf course at the Jasper Park Lodge, completed in 1925, and the bathhouse at Miette Hot Springs, completed in 1935. After the war was over, Jasper National Park became a major attraction and the rough and tumble townsite developed into a charming mountain village that is still beloved by 21st-century visitors from every corner of the globe.

EARLY VISITORS TO JASPER

EXPLORING THE TOWN OF JASPER

RANDY WILLIAMS

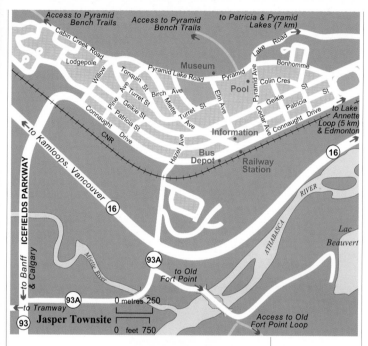

The town of Jasper is located approximately 420 kilometres northwest of Calgary, 380 km west of Edmonton and 30 km east of the British Columbia border. It is situated on the edge of a wide, open valley where the Athabasca and Miette rivers meet. Jasper has three entrances by automobile or bus — east bound through the Yellowhead Pass from B.C., westbound on Highway 16, and northbound on the Icefield Parkway from Banff National Park. The entrance through the Sunwapta Pass on the Icefield Parkway is thought by many to provide the most stunning scenery, but no matter how one approaches Jasper, the views of the surrounding Rocky Mountains are nothing short of spectacular. The town is also on the Canadian National Railway's transcontinental line; the train stops in town three times a week.

HISTORIC TRAIN

One of the most common observations about Jasper is that it has genuine small-town charm. This is probably because more than one quarter of the town's population is completely independent of tourism; Canadian National Railway employs hundreds of Jasper residents (the year-round population is approximately 5,400 people). Therefore, a sense of working community exists here that can't be found in most holiday destinations. Jasper is nonetheless an internationally recognized four-season attraction that sees more than two million visitors each year. It is the logical starting point for all kinds of adventures in the biggest of Canada's Rocky Mountain parks and one of North America's largest natural areas.

Although the townsite is small and humble in appearance, it does contain several points of historic interest. The beautifully designed Jasper Information Centre, on the main drag through town, is one of the best examples of rustic architecture to be found anywhere in Canada's national park system. Completed in 1914, the building was constructed of local fieldstone and timber and built to contain park administration offices, a small museum and the park superintendent's quarters. Up to that time, Jasper's architectural style had been characterized by tar-paper shacks and canvas tents. This building therefore helped to establish a tone for Jasper's development.

Today the building serves as the park's main information centre. This is the place to verify trail conditions and check in with park rangers before going on wilderness hikes or mountain climbing excursions. The Friends of Jasper National Park are also located here and their shop is the most reliable place to buy guide books,

topographical maps and park-specific souvenirs that aren't typical tourist items. This not-for-profit organization "promotes understanding, appreciation and respect for the natural ecosystems and cultural heritage of Jasper National Park and surrounding areas" through publishing, research, cultural preservation, educational activities and other projects. The Information Centre is open year-round; summer hours are 8:30 a.m. to 7 p.m. and off-season hours are 9 a.m. to 5:00 p.m.

JASPER RAILWAY STATION

Directly across Connaught Drive from the Information Centre is the charming railway station, constructed in 1925 (the original station had burned down) in the style of pre-World War I English country homes. The station was intended to serve the town, of course, but was also built with an eye toward bringing tourists to Jasper Park Lodge, then owned by CN Railway. The station is still a major stop for transcontinental trains and also serves as the town's bus station.

MUSEUMS, GALLERIES AND SHOPPING

Two museums offer nice rainy-day diversions and allow visitors to soak in some local history. An impressive gallery greets visitors to the Jasper-Yellowhead Museum on Pyramid Lake Road. The museum transports visitors to the days of fur trading, mountaineering, the coming of the railway and the formation of the national park. For those too timid to encounter animals in the wild, there is Jasper's Wildlife Museum. Here you can explore Alberta's natural beauty in the form of life-like habitats replicating the province's four natural regions: prairie, aspen parkland, mountain and northern forest.

BIGHORN SHEEP (BELOW); JASPER'S WILDLIFE MUSEUM, INSIDE WHISTLERS INN (BOTTOM)

Children will enjoy getting close to grazing elk, deer, caribou, pronghorns, beavers, coyotes, grizzly bears, black bears, moose and many others — especially because interacting with the real things in the park is both dangerous and expressly forbidden. The museum is located downstairs at Whistlers

SHOPPING IN JASPER
(ABOVE AND BELOW)

Inn, in the centre of downtown Jasper at the corner of Connaught Drive and Miette Avenue.

For those interested in learning more about the architecture and history of the townsite, the Friends of Jasper National Park offer a 90-minute historical walking tour of Jasper each evening during the summer. Times are posted at the Information Centre, which is where you will meet your guide. Donations for the tour are greatly appreciated.

The townsite has a full complement of gift shops, ranging from the usual T-shirt emporiums to wilderness sport outfitters to upscale merchants of unique jewellery and aboriginal crafts. One entire store is devoted to Mounties. All manner of excursions can be booked in town, whether you enjoy summer activities such as hikes, horseback rides, whitewater rafting and fishing or winter adventures like snowmobiling and cross-country skiing. And you can find virtually any kind of cuisine — Greek, Italian, Chinese, sushi, steak, seafood, coffee-house fare and the ubiquitous pizza and burgers.

FINE DINING AT JASPER PARK LODGE

DINING

Several Jasper restaurants have earned international reputations for their gourmet cuisine; the most famous of these is probably the award-winning Becker's Gourmet at Becker's Chalets, located five minutes south of Jasper townsite on the Icefields Parkway. Visitors can savour an exquisite view of Mt. Kerkeslin and the Athabasca River while enjoying fine continental-style dinners (served from 5:30 p.m. to 10:00 p.m.) such as lamb with nut crust, French brie in puff pastry, Morels Alexander, New York steak with mushroom sauce, sole paupiettes with nantua sauce, vegetable strudel, venison and daily pasta dishes. The breakfast buffet, served from 8:00 a.m. to 11 a.m., features egg dishes, home-baked treats and fresh fruit. Dinner reservations are recommended and can

be booked at (780) 852-3535. The restaurant and adjoining lounge are both non-smoking facilities.

TOP ATTRACTIONS

Many of the top attractions in Jasper National Park are just a short drive from the townsite. The Jasper tramway, just eight kilometres from town on Whistler's Mountain Road, is a must-see. Being whisked 2,285 metres up into Jasper's alpine tundra is an experience that will astonish all ages, and at the top there are unsurpassed views of glacial-fed lakes and rivers, six mountain ranges stretching up to 80 km away, and the Jasper townsite. Interpretive exhibits explain the alpine environment and a hiking trail leads to the summit of the mountain. From here, if you're very lucky, you may even be able to spot the snowcapped Mt. Robson, the highest mountain in the Canadian Rockies, though it is almost always shrouded in clouds.

The H.J. Moberly Bridge, just east of the townsite, takes you across the Athabasca River toward Lake Edith, Lake Annette and Jasper Park Lodge. The bridge is named for Henry Moberly, a factor for the Hudson's Bay Company who lived in the Jasper area from 1858 until 1931. Immediately after crossing the bridge, the road to Jasper Park Lodge branches to the right. A few kilometres along the road to the lodge, you will see an exit for lakes Edith and Annette on the left. Both spring-fed lakes are open for recreation year round. There are day-use areas that offer picnic sites, playgrounds and shelters in a beautiful setting. Enjoy a swim or just relax on the sandy beaches and open grassy areas. There are several excellent trails for quiet walks around the lakes, including the wheelchair-accessible Lee Foundation Trail, and Lake Edith also has bicycle trails.

JASPER TRAMWAY (TOP); JASPER PARK LODGE (ABOVE)

Jasper Park Lodge is just a little farther up the road. The lodge's location may have been the original site of Henry's House, the first permanent habitation in this part of the Rockies. In 1915, a tent camp was erected along the shores of emerald-green Lac Beauvert, and the camp eventually grew into the present-day lodge. Begun by the Grand Trunk Pacific Railway and long owned by the Canadian National

JASPER PARK LODGE AT NIGHT

119

DUCKS ON A LOG

Railway, the lodge was purchased by Canadian Pacific in 1988 and is currently managed by Fairmont Hotels & Resorts. The 1920s brought the construction of log bungalows for guests and the lodge's world-famous golf course, created by master architect Stanley Thompson. The original main building — the largest one-story log structure in the world — was destroyed by fire in 1952, and most of the original log cabins have long since been replaced with cedar chalets. Today, the lodge is a modern resort with boutiques, a sports lounge and gourmet dining facilities. The view is excellent, the accommodations are gracious, and it's well worth popping in for dinner or afternoon tea even if you are staying elsewhere.

ENJOYING THE OUTDOORS

**DAISY (INSET);
PYRAMID MOUNTAIN
(BOTTOM)**

Above the town of Jasper, a winding road leads to Pyramid Lake, where picnicking, fishing, boating and hiking are popular pastimes. To get there, turn right onto Cedar Avenue from Connaught Drive; as soon as you pass the Recreation Centre, this will become Pyramid Lake Road. The road climbs above town and meanders through a Douglas-fir forest. Pyramid Bench is studded with more than 20 small lakes left behind by glaciers. Watch for elk, deer and the occasional moose or bear. The road ends at breathtakingly beautiful Pyramid Lake, nestled at the base of Pyramid Mountain. A footbridge carries you to a small island in the middle of the lake, from which you can enjoy a spectacular view of the mountain — a striking Jasper landmark that shines an exquisite orange-red in the sun because of its iron-rich rock. Gasoline-powered motors are allowed on

the lake, and boats are available for rent at Pyramid Lake Resort. This in an excellent spot to try your luck at catching rainbow and lake trout or Rocky Mountain Whitefish. During winter, a lighted skating rink is maintained on the lake surface. Summer rental facilities include horse-back riding, boating, canoeing, windsurfing, fishing and sailing. Cross-country skiing, snowshoeing and ice-skating on Pyramid Lake in the winter make this location ideal for year-round fun.

PYRAMID LAKE

Thirty minutes from Jasper townsite, Mount Edith Cavell offers one of the most memorable half-day trips in the park. Indeed, few summits in Jasper can match it for rugged beauty. Edith Louise Cavell was a British nurse during the First World War who was executed by a German firing squad after hiding and aiding British soldiers who had become separated from their units; in 1916, this 3,363 metre peak was renamed in her honour. Travelling south from Jasper townsite, follow Highway 93A and turn right onto Cavell Road shortly after crossing the Astoria River. Switchbacks begin immediately, and this narrow, winding road is not suitable for travel by bus, trailers or large motor homes. Trailers can be left at the parking lot at the base of Cavell Road.

The road is closed to auto traffic during the winter months, when it becomes a popular cross-country ski trail.

GLACIER FRAGMENT IN MELT POOL, MOUNT EDITH CAVELL

At kilometre 15, the road ends at the Mount Edith Cavell parking lot, from which you can easily reach two short interpretive trails at the foot of the mountain's north wall. The Glacier Trail guides visitors through the mass of boulders, rubble, sand and rock flour left behind by the retreat of local glaciers and leads to a small, powder-blue lake and two remnant glaciers, the Angel and Cavell. This is

ATHABASCA FALLS

truly an otherwordly landscape with rocks scoured and scraped by passing ice, huge blue icebergs floating in the meltwater and an awe-inspiring view of both glaciers. It can be quite cold here even on summer afternoons, owing both to the altitude and the fact that the sun is largely blocked by the mountain. Another longer trail is perfect for flower lovers; it leads to picturesque, sub-alpine Cavell Meadows, which bursts into colourful life each July. The nearby Dune Wall is a popular multi-pitch climbing area, and the starting point for the Tonquin Valley trails is just up the road.

Also south of town are the Athabasca Falls, which are among the most spectacular and powerful in the Rockies. From Jasper townsite, head west out of town to the traffic lights and onto the Icefield Parkway. Turn right 31 km south at the junction with Highway 93A, then immediately turn left into the Athabasca Falls parking lot. The falls are just a few metres away; you should be able to hear the thundering water. The headwater comes from the Columbia Glacier, about 70 kilometres south, and pours into the Athabasca River, which here roars through a narrow gorge where rock walls have been worn away by the sheer force of the rushing water carrying sand and rock.

Visitors can view the falls and feel the spray from several vantage points. A self-guided trail actually takes you through abandoned river channels and old streambeds, providing an unparalleled look at the unique formations that result from the ancient struggle between water and rock. The site has parking and washroom facilities, paved trails, picnic areas, a gift shop and snacks. In the winter there is a cross-country skiing trail, and in the summer this is a starting point for whitewater rafting expeditions.

MOUNTAIN BIKING NEAR JASPER PARK LODGE

HIKING AND CAMPING

RANDY WILLIAMS

JASPER NATIONAL PARK

Jasper contains more than 1,200 kilometres of trails — a rugged backcountry trail system in addition to many paved trails and self-guided front-country trails for the less adventurous. First-time hikers and backpackers will want to visit the Friends of Jasper National Park at the Park Information Centre. The FJNP will lend you a hiking pack for the two-hour trek up the Old Fort Point Trail. The pack, which requires only a Visa or Mastercard deposit, contains guidebooks, interpretive pages, binoculars, a magnifying glass and a panoramic map of the summit. FJNP also offers a one-hour Junior Naturalist Program at Wapiti Campground that allows children between the ages of six and ten.

WAPITI CAMPGROUND

Hiking is one of the best ways to experience the mountains, enjoy unspoiled views and perhaps even see some wild animals in their natural habitat. But be sure to check the distance and level of difficulty before setting out, and always make sure you have the appropriate gear. Good footwear and layered clothing are a must, as it is colder at higher elevations. You should also be sure to pack a hat, sunglasses and sunscreen, a first aid kit and plenty of water. Registering with Parks Canada at the

BIGHORN SHEEP

Information Centre is a smart idea. Something as minor as a badly twisted ankle could potentially leave a hiker out in the wild overnight. Also be sure to check with Parks Canada for up-to-date trail conditions and maps.

Here are a few of the most popular trails around Jasper:

OLD FORT POINT TRAIL

The name "Old Fort" is most likely a reference to Henry House, the North West Company trading post that was once located just downstream. It's easy enough to picture fur traders climbing up to Old Fort Point for a panoramic view. The Point is a roche moutonnee, an exposed feature of bedrock modified by the convergence of two large glaciers, and is one of the highest such features in the Athabasca Valley. The trail passes through three distinct micro-climates, and bighorn sheep frequent the area. From the summit one has an unobstructed view of all the peaks surrounding the valley and a number of picturesque sights below, from Mount Edith Cavell in the south to Mount Bridgeland, the Victoria Cross Range, the limestone front ranges, Jasper townsite, Jasper Park Lodge and the surrounding lakes.

PYRAMID LAKE

RELAXING ON PYRAMID LAKE

A 13-kilometre round-trip hike from the town to Pyramid Lake and back, this hiking path climbs along an open hillside providing stunning glimpses of the Athabasca Valley. It's not uncommon to see bighorn sheep grazing on grass-covered slopes below the trail. The most scenic section is known as the "Pyramid Overlook," a 120-metre climb up a heavily wooded (mostly Douglas fir) ridge with frequent openings that offer breathtaking views. The trail eventually descends to the Pyramid Lake parking lot and begins a loop back to the townsite.

PATRICIA LAKE

A five-kilometre hike from the town to Patricia Lake and back, this loop gently climbs through mixed forest, with the most common trees being Douglas fir, aspen and pine. You will pass through a number of clearings with excellent views of the mountain ranges to the south before descending to the southernmost tip of Patricia Lake. The lake offers an ideal location for spotting beaver, deer, moose and a variety of birds.

THE WHISTLERS

The spectacular views at the top are still available to those who don't want to pay for the tram — or are afraid to ride it — on this seven-kilometre hike (each way) that climbs some 1,200 metres.

WHISTLERS CAMPGROUND

VALLEY OF FIVE LAKES

There are two hikes here — one from the town, starting at Old Fort Point, and the other beginning further down highway 93A. The shorter hike around the lakes is about five kilometres; from the town, add 10 km each way.

CAMPING

Overnight backpacking/camping hikes range from one-day trips (Watchtower Basin, Jacques Lake) to seven-day trips (the old Athabasca Pass) and should not be attempted casually. Three camping options are available in Jasper's backcountry: semi-primitive campgrounds, located in more heavily used areas where trails are better maintained, river crossings are bridged and campgrounds provide tables, tent pads, privies and fire boxes; primitive campgrounds, located in more isolated areas where trails are less frequently maintained, there are fewer bridges, trail signs and markers, and campgrounds provide only bear poles, pit privies and fire boxes; and wild areas where there are no trails, campgrounds or any other facilities. In remote regions, random camping is permitted but campfires are not allowed. Expert navigational skills are required to venture into these areas.

ATHABASCA PASS

Because of the threat of bears, campers should endeavour to keep campsites clean and free of food, garbage, coolers, cooking equipment or utensils. Some campgrounds provide bear poles, which are special cables or poles from which you can hang food and garbage high above the

TAKING THE PLUNGE

ground, where it will not prove to be a powerful draw for bears.

If there are no bear poles, lock food in the trunk of your vehicle or hang it four metres or higher from the ground and a metre from any side support such as a tree trunk. Choose a tree that is at least 90 metres downwind from your campsite sleeping area. Do not cook or eat in or near your tent. Clean utensils and put garbage in containers immediately after eating. Do not get food smells on your clothing or sleeping bag — sleep in clothing different from what you wear for cooking.

A Wilderness Pass, available at park information centres, is required to camp in the backcountry and safety is your own responsibility. To protect the environment and prevent overcrowding, quotas are maintained on most trails and campsites, so book early to avoid disappointment. The season for backcountry hiking and camping usually runs from mid-May to mid-October. If you have never lugged a heavy pack up a mountain trail before, you should probably consider a few short practise trips to build up experience and endurance. Remember, too, that differences in elevation and climate can affect your performance. Choose alternate trails or routes in case you need to change your plans due to adverse trail conditions.

For those who want to experience nature but aren't ready for the endurance test of backcountry hiking and camping, Parks Canada operates 10 campgrounds with a total of 1,772 sites in Jasper National Park. Reservations can be made for Pocahontas, Whistler's, Wapiti and Wabasso campgrounds on the Internet at www.pccamping.ca or by calling 1-877-737-3783. No other park campgrounds take reservations — campsites are available on a first-come, first-serve basis only and demand is heaviest between June and September. Serviced or "hook-up" sites are very limited in Jasper National Park and are only available at Whistler's and Wapiti campgrounds. Showers are available in Whistler and Wapiti campgrounds only. There are wheelchair-accessible sites in Whistler's, Pocahontas and Wabasso campgrounds. The only winter campground is Wapiti.

POCAHONTAS TRAIL

SKIING JASPER

RANDY WILLIAMS

MARMOT BASIN

Because Jasper is several hours from the closest major airport, it sneaks under the international radar for jet-setting resort spots. That's exactly what makes it a dream of a ski destination! At Marmot Basin, crowds of "beautiful people" haven't yet invaded, and the risk of standing in a long lift line is virtually non-existent.

As of 2005, Marmot Basin has a lift capacity of nearly 12,000 people per hour — but a typical snow season finds only 3,000 to 4,000 people on the slopes all day. There are nine lifts in all — one high speed quad, one quad chair, one triple chair, three double chairs, one T-bar, one platter and one Magic Carpet. A small snow-making machine blows a bit of white stuff at the base of the mountain when the season begins each fall, but man-made snow accounts for less than 1 per cent of Marmot's impressive powder. The mountain air is invigorating and the scenery spectacular. Marmot is located about 23 km southeast of Jasper, on Highway 93A. All "Ski Jasper" affiliated hotels have shuttle service to the chalets.

Marmot Basin offers a level of skiing for everyone, regardless of experience. The hill recently added several new runs — primarily advanced terrain, featuring some of the best adventure skiing and glade skiing in the Rockies — for a total of 84 named trails spread over more than

MARMOT BASIN

1,675 acres. Approximately 30 per cent are for novices, 30 per cent for people with intermediate skills and 40 per cent for experts. Various levels of runs can be reached from most of the lifts, so skiers of different abilities can enjoy a pleasant day together.

Marmot Basin operates three separate lodges on the mountain. Built in chalet style, the Paradise, the Eagle and the Caribou can accommodate all hungry skiers and tired après-skiers for meals and relaxation while on the mountain. There are lessons, ski and snowboard rentals, a daycare, mountain tours and group rates. And, as a yummy side note, all of the dining accommodations at Marmot are managed by the world-famous food service team from Jasper Park Lodge.

February is widely considered to be the best month for snow at Marmot Basin, but you might want to consider booking a ski trip a month earlier to take advantage of the annual "Jasper in January" festival. Visitors during the festival period can look forward to reduced rate lift tickets and special deals on lodging and other aspects of their vacation. The festival begins with a parade through Jasper townsite, followed by two weeks of events — both in Jasper and on the mountain — which typically include a snow sculpture contest, a chili cook-off and the Great Toboggan Race. Be forewarned, however, that January is usually the coldest month of the year.

SNOWBOARDING AT MARMOT

The longest "official" run at Marmot — from the top of the highest chair lift to the very bottom of the hill — is 5.6 km, or almost 800 vertical metres down. But if you hike to the absolute top of the mountain — an elevation of 2,600 metres — you can ski more than 900 vertical metres down to the bottom. Probably the most famous and challenging run at Marmot Basin is Charley's Bowl. The run has an astonishingly steep pitch somewhere between 45 and 50 degrees. The run is named after Charley Dupres, who died in an avalanche here many years ago. Other popular runs are Eagle East, Knob Peak and the High Traverse.

NORDIC NEAR MARMOT

NORDIC

Downhill skiing isn't the only game in town. There are over 200 km of cross-country trails in the Jasper area. The Tonquin Valley, just to the south and east of Jasper, is especially beautiful and is quite accessible. The silence of cross-country skiing in the pristine wilderness is an incredible experience. Even though many animals will be hibernating, you might want to invest in a bear-bell. Skiers can come upon animals too silently, and surprising a wild animal is in no one's best interest. If you don't intend to bring your own equipment, there are various places to rent whatever you require in the townsite.

MIETTE HOT SPRINGS

RANDY WILLIAMS

Turn-of-the-century bathers who wanted to experience the steamy, mineral-rich waters of the Fiddle Valley had to make a strenuous 17-kilometre trip by foot or on horseback. Modern travellers, on the other hand, can enjoy a pleasant drive up a winding road with spectacular views. Bighorn sheep are frequently spotted on the road, and when traffic is light, you might even see a black bear or two. The turnoff for the hot springs is 44 kilometres from Jasper townsite on Highway 16. The Miette Hot Springs Road is well paved, but also winding and narrow. Buses are permitted, but trailers and wide vehicles are advised not to use the road.

You should allow 60 minutes of driving time from the townsite; navigating the Miette Hot Springs Road takes 30 minutes and sometimes more due to traffic. Many people enjoy a swim or hike of one to two hours in duration, so a visit to the springs area can be accomplished in a long half-day. The best time to drive up to the hot springs is in the morning or late afternoon, when the road is least congested and the pool is quietest. There is a large picnic area near the facility and a café close to the pool, as well as a very good full-service restaurant in the adjacent Miette Hot Springs Bungalows.

The first park facility at the Miette Hot Springs, comprising a concrete pool and bathhouse, was built as a

ROCHE MIETTE (TOP); PUNCHBOWL FALLS (INSET)

Depression-era unemployment relief project between 1934 and 1938. A new multimillion dollar facility was built in 1986, approximately one kilometre from the original building. The natural springs, the hottest in the Canadian Rockies, produce water that must be cooled from a scalding 54° C to a soothing 39° C before being pumped into the pools at the Miette bathhouse. The facility includes two hot pools (one of which is fully accessible with a wheelchair ramp into the water), a cool pool that seems to be popular mostly with kids, and a poolside café, all of which afford breathtaking views of the scenic Fiddle Valley and the spectacular Ashlar Ridge.Visitors can rent swimsuits, towels and lockers, and warm showers are plentiful.

MIETTE HOT SPRINGS

From mid-May through the third week of June, the hot springs are open from 10:30 a.m. until 9 p.m. During peak season, from the end of June through Labour Day long weekend, the hours are 8:30 a.m. until 10:30 p.m. After Labour Day and on through the Canadian Thanksgiving long weekend, the hours are again 10:30 a.m.until 9 p.m. The hot springs — and the road up to them — are closed over the winter.

Several scenic hiking trails, ranging in length from 1.5 km to 40 km, are located in the vicinity of the Miette Hot Springs. One hike leads visitors through what's left of the old bathhouse. If you continue on past the ruins, you can see several locations where the hot mineral water bubbles up from the ground. Be careful: the high sulphur content of this untreated water makes it smell like rotten eggs, and it can be hot enough to cause burns.

Because this remote location is so peaceful, scenic and relaxing, you may want to consider staying at Miette. The adjacent bungalows are not exactly world-class accommodations on the order of Jasper Park Lodge, but they're charming in their own rustic way. They overlook the gorgeous Ashlar Ridge and the Fiddler Valley, are within walking distance of the hot springs, and offer easy access to all of the hiking trails in the area. There are ten cabins, all big enough to sleep most families, with kitchen units and fireplaces.

Several outlying buildings offer motel units with or without kitchenettes. Rooms have televisions, and guests have access to a playground, coin-operated laundry facilities and a barbecue pit with picnic tables. There is a fully licensed restaurant, where the staff is friendly and the food — steaks, pizza, Greek food, salads and other basic fare — is quite good. Lastly, the bungalow office features the inevitable souvenir shop and a smallish selection of groceries and other necessities, from firewood to toothpaste. Reservations are a must and can be booked at (780) 866-3750 during the facilty's six months of annual operation. The bungalows open in mid-May and close after the Canadian Thanksgiving long weekend (during which the restaurant offers a traditional Thanksgiving dinner).

JASPER EXCURSIONS

RANDY WILLIAMS

JASPER PARK COLLIERIES AND POCAHONTAS

Several other attractions are worth visiting but require more time to reach. At the base of Miette Hot Springs Road, visitors can explore the remains of a once-thriving mining town. Jasper Park Collieries came into being in 1908 when two prospectors staked claims at the foot of Roche Miette. Within two years, a major mining operation called Pocahontas was producing bituminous coal for railway steam engines and the nation's emerging industries. At the beginning of World War I, more than 50 families called Pocahontas home. Wartime demand for coal spurred production to an all-time high, and the company soon opened the Miette Mine across the Athabasca River near Bedson Ridge.

Before long, however, the war sealed the little mining town's fate. East of Pocahontas, the tracks of the old Grand Trunk Pacific Railway line were pulled up and sent to France for use in the war effort. Coal shipments now had to go west to Jasper before returning eastward along the old Canadian Northern line. The high cost of transport led to the mine's closure in 1919. Within two years, Pocahontas was a ghost town. Visitors can experience this history

131

by following an interpretive trail through the remaining ruins. They can reach scenic viewpoints from a series of foot trails and highways, and the Punchbowl Falls are just up a nearby hill. For those who would like a bit more information and guidance, the Friends of Jasper National Park offer a summertime interpretive hike that explores the remains of Pocahontas every Saturday during July and August at 2 p.m. There are also quaint bungalows for rent and a campground nearby that features flush toilets but no showers or hookups.

MALIGNE LAKE ROAD

A great day trip can be had on the Maligne Lake Road, from which one can see Hanging Valley Viewpoint, Maligne Canyon, Medicine Lake and Maligne Lake. Activities include

POKING ABOUT POCAHONTAS

sightseeing, walking, hiking, canoeing and whitewater rafting. The 46 km road, which is separated from the Banff/Jasper Highway by the rugged Maligne Range, follows the glacial valley separating this range from the neighbouring Queen Elizabeth Ranges. The H.J. Moberly Bridge, approximately five km east of Jasper townsite on Highway 16, will take you across the Athabasca River. From there, follow the signs to Maligne Road.

As you pass the road to Jasper Park Lodge, tune in your

MALIGNE CANYON

radio to AM 1490 (AM 1230 for a French-language broadcast) to hear a Parks Canada radio broadcast about early adventurers in this area. The drive will offer many opportunities for spotting wildlife including elk, moose, deer, bears, bighorn sheep and mountain goats. At kilometre six, a sign points left to a viewpoint. Take this exit to enjoy a panoramic vista of the Athabasca Valley, the townsite of Jasper, Pyramid Mountain, Whistlers Mountain and its tramway.

Maligne Canyon is approximately one kilometre farther along the road. Here, dazzling waterfalls plunge to depths of more than 50 metres through a steep limestone canyon. A one-kilometre round-trip interpretive trail winds its way from a picnic area across six bridges where you can feel the spray from the cascading Maligne River and gaze into the seemingly endless depths of the canyon. In winter, guided tours across the floor of the frozen canyon are available.

The next major attraction along Maligne Lake Road is Medicine Lake, a place of intrigue and aboriginal legend. Due to a unique underground drainage system in a network of underground caves, the water level of the lake varies from season to season; during the fall, it empties almost entirely. During the glacial runoff of summer, more than enough water is flowing into the lake from local streams to compensate for the drainage and Medicine Lake is in its full glory. But by September, the runoff has slowed to a trickle and the lake rapidly drains. The water resurfaces below Maligne Canyon, more than 17 kilometres downstream. Natives in the area once thought that spirits were responsible for the mysterious changes in these placid waters.

ICE CLIMBING IN MALIGNE CANYON

At road's end, you finally reach Maligne Lake, one of the most picturesque spots to be found anywhere in the Canadian Rockies. The lake was created when a landslide from the surrounding Opal Hills created a natural dam and caused the water to back up. At more than 22 kilometres, Maligne is the longest and the deepest lake in the Rockies and the second largest glacier-fed lake in the world. It is internationally famous for its deep azure colour and awe-inspiring views of the surrounding ranges. A one-and-a-half hour boat cruise takes visitors past glacier-pleated mountains to Spirit Island. Maligne Lake is a popular day-use area that offers superb fishing, canoeing, hiking, whitewater rafting and horseback riding in summer and cross-country skiing in winter. Although there are no overnight accommodations, the "Day Lodge" includes a gift shop and a restaurant offering light lunches, coffee, tea and fresh-baked breads, tortes, cookies and pastries.

MALIGNE RIVER

SUNWAPTA FALLS AND MOUNT ROBSON

Two final destinations, Sunwapta Falls and Mount Robson, are most often seen when visitors leave the park, either headed down the Icefields Parkway toward Banff (the falls) or over the Yellowhead Pass and into British Columbia (Robson). Sunwapta is a Stoney word meaning "turbulent river."

At the Sunwapta Falls, which are approximately 55 km south of Jasper townsite, the Sunwapta River abruptly changes course from northwest to southwest and cascades into a deep canyon. A good trail, which can be either hiked or biked, allows visitors to explore the nearby area or continue six kilometres on to Big Bend, 14 km to Athabasca Crossing or 25 km to Fortress Lake. Whitewater rafting on the Sunwapta River launches nearby. Seasonal accommodation, dining and picnic sites are available.

FORTRESS LAKE (ABOVE); WILDFLOWERS (INSET); BRITISH COLUMBIA (BOTTOM)

Located about an hour west of Jasper, Mount Robson Provincial Park is popular with backpackers and mountaineers. It's also a good place for canoeing, camping, day hiking and wildlife spotting. The mountain viewpoint on Yellowhead Highway 16 — complete with gas station, café, food and souvenir store, picnic site and telephone — is a good place for stretching your legs and using the bathroom facilities before embarking on the Coquilhalla, BC's swift toll highway to the coast.

Mount Robson is the highest peak in the Rocky Mountain chain, rising almost 4,000 metres from the

meadow base. Robson is considered a challenge for mountaineers from all over the world. Conquered first in 1913 by members of the Alpine Club of Canada, it is often a heart-breaker, as its history is dotted with failed and aborted climbs.

The Kain face, which is not visible from the highway side, includes a glacier and some precipitous cliffs. The dense blanket of clouds at the peak also makes for dangerous climbing. One must nearly circumnavigate the mountain to reach the peak; climbs last two or three days, with some snow and ice camping on the upper faces.

Various inns, motels, B&Bs and campgrounds can be found in and around nearby Valemount, B.C. If you are backcountry packing, rent or buy a "bear can" for your food and acquaint yourself with bear etiquette and safety guidelines. Register before you head in-country, and remember that most sites are first-come, first-served. The Berg Lake Trail, the most popular way in, is considered a two-day trek. Three front-country sites exist inside the park, and another (Emperor Ridge) is located outside — just 1,000 metres from the Yellowhead Highway viewpoint of Mount Robson.

EXPLORING EDMONTON

JANICE MACDONALD

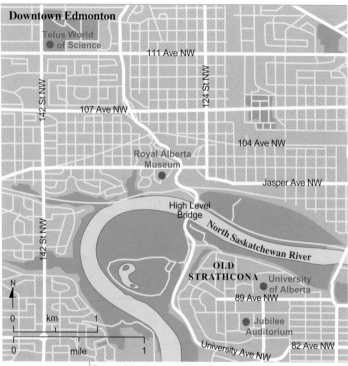

Downtown Edmonton

Telus World of Science
111 Ave NW
142 St NW
124 St NW
107 Ave NW
104 Ave NW
Royal Alberta Museum
Jasper Ave NW
High Level Bridge
North Saskatchewan River
142 St NW
OLD STRATHCONA
University of Alberta
89 Ave NW
Jubilee Auditorium
University Ave NW
82 Ave NW
N
0 km 1
0 mile 1

Located in the geographical centre of the province of Alberta, Edmonton is considered the most northerly major metropolis in Canada. It is home to world-class symphony, ballet and opera companies, more theatres per capita than anywhere else in the country, hockey, football and baseball teams, and a series of festivals that keep most Edmontonians in town through the summer. It's easy to see why so many visitors to Edmonton find a way to return time and again…or permanently. Air travellers arrive from the Edmonton International Airport, located 15 minutes to the south. Many visitors arrive from Calgary, travelling north along the

EDMONTON SKYLINE

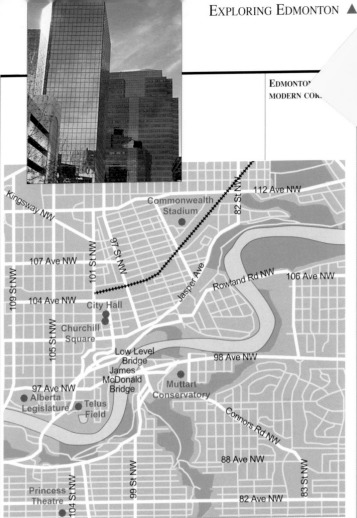

Queen Elizabeth II Highway (formerly Highway 2), often en route to the Alaska Highway. The Yellowhead Highway links Edmonton, the capital of Alberta, to Saskatoon to the east and Jasper to the west.

Nestled in aspen parkland, Edmonton is bisected by the North Saskatchewan River, and the entire river valley and adjacent ravines are designated park area. The foresight of city planners means that Edmonton has more connected green area than any city in North America, including New York's Central Park and Boston's Ribbon of Green. Trails connect the parks, and it is not unusual to see joggers, cyclists, walkers and inline skaters sharing the river valley in the milder months. In the winter, they trade in their wheels for cross-country skis.

CYCLING IN THE VALLEY

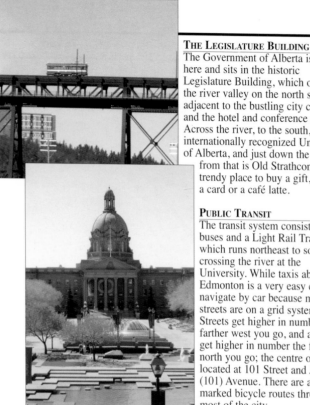

THE LEGISLATURE BUILDING

The Government of Alberta is located here and sits in the historic Legislature Building, which overlooks the river valley on the north side, adjacent to the bustling city centre and the hotel and conference area. Across the river, to the south, is the internationally recognized University of Alberta, and just down the road from that is Old Strathcona, the trendy place to buy a gift, a book, a card or a café latte.

PUBLIC TRANSIT

The transit system consists of buses and a Light Rail Transit, which runs northeast to southwest, crossing the river at the University. While taxis abound, Edmonton is a very easy city to navigate by car because most streets are on a grid system. Streets get higher in number the farther west you go, and avenues get higher in number the farther north you go; the centre of town is located at 101 Street and Jasper (101) Avenue. There are also well-marked bicycle routes through most of the city.

LIGHT RAIL TRACK OVER DOWNTOWN EDMONTON (TOP); ALBERTA LEGISLATURE (ABOVE) AND MUTTART CONSERVATORY (BELOW)

WEST EDMONTON MALL

Serious shoppers are going to want to see West Edmonton Mall, which is cunningly located in the west end of Edmonton. Curious questers and science buffs will be delighted to experience the Royal Alberta Museum and the Telus World of Science (formerly the Odyssium). Plant lovers will revel in the pyramids of the Muttart Conservatory and the Devonian Botanical Gardens. The historically minded can head to Fort Edmonton Park or the Ukrainian Cultural Heritage Village, pausing to see the bison in Elk Island National Park. For visitors, Edmonton is a city for all seasons. Festival season begins at the end of June; fall weather and foliage is glorious; and the blue skies and access to the mountains make winter vacations a brilliant adventure.

A FUR TRADING POST GROWS UP

JANICE MACDONALD

THE FUR TRADE & GOLD RUSH

In the 17th, 18th and early 19th centuries, the fur of the lowly beaver was prized for making the top hats so popular in Europe. Fur traders realized that it was efficient to build fur-trading forts and posts near where the Native trappers lived. After 1821, when the North West Company and the Hudson's Bay Company (HBC) merged, Fort Edmonton became the centre of a fur-trading region that stretched from the United States border to as far north as it was possible to go, and was bordered on the west by the Rocky Mountains.

Fort Edmonton was responsible for making the shallow-draft inland cargo boats known as York boats and for supplying the HBC traders with pemmican (dried buffalo meat), as well as for trading with the local Cree and Blackfoot tribes. Today's Fort Edmonton Park is not situated on any of the four or five original sites for Fort Edmonton, but is a life-sized replica of the fort as it appeared in the late 1840s. Alberta's Legislature Building sits on the land where the actual Fort Edmonton last stood.

FORT EDMONTON PARK

ARCHWAY TO historic OLD STRATHCONA

139

JOHN WALTER'S HOUSE

WAYNE GRETZKY STATUE

In the 1890s, gold was discovered in the Klondike region of the Yukon, and Edmonton became the southern provisioning post for those with gold fever hoping to strike it rich. People today think of it as the "Gateway to the North" — starting point of the Alaska Highway for those who are seeking great scenery and adventure.

STRATHCONA

The mighty North Saskatchewan River, which was the highway for the early fur traders, formed the boundary between the two small rival towns of Edmonton and Strathcona, which later joined to become the city of Edmonton. Several bridges now connect the south side of the city with the north, but once upon a time, the only way across meant using the ferry run by John Walter. This prominent citizen's original home is a historic site and can be found next to the Walterdale Bridge. Other important people have also been commemorated by the naming of buildings, parks and neighbourhoods (e.g. Frank Oliver, George MacDougall and Laurent Garneau). Edmonton, however, was named after the English hometown of Hudson's Bay Governor George Simpson. Strathcona commemorates the lord who is most famous for hammering in the last spike of the Canadian Pacific Railway.

OIL & DINOSAURS

In 1947 oil was found at the well known as Leduc #1, and the boom began. The oil industry is now one of the mainstays of the Alberta economy. Where there is oil, there are usually dinosaur fossils. Some of the greatest finds have turned up in Alberta, and some significant fossils have emerged from the clay of the North Saskatchewan River valley. A replica of a friendly Edmontosaurus can be found in the Royal Alberta Museum, next to Edmontonia, a small ankylosaur.

SPORTS

Edmonton has long been known as the City of Champions. In football, the Edmonton Eskimos have often won the prestigious Grey Cup; in hockey, the Edmonton Oilers (under the captaincy of Wayne Gretzky) won the Stanley Cup a record five times in seven years; in baseball, the former Edmonton Trappers took the Pacific League pennant various times. A lacrosse team and AA baseball team are now on board, and the Alberta and Canadian champion curlers led by Randy Ferbey are based here, as are many Olympic and world-class athletes. Edmonton has hosted the Commonwealth Games, the World Universiade Games and the 2001 World Track and Field Games, as well as a myriad of other sporting events.

SHOPPING

JANICE MACDONALD

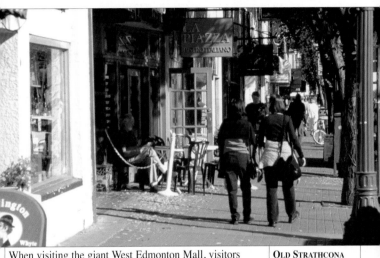

When visiting the giant West Edmonton Mall, visitors should wear their most comfortable shoes, because walking on marble and concrete can be very tiring. Comparison shopping works well here, because almost every major retail chain is represented; some of the chains have two or three stores in the complex. When the urge to shop begins to wane, visitors can find plenty of coffee bistros and restaurants dotted throughout the mall.

OLD STRATHCONA

For a different kind of shopping experience, visitors can head to Old Strathcona, famed for its trendy little boutiques and one-of-a-kind stores. Funky shoes, beads, knick-knacks, t-shirts, books, cards, independent label CDs, antiques, duvets, vintage clothing, small designer clothing, natural and organic foods, ethnic groceries, bakeries, tarot readings, and exotic pets can all be found here. In the summer months, street salesfolk will braid your hair, henna your palm or serenade you. Old Strathcona runs along Whyte (82 Avenue) for about six blocks, and is two to three blocks wide. There's a full afternoon's browsing here, and you can cap it off on either end with lunch or an early supper at one of the many great restaurants in the area. If you visit on Saturday

OLD STRATHCONA

MERCHANDISE ON WHYTE AVE.

141

ART IN THE GALLERY DISTRICT

morning, be sure to arrive early and visit the Strathcona Farmers Market, where you will find everything from fresh flowers to Quillows. If you're looking for unique gift ideas, look no further.

THE GALLERY DISTRICT

Where Jasper Avenue curves on its westernmost access, at 124th St., is known unofficially as the Gallery District. Several times in the year there is a gallery walk and you can sample hors d'oeuvres as you go from one gallery to the next. Many well-known artists are represented here, and some great new artists can be discovered.

DOWNTOWN

The downtown core has been built with occasional inclement weather in mind. If you want to stay indoors, you can shop from Edmonton Centre, through to Eaton Centre, and continue into Manulife Place. The Bay and Holt Renfrew are two of the larger stores on this route, with representatives of upmarket chains between them. Often there will be entertainment from some of the city's finest musicians, making shopping a multi-sensory pleasure. A farmer's market is available on sunny weekends between May and October, on 104th Street, between 102 and 103 Avenues. In inclement weather, they move into the Revillon Building next door.

Edmonton is known for its reading public and its fine bookstores. Audrey's Books is located downtown, right on Jasper Avenue. Greenwoods Books is in Old Strathcona. Laurie Greenwood's Volume II is in the 124th Street Gallery District. A rather pleasant Indigo Books is situated with other big box stores in South Edmonton Common on the outer reaches of the city, and most malls have a Chapters or a Coles. Think about purchasing a local book for a souvenir. Alberta has more than its share of award-winning writers, for both adults and children. Several wonderful second-hand bookstores are also found here, among them the Edmonton Book Store, Athabasca Books and The Wee Book Inn.

Another distinctly western purchase would be Saskatoon preserves or syrup. Some of the best places to shop are Debaji's Groceries and the SunTerra Market, where the foodstuffs are laid out as beautifully as in a Cézanne still life. Both have eat-in areas, which is a good thing, since no matter what the time of day, a visit to either will make your mouth water.

THE BAY

TOP ATTRACTIONS

JANICE MACDONALD

FORT EDMONTON PARK

Nestled in the river valley next to the Quesnel Bridge, Fort
Edmonton Park celebrates the history of Edmonton,
starting with its roots in the fur trade. The fort is a life-
sized replica of the building as it appeared in 1848, when
John Rowand was chief factor, and shortly after a visit by
the celebrated artist Paul Kane. A steam train takes visitors
to the fort, and from there they walk forward through
history. After passing through the fort and Native
settlement, they find themselves on 1885 Street, where
historic buildings and replicas line the dirt road. Turning
the corner onto 1905 Street, they can see the trolley tracks
and other signs of municipal development. The post-war
period of 1920 Street takes visitors all the way back to the
train station where the visit started. There are interpreters
on hand in almost all the buildings, dressed in period
costumes and performing period chores while talking
about the history of the place. Visitors should allow
themselves a full day, and wear good shoes and a hat.
Lunch is available at various restaurants on 1885 and 1905
Street. Overnight accommodation is available at the Hotel
Selkirk in the park.

WEST EDMONTON MALL

The West Edmonton Mall (WEM) was once listed in the
Guinness Book of World Records as the largest shopping
centre in the world. More than a kilometre long and three
blocks wide, it covers the equivalent of 48 city blocks. In
addition to the more than 800 shops and services, there is
an indoor amusement park; a five-acre indoor water park;

FORT EDMONTON

143

an NHL-sized ice rink, where visitors can skate, watch figure skating lessons, or catch an Edmonton Oilers practice; and a lagoon where visitors can see a sea lion show or a scale model of Columbus's Santa Maria, or go on a deep sea adventure in one of the four real submarines. There is also a bingo hall, a casino, a chapel, an 18-hole miniature golf course, a hotel (with theme rooms), 26 cinemas (including a 3-D Imax theatre), a fire-breathing dragon, bungee jumping, a dinner theatre, nightclubs, restaurants and six major department stores. WEM also has the largest parking lot in the world — and most Edmonton hotels have shuttle services to the mall.

WEST EDMONTON MALL (TOP), POST OFFICE IN OLD STRATHCONA (RIGHT)

OLD STRATHCONA

Once the main street of the town known as Strathcona, Whyte Avenue was left pretty much to itself after the inception of Edmonton as a city. Rediscovered in the mid-'70s and preserved with an eye to maintaining some of the important landmarks, it has become a trendy avenue of boutiques, restaurants, bistros and bookstores wedged in among long-established family businesses. Visitors can take in an indie film at the Princess Theatre, eat at one of the restaurants housed in the Old Post Office, window shop or be entertained by a busker. Old Strathcona is home to the popular Edmonton Fringe Theatre Festival in August, but is in vogue year round as a place to see and be seen.

PRINCESS THEATRE, OLD STRATHCONA

TELUS WORLD OF SCIENCE (FORMERLY, THE ODYSSIUM)

More than half a million people a year visit this hands-on museum and discovery space. The building was designed by Douglas Cardinal and is a work of art in itself. Inside the swirling shape is housed an IMAX

theatre, a planetarium star theatre with the most comfortable seats in the city, several galleries of space and science material, and two changing galleries for travelling exhibits. Visitors can watch people make comets and other science demonstrations, have their pictures taken as space-walking astronauts or aliens, examine forensic evidence in a police investigation, or race some of the fastest animals in the world. Numerous adventures await the visitor. In the evening, visitors can join stargazers at the observatory (southeast on the grounds), free of charge.

TELUS WORLD OF SCIENCE

THE ROYAL ALBERTA MUSEUM

Just west of the downtown core, perched on the north bank of the river, is one of the most popular museums in Canada. The focus is divided evenly between natural and human history. On May 24, 2005, it was designated the Royal Alberta Museum by Her Majesty Queen Elizabeth II.

On the main floor to the right is Wild Alberta, where visitors can find a dynamic presentation of renowned life-size dioramas of animals indigenous to the province. The lower left gallery is reserved for travelling and special exhibits. Upstairs, to the left, is the lavish and thought-provoking Syncrude Gallery of Aboriginal Culture, which takes visitors from the earliest time of humans in the area through to both the celebrations and the tragedies of contemporary Native Canadians. The Natural History Gallery, upstairs to the right, features geology displays, a dinosaur room, the Bug Room where visitors can get down with the creepy crawlers, and a collection of birds and beasts of Alberta.

Film society films and scholarly lectures are also organized in the Museum Theatre, to the right of the foyer. There is a restaurant in the museum, a good gift shop, and plenty of places to sit and rest. The Provincial Archives are attached to the museum building.

COUGAR EXHIBIT AT THE ROYAL ALBERTA MUSEUM

The sandstone building across from the entrance to the museum is Alberta House, where governmental entertainments are conducted. Tours are not usually available.

THE ALBERTA LEGISLATURE

The Legislature Building offers free and informative tours several times daily. When the government is in session, a chamber or two may be out of bounds, but most of the building is open to the public. Visitors can see Alberta's original mace built of toilet floats and odds and ends; the shower spot, where an aural illusion allows you to hear the rotunda fountain as if it were water flowing on your head; the paintings of former premiers and lieutenant-governors, and the

ALBERTA LEGISLATURE

palm trees sent as a gift from the state of California. The stained glass windows were unveiled during the 2005 royal visit of Queen Elizabeth II. The grounds, including the reflecting pool and the northern fountain gardens, are also worth a walkabout. The southern lawns are a favourite place for wedding photos in the summertime and for skating in the winter.

THE ARTS DISTRICT

The centre of the city around Sir Winston Churchill Square (itself the location of various festivals and events) has been dubbed The Arts District, and for good reason. Here visitors will find City Hall, which lends its central foyer to choral events, readings and community gatherings; and its outdoor reflecting fountain to winter skating and summer splashing.

If you think of City Hall as twelve o'clock on the clock face that is Churchill Square, then the Art Gallery of Alberta can be found at two o'clock. It has a good collection of the Group of Seven, a very decent modern collection, a hands-on children's gallery that makes everyone happy, and fascinating touring collections. All the teak found in the building was harvested from one tree. A new gallery is presently in the works.

ART GALLERY OF ALBERTA (RIGHT); CHURCHILL SQUARE (BELOW)

THE EDMONTON ART GALLERY

art is for everyone

At four o'clock is the Francis Winspear Centre for music, considered one of the finest and most acoustically perfect concert halls in North America. Check what is playing, and go no matter what it is, the hall itself is worth seeing, but everything sounds better in the Winspear.

Five o'clock on the Arts District clock belongs to the Citadel Theatre, the largest theatre complex in Canada, which houses three theatres and a cinema, a theatre school, bookstore, restaurant and bar, as well as the Lee Pavilion tropical garden, a place where it's easy to remember that winter doesn't last forever.

At six o'clock is the

Stanley Milner Library, the main branch of the Edmonton Public Library system. And at nine o'clock you will find the City Centre Mall, which houses the CBC broadcasting centre, a three-level shopping mall, several business towers and two hotels attached. A complex system of overpasses and underground walkways connects most of downtown Edmonton, and this is one of the starting points.

WINSPEAR CENTRE

THE MUTTART CONSERVATORY

The four pyramids seem like an anomaly in this northern city. They were not built as a tribute to Ahkenaten, but to house Edmonton's horticultural conservatory. Nestled in the river valley, three of the pyramids contain separate climates: arid, temperate and tropical. The fourth is reserved for rotating shows: spring bulbs, orchids, and Japanese gardens. In the centre of the pyramids are a sunny tearoom and gift shop. There are benches in all the pyramids; locals find the conservatory a nice place in which to take a break, especially in the winter months.

THE RIVER VALLEY

The river valley system includes two ski hills, six golf courses, one driving range, 29 day campsites, an equine centre, two outdoor pools, 70 staircases, 95 viewpoints, six toboggan hills, and 63 bridges. If you include the ravines in the system, you can add to these an overnight campsite, another ski hill, off-leash dog parks, and miles of walking, cross-country skiing, biking, and general-purpose trails.

MUTTART CONSERVATORY

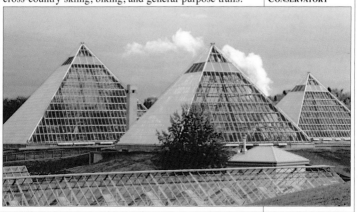

DINING

JANICE MACDONALD

FINE ALBERTA DINING

HIGH LEVEL DINER AND CREPERIE (BELOW)

In Edmonton, it is possible to dine out on any budget.

EXCLUSIVE

To mark a very special occasion (or if money is no object), the urge for the best of Alberta beef can be satisfied downtown at Hy's Steak Loft. The décor is stylish Art Deco, the service is magnificent and the food is sublime. The beef in Alberta is grain fed, as opposed to the corn-fed beef of the U.S., so there is a distinct difference in taste. Jack's Grill is equally wonderful, and a hotly guarded southside Edmonton secret. It's intimate, with delightful idiosyncratic design, and the food is nouvelle cuisine in presentation but generous in amount. The menu changes regularly and the specials are a treat. Another gustatory treat, coupled with fantastic scenery, is La Ronde, the rotating restaurant atop the Chateau Lacombe. One of the newest and best of Edmonton's restaurants is The Hardware Grill. It has appeared in a heritage building that used to be Edmonton's premier hardware store, the W. W. Arcade. To commemorate the landmark, hammers for door handles and other idiosyncratic décor abound. The food aims to create international stylings of indigenous ingredients: venison, salmon and, of course, Alberta beef. The service is superb; this is the home of the server voted Edmonton's best several times running.

AFFORDABLE

A more regularly affordable attraction is the High Level
Diner, found near the bridge of the same name.
Consistently voted the best for vegetarian food, the
restaurant offers enough variety to satisfy a carnivorous
palate as well. This is also a fantastic place for
breakfast, late-afternoon coffee and people-watching
from the terrace. Interesting local art changes regularly
on the walls. Along the same lines is The Upper Crust,
located two blocks away and now featuring a new
space for literary readings. Catering is also available.
Packrat Louie's is a trendy place to meet to eat in the
heart of Old Strathcona, and, if you're downtown, East
Bound provides a nice mix of sushi and western cuisine
offered amid serene décor.

INTIMATE

For intimate dinners, The Creperie has long been an
outstanding restaurant, while The Red-Ox Inn is also
perfect for that special date. Reserve here ahead of
time, since seating is limited.

ETHNIC

Edmonton has a wide
variety of ethnic
restaurants. The Mirama
downtown offers Chinese
dim sum on weekend
mornings. The Happy
Garden in Parkallen serves
up terrific Sichuan cuisine.
Vietnamese food, great
service and the best lunch
deal in town can be found
at Bach Dang, on the edge
of Old Strathcona. The
Fantasia Noodle House on
Jasper Avenue has a daily

PACKRAT LOUIE'S
(ABOVE); THE
CREPERIE (BELOW);
BARB AND ERNIE'S
(BOTTOM)

149

lunch special that will hold you long past suppertime. Dining at the Mikado, either at the sushi bar or in one of the private rooms, is consistently fine. Julio's Barrio offers Baha Mexican fare. The Sherlock Holmes pub has a wide selection of beers, and a menu of scotch eggs, steak and kidney pie and ploughman's luncheons. The Bulgogi House has long satisfied the urge for Korean cuisine, although there are now plenty of competitors. Grub Med, found in a small neighbourhood strip mall, is one of the best Greek restaurants this side of Athens. New Asian Village's South Indian lunch buffet offers plenty of selection. The entrance to Sceppa's Pizza is, disarmingly, around the back, but a wonderful Italian feast awaits you inside. Then there's Barb and Ernie's, a German restaurant with a standard menu that includes wild boar and the best rouladen and spätzle this side of the Harz Mountains. Ernie, who plays mein host with great verve and charm, makes sure all are welcome, and there is often a lineup for weekend brunches. If you're a fan of eggs Benedict, you'll understand why.

SHERLOCK HOLMES PUB (TOP); BILLINGSGATE FISH MARKET (ABOVE)

OTHER

Lunch at Colonel Mustard's and you'll feel like you've been transported into the kitchen of a cook who really cares for you. Located near the museum and the gallery district, the restaurant serves great soups, sandwiches and hearty desserts. Max's Light Cuisine offers new vegetarian entrees every day for lunch and early diners. The Old Spaghetti Factory is always a favourite, with locations both downtown and in West Edmonton Mall. Any of the Earl's, Joey Tomato's and East Side Mario's restaurants offer a wide selection of good food.

FAST FOOD

If you're looking for fast food and haven't made up your mind, the shopping malls offer a variety of outlets in their food courts. Two of the best are at Southgate Centre and Kingsway Garden Mall. Joey's Only Seafood offers all-you-can-eat fish and chips on Tuesdays. You can eat in or take out at the lighthouse of the Billingsgate Fish Market. Tokyo Express offers very reasonable prices and quick service, as does its counterpart, Mongolian Express.

Col. Mustard's Sandwich Canteen
FRESH FOOD • CATERING • EAT IN • TAKE OUT

CITY OF FESTIVALS

JANICE MACDONALD

As the trees begin to bud, festival season starts, and it doesn't end until white shoes go back in the closet.

CHILDREN'S THEATRE FESTIVAL, JAZZ FESTIVAL AND THE WORKS

The International Children's Theatre Festival begins in May, featuring theatre troupes from around the world, while the Dreamspeakers Festival promotes and celebrates native arts. June kicks off what seems like one long, continually transforming festival. The Yardbird Jazz Festival and The Works Visual Arts Festival begin almost simultaneously in late June and slide into July. Jazz venues can be found all over town, large and small. Local galleries and downtown foyers and mezzanines help host the art works.

HERITAGE DAYS

NINE LIVES BY KEN MACKLIN (BELOW), AT THE WORKS VISUAL ARTS FESTIVAL

STREET PERFORMERS
FESTIVAL

KLONDIKE DAYS

STREET PERFORMERS FESTIVAL

As you hear the last wailing note from a saxophone, the Street Performers Festival takes up residence in Sir Winston Churchill Square. Come prepared with plenty of loonies and toonies ($1 and $2 coins) in your pockets, as the jugglers, clowns, fire-eaters, and buskers pass the hat after each performance.

KLONDIKE DAYS

Klondike Days, the grandaddy of Edmonton summer festivals, takes place in mid-July, with a trade show from a visiting country, an enormous midway of rides, games of chance and cotton candy at the fairgrounds, and varied events (raft races, beard growing, bathtub races, Sunday Promenade) both downtown and about town. Celebrating the 1890s, when Edmonton was the gateway to the Yukon gold rush, every bar becomes a saloon for ten days, and your bank teller might be dressed as a dance hall girl while your waiter looks for all the world like a card shark. Take advantage of one of the myriad pancake breakfasts around town and enjoy Tom Thumb doughnuts as you stroll the midway.

HERITAGE DAYS

Heritage Days, celebrating the city's diverse multicultural mosaic, takes place the first weekend of August in Hawrelak Park and coincides with the annual civic holiday. Some 80 tents and stages and, most importantly, kitchens, are set up for two days of partying. Wear sunscreen, and if you don't bring a hat, buy a sombrero, beret, coolie hat, tam-o'-shanter or Stetson while you're there.

EDMONTON FOLK FESTIVAL

The Edmonton Folk Music Festival takes place in Gallagher Park, the river valley's natural amphitheater, and provides four nights and two full days of music in both workshop and concert form. Indulge your "inner hippie" and layer your clothing in order to enjoy both day and night temperatures. There are several stages, a beer tent, a craft tent, a kids' area, and great kiosks where you can rent a washable plate. You are welcome to bring your own food, but this is the best place to find elephant ears, a concoction of fried dough and sugar. Sunscreen, a water bottle and a hat are essential. This festival is rarely rained on. The sunsets over the city skyline add a light show to the evening concerts. Tickets go on sale June 1 each year, and are sold out well before the event, although you should pay attention to online message boards that the Festival maintains for people looking to buy and sell tickets.

If you're too late to get tickets to the Folk Fest, don't miss the colourful parade down Jasper Avenue of the Cariwest Festival, which also takes place that weekend. Churchill Square rings with the pitch of steel drum bands, making the summer evenings even hotter.

FRINGE FESTIVAL & OTHER EVENTS

The Fringe Theatre Festival is the place to be in mid-August. This event takes over the Old Strathcona district, closing one side street completely and creating theatres out of every spare space. Buy tickets in advance at a slight premium or risk lining up only to see "sold out" signs on popular shows. Buskers and other street entertainers round out the picture, which wouldn't be complete without green onion cakes with hot sauce on the side.

DETAIL FROM *BUFFALO TWINS* **BY LEWIS LAVOIE**

Symphony Under the Sky, the classical and contemporary music festival in the amphitheatre of Hawrelak Park, takes place during the five evenings over the Labour Day weekend, as a kind of grand finale to the summer of festivals. Come hear the 1812 Overture as it was meant to be heard — out of doors and complete with cannons.

The Edmonton International Film Festival revs up in October, bringing independent films and filmmakers from all over the world. Cinemas in several places in town host some great films and fascinating directors. Everyone from Bill Forsyth to John Waters has come to speak and schmooze.

On New Year's Eve, First Night takes place downtown both indoors and outdoors. It's a dry party with entertainments for all ages, complete with ice sculptures, a parade, mask-making, concerts and free transit for everyone wearing a First Night button. Dress warmly and take frequent indoor breaks.

FRINGE FESTIVAL

Excursions from Edmonton

Janice MacDonald

WINTER AT ELK ISLAND NATIONAL PARK (TOP) AND THE BOARDWALK (ABOVE)

ELK ISLAND NATIONAL PARK

Less than one hour's drive east of Edmonton is one of Canada's smallest national parks, Elk Island. Concerned residents have turned the island into a 500-square-kilometre refuge for elk. Elk Island is also home to about 400 head of plains bison, which are the animals you will see as you drive through the park and buffalo paddock. A smaller herd of wood bison is kept south of the highway on land that is not visitor accessible. The herds are isolated from each other to keep the two from mating, as they have done in Wood Buffalo National Park. All pure plains bison in North America (about 100,000 in parks and zoos) can be traced back to the 50 that remained on Elk Island out of an original 400 delivered by Montana ranchers.

Remember that bison and all other animals have the right of way in this park. The animals seem to think that the cross-country ski and hiking trails were built for them to wander on, and they can appear without warning. Most hikers and skiers wear bells. Bison are herbivores, but they are also territorial; their hooves are extremely sharp, and they can butt and trample you to death. While they can and

do turn up all over the park, in picnic sites and along walking trails, you can be assured of a sighting in the paddock, where various shaggy beasts are corralled specifically for viewing purposes. They don't much like the sandy beach area of Astotin Lake.

ELK ISLAND NATIONAL PARK

The combination of aspen parkland and boreal forest is a result of previous glaciation, which created a "knob and kettle" land formation. There are more than 250 lakes, marshes and wetlands found in the park. While low in oxygen, the lakes are very rich in nutrients, making them bird havens. There are more than 230 species of birds found in the park and 44 species of mammals.

UKRAINIAN CULTURAL HERITAGE VILLAGE (BELOW AND BOTTOM)

The mandate for this national park is one of accessible conservation. There are 60 kilometres of cross-country ski trails, a boardwalk nature trail, and a sandy beach on Astotin Lake for windsurfing, non-motor boating and sandcastle building. A campsite is nearby, and several group and individual picnic sites dot the area. A radio tour can be accessed by dialling in to the local frequency; it describes local flora and fauna to be observed, depending on the season. Another thing to see near Astotin Lake is a Ukrainian settler's house.

UKRAINIAN CULTURAL HERITAGE VILLAGE

If you find this intriguing, you'll enjoy a visit to the nearby Ukrainian Cultural Heritage Village. Open from May 15 until Labour Day, this historic open-air museum is a provincial heritage site. Role-playing interpreters can be found in all the buildings, demonstrating the hardships and triumphs of the Ukrainian settlers who came to the area between 1892 and 1930. The grounds can be covered in an afternoon, and a kiosk serving perogies and kielbasa is located near the entrance to the park. Visitors are also welcome to bring a picnic lunch, but no food can be taken into the park itself, which you reach by traversing a long wooden bridge.

THE REYNOLDS-ALBERTA MUSEUM

Located in nearby Wetaskiwin (Cree word for "hills of peace," although people now say jokingly that it stands for "town of many car dealerships") this

155

PART OF THE
COLLECTION OF THE
REYNOLDS-ALBERTA
MUSEUM

museum, which opened in 1992, is the byproduct of a lifetime of collecting by Stanley G. Reynolds, who was a car dealer in Wetaskiwin. He struck an agreement with the Alberta government, offering his vast collection of cars, trucks and farm vehicles if it would build a museum. The result is a fascinating visit through the history of the automobile and motor vehicles in general. The museum has many hands-on displays, and examples of how restoration is done. There is a cafeteria on site, and the adjoining Aviation Hall of Fame is worth a good half-day's jaunt. If you return via Highway 2A, Millet offers an opportunity to scrounge the antique shops and have an ice cream cone.

THE DEVONIAN BOTANICAL GARDENS

Established and maintained by the University of Alberta, the northern-most botanical garden in North America is found due west of the city, about 15 minutes out of town. Bring along a picnic lunch or buy it at the Bean in the Garden concession. There are more than 32 hectares of diverse gardens and another 44 hectares of preserved areas, so give yourself at least an afternoon to walk and explore. There are cinder trails and an extended concrete path for wheelchair and stroller ease. A complete Japanese garden, a butterfly house, a native garden, an alpine garden, an ancient herb garden and even a garden of poisonous plants are among the treats. The Devonian Botanical Garden is open from May until December, and many crafts and horticultural activities are scheduled. The ticket booth people will tell you what special things to look out for that day. The gift shop is a terrific place to purchase one-of-a-kind items for both souvenirs and thoughtful presents.

LACOMBE CHAPEL

FATHER LACOMBE CHAPEL

The city of St. Albert is five minutes north of Edmonton along the St. Albert Trail and is home to the oldest building in Alberta, Father Lacombe Chapel. The candles and incense in the simple log building evoke earlier, hardier times. Special events and demonstrations take place from May 15 through the summer months until Labour Day. Tours of the chapel and historic Mission Hill are given in English and French, in deference to the strong Métis community that founded the city of St. Albert.

DRUMHELLER & WATERTON

DRUMHELLER & THE BADLANDS

GILLIAN STEWARD

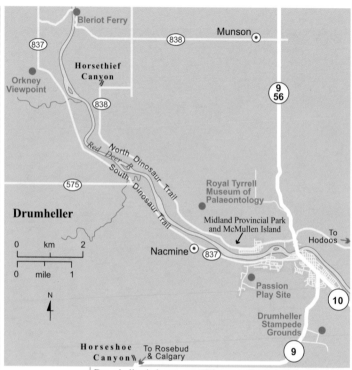

FOUNTAIN AT ROYAL TYRRELL MUSEUM

Drumheller is known as "Dinosaur Capital of the World," so history has a long reach here — about 225 million years. In the early days, the giant reptiles of the Triassic period roamed the area, living, birthing and dying in a huge, tropical swamp that has long since disappeared and been replaced by treeless prairie and deep, dry canyons of sculpted cliffs and bizarre rock formations. Fortunately, the descendants of those early dinosaurs left a lot of bones, eggs and other fossilized remains scattered across their former home. And it is this paleontology treasure trove that has put hardy Drumheller, about 150 kilometres northeast of Calgary, on the map.

HISTORY

Tucked in a canyon and strung along the Red Deer River, this town of almost 8,000 souls is named after

ATLAS MINE

Samuel Drumheller, a farmer, rancher and coal mine operator who arrived in the early 1900s from the United States. But that is relatively recent history. Before European and American settlers arrived, the area was home to the powerful Blackfoot Nation, one of the most revered Plains Indian tribes. The buffalo were plentiful then too. Explorer John Palliser wrote that the plains above the Red Deer River were "black with buffalo" when he passed through this area between 1857 and 1859.

Rich deposits of coal lured thousands of coal miners to the 139 mines in the valley, and although the last one closed in the 1950s, coal mining is still very much on the minds of older residents here. So much so that the Atlas Mine has been fully restored and turned into a tourist attraction. Alongside the coal mines, homesteaders seeking rich, fertile soil established grain farms in the region.

Cattle herds replaced the buffalo. After the coal mines closed, Drumheller found it had become a minor hub of oil and gas exploration. There is also a federal penitentiary located here.

But it was in 1985 when the Royal Tyrrell Museum opened just outside Drumheller that this town at the bottom of a canyon realized dinosaurs were its destiny. The town's new-found fame is evident everywhere you look. Sculptures and murals of dinosaurs dot streets and buildings. And where else would a Best Western Hotel be called the Jurassic Inn?

JURASSIC INN (BELOW); THE 150-FOOT T-REX (INSET)

EXPLORING DRUMHELLER

The town lies at the bottom of a wide, dry canyon slit through the middle by the muddy Red Deer River. It's a little green oasis of poplar and cottonwood trees where many of the town's original buildings still grace the main street. Elegant brick homes are interspersed with the smaller homes of former coal miners. And the world's largest dinosaur towers over everything. The dinosaur, a 150-foot T-Rex attached to the Visitors Information Bureau also offers the best view in town — if you're game enough to climb the 100 steps inside ($3 admission fee).

Once you've navigated the colourfully decorated insides of the roaring T-Rex, you'll be treated to an almost 360-degree view of the town, the river, the canyon walls that surround

159

it, and the wide, wide sky that rises from the tops of the canyons. Just across the street from the T-Rex, a large grassed park with a fountain and picnic tables provides the perfect rest stop. On the main street there are several stores that sell mementos and souvenirs. On your way to the Royal Tyrrell Museum you'll pass the Fossil Shop which sells fossils and other dinosaur-related items.

INSIDE THE FOSSIL SHOP (TOP); STAVROS FAMILY RESTAURANT (ABOVE)

There are several restaurants in Drumheller, including Stavros Family Restaurant and Fred and Barney's Family Restaurant. The Whistling Kettle, across from the big T-Rex, is famous for its pie. If you're planning to stay overnight, there are lots of B&Bs to choose from, as well as a Best Western Hotel, Travelodge and Super 8 Motel. RV parks and campgrounds are also available.

If you're looking for evening entertainment, check out the Rosebud Dinner Theatre in the Hamlet of Rosebud, a 25-minute drive southwest of Drumheller. Tickets include a delicious country buffet served in the historic Mercantile Building. Following the meal, guests walk to the Opera House to enjoy a lively theatrical performance. The Rosebud Theatre is open most of the year.

If you are visiting Drumheller during the first two weeks of July, take in the annual Passion Play. Now in its eighth year, this grand outdoor production brings together 150 amateur actors, 175 choristers and 700 volunteers from the community and surrounding area to work behind the

PASSION PLAY

scenes. The spectacle depicts the life and times of Jesus and takes place in a natural rock amphitheatre that seats 2,300. Reservations are a must since the Passion Play is usually sold out by May. Not surprisingly, Travel Alberta named the Passion Play one of the province's top cultural attractions.

THE ROYAL TYRRELL MUSEUM

Nestled amid the sculpted cliffs of the stark and imposing badlands just outside Drumheller, the Royal Tyrrell Museum looks as though it has been part of the landscape forever. But it is a relatively new museum, opened in 1985, that specializes in a relatively new science: the science of the dinosaur. Nevertheless, the Royal Tyrrell already houses the largest collection of dinosaur fossils to be found anywhere in the world.

Of course it helps that the Royal Tyrrell is located in the richest fossil beds in the world. But no one had any inkling of this rich resource until 1884, when geologist Joseph Burr Tyrrell made Canada's first important dinosaur find. He wasn't looking for dinosaurs but for coal in the Red Deer River Valley when he came across the partial skull of a huge animal later named Albertosaurus (meaning "reptile from Alberta"). A close relative of *Tyrannosaurus rex*, Albertosaurus was a large, flesh-eating dinosaur that thrived in the region some 75 million years ago.

We now know that 10 percent of all dinosaurs, in terms of species, come from Alberta. These "terrible lizards" left so many fossilized remains that Dinosaur Provincial Park, located about 200 kilometres southeast of the museum, has been designated a UN World Heritage Site. Alberta is also home to another important resource: Dr. Philip Currie, head of dinosaur research at the Tyrrell, is now recognized as the leading authority on prehistoric predators. In June 1990, Queen Elizabeth visited the museum and thought it was so terrific she bestowed the Royal designation.

As you approach the Royal Tyrrell, try to imagine the lush swamp that once covered the area and the huge beasts that inhabited it. Two hundred million years ago a *Tyrannosaurus rex* might have savagely killed prey with its six-inch dagger-like teeth right where you park your car in the Royal Tyrrell's ample parking lot. As you approach the entrance, three life-size replicas — including the ferocious

THE MUSEUM'S
T-REX

Albertosaurus — will greet you. Kids (and adults) love having their photo taken with these ancient monsters.

Once inside, you will enter the dinosaur gallery, which features dramatic lighting and colourful background murals. There are two rhino-like Chasmosaurs preparing to lock horns in a prehistoric face-off. The display of dinosaurs from the Jurassic Period (213–144 million years ago) begins with an eight-metre-long, armour-plated Stegosaurus, its deadly spiked tail poised to ward off predators. Nearby, its arch-enemy, a 12-metre-long predator called Allosaurus, attacks its prey while a long-necked giant called Camarasaurus feeds from the top of a tree, as it did some 140 million years ago.

Dinosaurs lived during the Mesozoic Era, which is divided into three periods: the Triassic (248–213 million years ago), the Jurassic (213–144 million years ago) and the Cretaceous (144–65 million years ago). The Royal Tyrrell's collection of Jurassic dinosaurs, most of which come from Montatna and Wyoming, is impressive, but its reputation rests on its Cretaceous fossils which were all discovered locally.

During the past decade we have become used to seeing life-sized replicas of dinosaurs and virtually real dinosaurs in movies and TV programs. So it's important to remember that the Royal Tyrrell is not a theme park but an internationally recognized research centre and fossil archive. You will see a lot of dinosaur skeletons, composed of replicated dinosaur bones since the fossilized bones are so heavy. And a lot of fossilized smaller creatures — everything from tiny insects to fish.

You will also be able to look through a wide picture

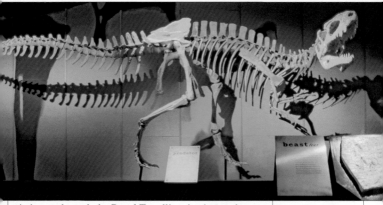

window and watch the Royal Tyrrell's scientists as they chip away at the latest fossils brought in from various digs in Alberta and other parts of the world. You can walk through the Paleoconservatory, which features more than 600 plants and trees that dinosaurs would have fed on. Who would have thought that harmless-looking potted fern in your living room was once a favourite dinosaur snack? If you're looking for something a little more whimsical, be sure and visit the Burgess Shale exhibit. In this imaginative diorama, you will feel as though you are underwater along with some bizarre little creatures that look as though they are straight out of a dream, but in fact thrived in the great sea that once covered Alberta.

For those who want more than the museum experience, consider a trip to the museum's field station in Dinosaur Provincial Park; or Royal Tyrrell's invitation to join day digs, weeklong digs, kids camps and other programs. It's a

DENIZEN OF THE MUSEUM

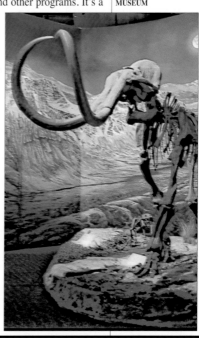

chance to get out in the field and work with the scientists as they search for dinosaur fossils. Programs are available for children as young as 4, as well as youth, adults and seniors. Some of the programs require reservations; for others you can simply sign up when you visit the museum.

The Royal Tyrrell is an engrossing museum, so plan to spend at least a day there. If you're heading out from Calgary it will take you about two hours by car. There's a well-stocked, large cafeteria at the museum and plenty of shaded picnic tables outside. The museum is open all year round, although hours vary depending on the season. During the winter months the museum is closed Mondays. Admission prices are: Adults, $10.00; seniors, $8.00; youth, $6.00; children six and under are free. Family passes are available for $30.

BADLANDS

Alberta's badlands can best be described as a miniature version of the Grand Canyon. Similar in appearance, they seem to have been carved out of the prairie itself, which is in fact the case. With the retreat of the last glaciers around 18,000 years ago, immense amounts of water were released to carve large and intricate drainage channels through the soft rock. Over time, these channels have been sculpted and molded by wind and water into the intricate, and almost eerie, landscapes we see today.

BADLANDS LANDSCAPE: AT NIGHT (TOP), AND HOODOOS (ABOVE)

Newcomers are never ready for the badlands. You're travelling across the flattest of prairies when the ground abruptly opens up into a wide, beautiful canyon. The badlands bring a little of the southern desert to the Alberta plains. In spring, the desert comes to life as the prickly pear and pincushion cactus explode into fiery yellow and red flowers. Since most of our badlands are located along river valleys, they form an oasis for local birds and wildlife. Pronghorn antelope and mule deer peer at you from a safe distance and an endless variety of birds roost in the trees lining the river.

Wander away from the shoreline and the climate quickly changes. The ground immediately dries and cracks. The plants eke out a tough existence in this wild and dry land. The landscape is stark — almost moonlike. In fact, one area of Dinosaur Provincial Park is known as the Valley of the Moon. You have stepped into a wondrous new world — a world that begs to be explored. Be cautious though! Many badlands, including the Drumheller and Dinosaur park areas, are underlain by a bentonite clay soil that swells and forms a completely frictionless surface when wet. In addition, the clay causes flash floods through this normally dry valley. Luckily, rainfall is rare in this near-desert area.

Unfortunately, the name "badlands" tends to drive away tourism. Who in their right mind, would want to visit an area described as "bad"? In reality, the badlands are an area of incredible beauty and stark character. The name "badlands" was actually a mistranslation of a French term used to describe similar areas — *mauvaises terres a traverser* or simply "bad lands to cross." This is a very apt description as the badlands are indeed difficult to cross by walking in a straight line. However, if you don't mind a meander, they provide endless opportunities for exploring.

WATERTON LAKES NATIONAL PARK

CHRIS MORRISON

Waterton Lakes National Park in the Canadian Rockies is renowned as a place where the mountains meet the prairies. Located in the southwest corner of Alberta, it features a combination of rich alpine terrain, woodlands, grasslands and aquatic environments all crammed into just 525 square kilometres.

The four main lakes, Upper, Middle and Lower Waterton and the Maskinogne, can all be seen from the comfort of an automobile. The 11-kilometre-long Upper Waterton Lake is the deepest in the Rocky Mountains at 148 metres.

PLANTS AND ANIMALS

Waterton's distinctive geographic features and biodiversity attract some 300,000 visitors a year — the majority of whom come in the summer months. Because Waterton receives more precipitation than anywhere else in the province, it boasts more plant life than either Banff or Jasper: 960 species of plants, including over 50 nationally rare plants.

Waterton is also home to over 250 species of birds and 60 species of mammals. And while the park is also the second

WATERTON NATIONAL PARK

BIG HORN SHEEP

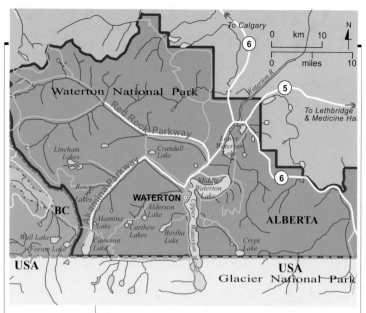

BEARGRASS

windiest place in the province (the Crowsnest Pass is first), this climate does not deter visitors from experiencing the mountain vistas, pine-scented air and magnificent lakes.

The diversity of the park gave rise to recognition in 1932 when, with adjacent Glacier National Park in Montana, the area became the world's first International Peace Park. Sixty-three years later, in 1995, the peace park was made a United Nations World Heritage Site in recognition of its outstanding global value.

Visitors can learn more about these designations in the park's townsite, just eight kilometres from the park's entry gate. It is almost impossible to get lost driving in the park. The road to the townsite must be retraced to exit the park, and the two main side roads — Red Rock Canyon Parkway and Akamina Parkway — must also be retraced.

CAMPGROUNDS

There are four front-country campgrounds in the park. Two campgrounds are in the town, from which a walk of a few minutes will get you to Upper Waterton Lake. The larger of these accommodates both tents and recreational vehicles; wheelchair-accessible toilet/shower facilities are provided. A number of camp kitchen/shelters located throughout the campground offer picnic tables and central stoves, with wood available for purchase at nearby stores.

The smaller campground, along the shore of Cameron Creek, accommodates only walk-in tenters, who must leave their vehicles in a nearby parking lot. Toilet/shower facilities are close at hand, as is a camp kitchen. Neither of the town's campgrounds provides protection from the wind, but their proximity to amenities such as a grocery store, liquor store, post office, movie theatre, restaurants, shops and an interpretive theatre make them attractive to many visitors.

If you hanker for a more rustic camping experience, two other campgrounds are available. Crandell

campground on Red Rock Canyon Parkway and Belly River campground off the Chief Mountain Highway offer more secluded and forested campsites for both tenters and RVs.

HIKING AND CAMPING

There are more than 160 kilometres of trails in the park. Some trailheads begin from the town; some require driving to access. Free maps of trail locations are available from the visitor information centre.

INDIAN PAINT BRUSH

The Bear's Hump trail, which begins behind the visitor information centre, is a steep but short (1.2 kilometre) climb which ends in spectacular views of the Waterton lakes and Glacier National Park. There are two wheelchair accessible trails. One circles the town along the lakeshore, leading to Cameron Falls before returning to the lake. The other is the Linnet Lake loop path, starting at the Middle Waterton lake boat launch. Interesting interpretive plaques are located along the way.

Allow a full day to experience one of the most popular and unusual trails, known as Crypt Lake. It begins at the town's marina, from which a boat takes hikers to the east side of Upper Waterton Lake. The trail climbs 8.7 kilometres to Crypt Lake, which can only be seen after crawling through a naturally-occurring 20-metre tunnel which passes through a sheer rock wall.

The Lakeshore and Bertha Lake trail also begins in the town. Hikers can branch off to Bertha Falls and Bertha lake, or continue south some 13 kilometres along the western shore of Upper Waterton Lake, across the international boundary to Goat Haunt in Glacier National Park.

RED ROCK CANYON

Since recently imposed conditions/restrictions may apply to those hiking across the international boundary, check at the visitor information centre before setting out. From Goat Haunt there are three options: return to Waterton by boat, with reservations recommended, especially during July and August; return on foot; or continue south more than 45 km to the Swiftcurrent Valley. Time spent waiting for the boat can be used to investigate the ranger station interpretive display and a peace park display at the boat dock.

A drive along the Red Rock Parkway will give you access to another set of trails. At the end of this 15-km parkway, a short self-guiding nature trail loops along Red Rock Canyon offering interesting views of Blakiston Creek's erosional effects. A one-kilometre walk to Blakiston Falls winds through forest to the thundering spectacle. The canyon is also the starting point for several longer, strenuous hikes which range from 11 to 36 kilometres.

A variety of trails begin off the 16-kilometre Akamina Parkway which leads to Cameron Lake. Trails to Crandell Lake,

CARTHEW LAKES

Rowe Lakes and Lineham Lake all begin from this roadway where route maps are posted and limited off-road parking is provided. Wall Lake trailhead also begins from this road and is an easy and pleasant hike suitable for families with young school-aged children.

Overnight backcountry camping sites are available at a variety of destinations in the park but registration fees are required and group size limited. Details are available at the visitor information centre.

At Cameron Lake, day visitors will enjoy the lakeshore walk trail which winds close to the water, while serious hikers will find the Alderson-Carthew trail, which begins on the eastern shore of the lake, one of the most spectacular and demanding trails in the park. A shuttle service to Cameron is available for those who take this 20-km hike, which ends at the Waterton townsite.

OTHER POINTS OF INTEREST

Perched above the town on a knoll overlooking two of the lakes is the impressive Prince of Wales Hotel, built in 1927 by the Great Northern Railway. It is a must-see both for its architecture and its designation as a National Historic Site. Visitors enter the hotel to a dark lobby but are immediately drawn to the striking views of the fjord-like lakes from the two-story high windows. Wander through the gift shop, take high tea in the lobby, have a drink in the Windsor Room or a meal in the dining room.

The town provides a visitor information centre, a peace park pavilion, a tiny heritage museum, several bars and restaurants, a grocery store, gas stations, a movie theatre, equipment and souvenir shops, tennis courts, horseshoe pits and a marina from which scheduled excursion boat trips are available. A stroll around the town, either on the streets or on the lakeshore trail, is rewarding. Don't miss the much-photographed Cameron Falls, which tumbles over some of the oldest rocks in the Rocky Mountains, spilling into Cameron Creek.

UPPER WATERTON LAKE

Just east of the town proper lies an 18-hole golf course, one of the oldest in the Rockies, which is open from mid-April to mid-October. Horses are also available for trail riding by the hour, half day or full day.

LISTINGS: CONTENTS

Getting There	170		Museums	192
CALGARY			Professional Sports	192
By Air	170			
By Car	170		BANFF	192
By Bus	170		Top Attractions	192
			Nightlife	193
EDMONTON			Arts	193
By Air	170		Museums	193
By Car	170			
By Bus	170		COLUMBIA ICEFIELD	193
Travel Essentials	170		JASPER	193
Money	170		Top Attractions	193
Passports	171		Museums	194
Customs	171			
Taxes	171		EDMONTON	194
			Top Attractions	194
Getting Acquainted	171		Museums	195
Time Zone	171		Professional Sports	195
Climate, Rain and Snow	171			
Guides and Information	172		DRUMHELLER	195
			WATERTON	196
Getting Around	173			
Public Transit	173		**Outdoor Recreation**	196
Cars and Rentals	173		Kananaskis	196
Tours	174		Banff	197
			Columbia Icefield	197
Accommodation	175		Jasper	197
Calgary	176			
Kananaskis Country	177		**Shopping**	197
Banff	178		Calgary	197
Lake Louise	180		Banff	199
Columbia Icefield	180		Jasper	199
Jasper	180		Edmonton	199
Edmonton	181			
Waterton	182		**Festivals**	200
Drumheller	183		Calgary	200
			Kananaskis Country	201
Dining	183		Banff	201
Calgary	183		Jasper	201
Banff	185		Edmonton	201
Lake Louise	187			
Columbia Icefield	187		**Excursions**	202
Jasper	187		Elk Island National Park	202
Edmonton	187		Father Lacombe Chapel	
Drumheller	189		Provincial Historic Site	202
			Kicking Horse Pass and	
Attractions	189		Yoho National Park	203
CALGARY	189		Kootenay National Park	203
Top Attractions	189		Reynolds-Alberta Museum	203
Music & Opera	190		Ukranian Cultural Heritage	
Theatre	190		Village	203
Dance	191			
Clubs	191		**Index**	204

GETTING THERE

CALGARY

The Gateway to the Rockies, Calgary is well served by air and land routes.

BY AIR

The Calgary International Airport is located north of Calgary, approximately 20 minutes from the downtown core. In this location since 1956, the current terminal opened in 1977. Since 1992 it has been operated by the Calgary Airport Authority and is currently undergoing major renovations and expansion to improve its facilities and keep up with a growing city. It is a hub for regional, national and international travel as well as cargo transportation.

  More information can be found at www.calgaryairport.com

BY CAR

Two major highways connect Calgary to the rest of Alberta, Canada and the United States. Highway 1, the TransCanada, runs east-west across the centre of the city. It is called 16th Ave. N. in the city limits, and is the major link to the rest of the country. Traveling westward, Highway 1 leads to the Rockies and Banff. The main north-south route is Highway 2, linking Calgary to Edmonton in the north, and the United States in the south.

BY BUS

Visitors from U.S. and Canadian cities can get to Calgary on Greyhound buses. The station is located at 850 16 St. S.W. and you can call 403 265-9111 or 1-800-661-8747 in Canada, 1-800-231-2222 in the U.S., www.greyhound.ca. Red Arrow coach services also provide transport between Calgary, Edmonton and Fort McMurray. 101, 205 9th Ave. S.E. Calgary, AB T2G 0R4; 403 531-0350 or 1-800-232-1958; Fax: 403 264-1004, Email: info@redarrow.pwt.ca, www.redarrow.pwt.ca

EDMONTON

BY AIR

The Edmonton International Airport is located 15 minutes south of the city limits on Highway 2. It is Canada's most northerly international airport and has undergone much development and expansion since the Edmonton municipal airport was closed to general air traffic several years ago. More information can be found at www.edmontonairports.com

BY CAR

Two major highways connect Edmonton to the rest of Alberta and Canada. Highway 16 runs east-west across the centre of the city. It is the major link to Jasper and the Rocky Mountains. The main highway south is Highway 2, redubbed the Queen Elizabeth II Highway, with royal purple road signs to commemorate Alberta's centennial in 2005, linking Edmonton to Calgary. Towards the north there are various routes to Peace River, Fort McMurray and Northern Alberta.

BY BUS

Visitors from U.S. and Canadian cities can get to Edmonton on Greyhound buses. The station is located at 10324 103rd St. and you can call 780 413-8747 or 1-800-661-8747 in Canada, 1-800-231-2222 in the U.S., www.greyhound.ca

  Red Arrow coach services also provide transport between Calgary, Edmonton and Fort McMurray. 10014 104th St. Edmonton, AB; 780 425-0820 or 1-800-232-1958, Email: info@redarrow.pwt.ca, www.redarrow.ca

TRAVEL ESSENTIALS

MONEY

Canadian cash consists of $1 (loonies) and $2 (toonie) coins and differently coloured $5, $10, $20, $50, $100 and $1,000 bills. Main branches of Canadian chartered banks can exchange foreign currency, although small local branches may not exchange currency other than U.S. dollars directly. Banking hours in general are 9:30 a.m. to 4:30 p.m., Monday to Friday, with extended hours and weekends at some branches. Most banks have automatic teller machines posted in various locations around cities and towns; these can be accessed 24 hours a day with bank cards on international banking networks such as Cirrus, Plus and Interac. Currency can also be exchanged at the many commercial money exchange outlets in each city and town.

  Most businesses accept all major credit

cards such as American Express, Diners Club, EnRoute, MasterCard and Visa. Smaller businesses, however, may accept only one or two of these cards. Traveller's cheques can be cashed in major hotels, some restaurants and large stores.

PASSPORTS

Citizens and permanent residents of the United States can cross the border with a birth certificate and photo ID or a passport. A current U.S. driver's license is not accepted as proof of citizenship. Naturalized American citizens should carry naturalization certificates. Visitors from countries other than the United States must have a valid passport and may require other documentation such as a visa or alien card allowing entry. Check with the nearest Canadian Consulate well in advance of travel.

CUSTOMS

Arriving

Travellers entering Canada must declare all goods. Reasonable amounts of personal effects and food are admitted free of duty. Special restrictions or quotas apply to certain specialty goods, especially to plant-, agricultural- and animal-related materials. Each visitor that meets the age requirements of the province or territory where they enter Canada (18 years in Alberta) may bring into Canada up to 40 ounces (1.1 litres) liquor or wine, or 288 ounces (8.5 litres) of beer or ale. Visitors over the age of 19 may also bring up to 50 cigars, 200 cigarettes and 7 ounces (200 grams) of tobacco. Revolvers, pistols and fully automatic firearms are not allowed into Canada. All other weapons (such as hunting rifles and shotguns) must be declared. For information contact:
Revenue Canada, Customs and Excise, Regional Office, 3033 34th Ave. N.E. Calgary, AB T1Y 6X2; 403 292-4613, 1-800-461-9999; Fax: 403 292-4840. www.cbsa-asfc.gc.ca/travel/visitors-e.html

Departing

Before visiting Alberta, contact a U.S. Customs office, where copies of the U.S. customs' brochure "Know Before You Go" are available, to find out customs rules for entering or re-entering the United States. Visitors from other countries should check their own customs regulations before leaving home as well.

TAXES

The Federal Goods and Services Tax (GST) of 7% is applied to most goods and services. Visitors from outside Canada can obtain a GST rebate on most goods taken out of Canada and on accommodation for a stay of less than 30 days. For an instant GST rebate of up to $500 upon exiting Canada, submit receipts and a one-page form to participating duty-free shops. Alternatively, visitors can have original receipts validated by duty-free shop staff or customs officials, and file for a GST rebate (reimbursement by cheque) when they return home. Visitors departing by air, rail, charter-bus or ferry must include boarding passes or a carrier ticket with the claim. There is no Provincial Sales Tax charged in Alberta, however a non-refundable 7% P.S.T. is levied in British Columbia on all retail purchases. For more information or assistance, call 920 432-5608 (outside Canada) or 1-800-668-4748 (inside Canada) or go to http://www.cra-arc.gc.ca/visitors-e.html

GETTING ACQUAINTED

TIME ZONE

All of Alberta and a slice of British Columbia, including the locations mentioned in this publication, are in the Mountain Time Zone. It observes Mountain Standard Time during the winter (November to April), and Mountain Daylight Saving Time during the summer (May to October).

CLIMATE, RAIN AND SNOW

These are the average high and low temperatures in Banff (source Environment Canada, based on data from 1881 to 1990):

January	-14.9°C to -5.3°C
	5.0°F to 23°F
February	-11.3°C to 0.1°C
	12°F to 32°F
March	-7.9°C to 3.8°C
	18°F to 39°F
April	-2.8°C to 9°C
	27°F to 48°F
May	1.5°C to 14.2°C
	35°F to 58°F
June	5.4°C to 18.7°C

	42°F to 66°F
July	7.4°C to 22.1°C
	46°F to 72°F
August	6.8°C to 21.6°C
	44°F to 71°F
September	2.7°C to 16.1°C
	37°F to 61°F
October	-1.1°C to 10.1°C
	30°F to 50°F
November	-8.2°C to 0.5°C
	17°F to 33°F
December	-13.8°C to -5.3°C
	7°F to 23°F

Average Annual Rainfall:

281.2 mm (11 inches)

Average Annual Snowfall:

243.8 cm (96 inches)

GUIDES AND INFORMATION

Alberta has established a Visitor's Info Network with Visitor Info Centres in many communities to assist travelers throughout the province. Travel Alberta's official web site can be found at www.travelalberta.com. Visitors can call 1-800-252-3782 (1-800-ALBERTA) in North America and 780 427-4321 internationally for reservations and help with accommodations and other travel plans. E-mail: travelinfo@travelalberta.com

CALGARY

• Tourism Calgary. Information locations at 220 8th Ave. S.W.; Eau Claire Market, 200 Barclay Parade S.W.; and at the Calgary International Airport. Administration located at 200-238 11th Ave. S.E., Calgary, AB T2G 0X8; 403 263-8510, 1-800-661-1678; Fax: 403 262-3809, www.tourismcalgary.com. Source for current information on the Calgary Area, guides and maps. Visitors can make reservations for many accommodations, sightseeing, transportation and outdoor adventures.

KANANASKIS COUNTRY

• Barrier Lake Information Centre, Highway 40, Kananaskis; 403 673-3985, www.cd.gov.ab.ca/enjoying_alberta/parks/featured/kananaskis/flashindex.asp. Information on all of Kananaskis Country, guidebooks, maps and trail information available. Also cross-country ski tours, guides

and lessons.
• Tourism Canmore, 907 7th Ave., Canmore; 403 678-1295 or 1-866-226-6673 (1-866-CANMORE); Fax: 403 678-1296, www.tourismcanmore.com

BANFF / LAKE LOUISE

• Banff & Lake Louise Tourism, 224 Banff Ave., PO Box 1298, Banff, AB T1L 1B3; 403 762-8421; Fax: 403 762-8163, Email: info@banfflakelouise.com. www.banfflakelouise.com. Source for current information on Banff and the Canadian Rockies including tours, outdoor adventure and accommodation.
• Banff Weather Office: 403 762-2088.
• National Park Warden Service: 403 762-1550
• Avalanche Bulletin: 403 762-1460.
• Lake Louise Visitor Centre, Lower Lake Louise, Box 213, Lake Louise, AB T0L 1E0, 403 522-3833; Fax: 403 522-1212.

JASPER

• Jasper Information Centre, 500 Connaught Drive, P.O. Box 98, Jasper, AB T0E 1E0; 780 852-3858; Fax: 780 852-4932, Email: jaspercc@incentre.net, www.jaspercanadianrockies.com. Obtain information on trail conditions, check in before embarking on wilderness hikes or mountain climbing excursions. Friends of Jasper National Park located here.

EDMONTON

• Edmonton Tourism, 9990 Jasper Ave. Edmonton, AB T5J 1P7; 780 424-9191, 1-800-463-4667, Email: info@edmonton.com, www.edmonton.com/tourism. Information on attractions and events in the Capital Region.

DRUMHELLER

• Drumheller Regional Chamber of Development & Tourism, 60 1st Ave. W., Box 999, Drumheller, AB T0J 0Y0; 403 823-8100, 1-866-823-8100; Fax: 403 823-4469, Email: tourisminfo@drumhellerchamber.com, www.traveldrumheller.com. Information is available on attractions, accommodation and more.

WATERTON

- Parks Canada Visitor Information Centre, Box 200, Mount View Road, Waterton Park, AB T0K 2M0; 403 859-5133. Email: waterton.info@pch.ca, www.parkscanada.pch.gc.ca/waterton
- Chamber of Commerce & Visitors Association, Box 55, Waterton Lakes National Park, AB T0K 2M0; 403 859-2224; Fax: 403 859-2650, E-mail: waterton.info@pch.gc.ca, www.watertonchamber.com. Both services offer information and advice on what to do in the area, accommodation, safety in the outdoors and outdoor recreation.

GETTING AROUND

PUBLIC TRANSIT

CALGARY

The Calgary Transit system is a network of buses and Light Rail Transit (LRT) trains. Fares for travel during a 90-minute time period are Adults $2 and Youth $1.40. You can connect between buses and trains (commonly referred to as the C-Train) in any direction for any distance during this time; stopovers are allowed. Be sure to ask for a transfer from the driver if you are changing buses in order to have proof of payment. Day passes cost $5.60 adults/$3.60 students. Books of tickets are available (10 for $17.50) at many convenience, grocery and drug stores around the city. It is worthwhile to note that in the downtown core along 7th Avenue S.W. the C-Train is a free-fare zone and no tickets are required. Buses and trains on most routes run from 5-6 a.m. to 12-1 a.m. Drivers carry no change, so bring exact fare. Tickets for the C-Train are available from machines on train platforms and tickets from books and day passes must be validated before traveling. Many C-Train stations have "Park & Ride" zones where cars can be left. Schedules are available at the Calgary Transit Customer Service Centre at 240 7th Ave. S.W. Calgary, and online at their web site: www.calgarytransit.com. Each bus stop or station has a 4-digit code that can be used to find specific information. The Tele-ride service (403 974-4000) allows you to call in and, using an automated system, request the next bus times for routes in the city.

Many buses are wheelchair accessible with low floors. Telephone services are available for the hard of hearing at 403 268-8087. For further information, call 403 262-1000.

EDMONTON

The transit system in Edmonton is a comprehensive network of buses and a Light Rail Transit system that runs north-east to south-west. Adult fare is $2.00 and youth (6-17) $1.75. Day passes are available for $6.00 and a variety of ticket books (10 for $16.00) and monthly passes are available for sale at more than 200 locations including kiosks and convenience stores around the City. You can transfer between buses and LRT using a transfer obtained from your bus operator. Fares are valid for a 90-minute period. Tickets for the LRT can be purchased at automatic machines on train platforms. Information on schedules and services can be obtained at www.edmonton.ca, or by calling the Bus Link service at 780 496-1600. The customer service centre, open weekdays, is located in the Churchill LRT station and can be reached at 780 496-1611.

Many routes are serviced by low floor buses and a Disabled Adult Transit Service (DATS) is available. Contact 780 496-4570 or Email: dats@edmonton.ca for further information.

CARS AND RENTALS

Most foreign drivers' licences are valid in Alberta. Check with an Alberta Motor Vehicle Registry to find out specific requirements. Visiting motorists should bring registration documents and have insurance in place before driving. Insurance is available as an option in most car rental contracts, and Visitor to Canada Insurance can be purchased through the Alberta Motor Association (AMA), www.ama.ab.ca. They can also provide information on route planning, road conditions and maps. United States motorists should have a Canadian Non-Resident Interprovince Motor Vehicle Liability Insurance Card, available only in the U.S. For more information or to obtain a copy of the "rules of the road," contact The

Alberta Traffic Safety Initiative at Alberta Transportation, Main Floor, Twin Atria, 4999 98th Ave., Edmonton, AB T6B 2X3; 780 422-8839; Fax: 780 422-3682, www.saferoads.com

Speed limits within Alberta are 50 km/h (30 mph) unless otherwise posted. The use of seatbelts, child restraints and motorcycle helmets is mandatory. Residents also believe in the pedestrian's right of way. Distances, speed limits and fuel measurements are indicated in metric units. To convert kilometres to miles, multiply by 0.6; to convert miles to kilometres, multiply by 1.6. One litre equals about 1/3 of an American gallon or 1/5 of an Imperial gallon.

CALGARY
- Alamo, Calgary International Airport; 403 543-3985, 1-800-462-5266, www.alamo.com
- Avis, 211 6th Ave. S.W., Calgary, AB T2P 1K2; 403 269-6166, 1-800-272-5871; Calgary International Airport; 403 221-1700, 1-800-675-0185, www.avis.com
- Budget, 724 6th Ave. S.W., Calgary, AB; 403 226-1550; Calgary International Airport; 1-866-799-7968; www.budget.com
- Enterprise, 1935 McKnight Blvd. N.E., Calgary, AB T2E 6V4; 403 216-3426; 1-800-736-8222, www.enterprise.com
- Hertz, 117 5th Ave. S.E., Calgary, AB; 403 223-8366; Fax: 403 233-7730, 1-800-263-0600; Calgary International Airport; 403 221-2970, 1-800-263-0600, www.hertz.com
- National Car Rental, Calgary International Airport; 403 221-1690, 1-800-227-7368, www.nationalcar.ca
- Thrifty, 123 5th Ave. S.E., Calgary, AB T2G 0E3; 403 262-4400, 1-800-367-2277; Fax: 403 233-0592; Calgary International Airport; 403 221 1961, 1-800-847-4389, www.thrifty.com

TOURS
The following is a sample of the many tour operators offering excursions in Calgary, the Rockies and surrounding areas in Alberta. Many of them offer specialty excursions, and cover more than one part of the province.
- Brewster Transportation and Tours. Guided sightseeing tours for Calgary, the Rockies, Edmonton and other locations in Alberta, plus Airporter Services. 1140 Gopher Street, Banff, AB T1L 1J3; 403 762-6700, 1-877-791-5500, Email: feedback@brewster.ca, www.brewster.ca
- Brewster Rocky Mountain Adventures. Offering horseback adventures from day trips to longer journeys. PO Box 370, Banff, AB T1L 1A5; 403 762-5454; Fax: 403 673-2100, Email: horses@brewsteradventures.com, www.brewsteradventures.com
- Creative Journeys. A wide variety of guided tours in Calgary, the Rockies, the Badlands and the Prairies. Offer specialized outings including historical walking tours and craft and gallery tours. 1702 34 St. S.E., Calgary, AB T2A 1A3; 403 272-5653; Fax: 403 272-1151; Email: cjdeneve@creativejourneys.com, www.creativejourneys.com
- Canada West Tours and Adventures. Provide tours and activities in Western Canada. Specializing in custom-designing tours and focusing on special interests such as birdwatching or zoology. Box 61215, Kensington PO, Calgary, AB T2N 4S6; 403 283-1131; Fax: 403 270-1830, Email: canadawt@canadawesttours.com, www.canadawestjourneys.com
- Canadian Mountain Holidays. One of the world's largest operators of Heli-Skiing and Heli-Hiking adventures. PO Box 1660, Banff, AB T1L 1J6; 403 762-7100, 1-800-661-0252; Fax: 403 762-5879, Email: info@cmhinc.com, www.cmhmountaineering.com
- Canadian Rockies Rafting Company. Whitewater rafting trips on the Bow and Kananaskis Rivers. PO Box 8082, Canmore, AB T1W 1A1; 403 678-6535, 1-877-226-7625; Fax: 403 609-2335, Email: canrock@telusplanet.net, www.rafting.ca
- Curries Guiding / Beyond the Beaten Path. Exciting tours and activities in the outdoors including hiking, fishing, canyon walks, dog sledding and snowmobiling. Box 105, Jasper, AB T0E 1E0; 780 852-5650; Fax: 780 852-5670, Email:

curries@telusplanet.net,
www.jasperoutdooradventure.com

- Discover Banff Tours Ltd. Interpretive tours of Banff, Lake Louise, the Columbia Icefields and more. Small Groups. P.O. Box 1566, Banff, AB T1L 1B5; 403 760-5007, 1-877-565-9372; Fax: 403 760-7651, Email: info@discoverbanfftours.com, www.banfftours.com

- Explore Holidays Inc. Offer camping, hiking, biking and motorcoach tours in areas including the Rockies, Waterton and Calgary. 743 Railway Ave, PO Box 607, Canmore, AB T1W 1P2; 403 609-4101; Fax: 403 609-4102, Email: exploreholidays@shaw.ca, www.exploreholidays.com

- Geo-Spirit Tours. Theme tours offered in Calgary and Area on topics such as birding, geology and the natural landscape. Box 20185 Bow Valley, Calgary, AB T2P 4L2; 403 815-1482; Fax: 403 281-8807, Email: geospirit.tours@cadvision.com, www.geospirittours.com

- Howling Dog Tours offer dog sledding tours. P.O. Box 8055, Canmore, AB T1W 2T8; 403 678-9588; 1-877-364-7533, Email: mushing@telusplanet.net, www.howlingdogtours.com

- Hummer Tours. Trips into the backcountry, tours and more. Sundre, AB T0M 1X0; 403 638-8090, 1-877-894-9378; Fax: 403-638-8092, Email: info@purewest.com, www.canadianrockies.net/hummertours

- Hydra River Guides. White water rafting trips to the world famous Kicking Horse River. 211 Bear St., PO Box 778, Banff, AB T1L 1A8; 403 762-4554, 1-800-644-8888, Email: info@banffadventures.com, www.banffadventures.com

- Lake Minnewanka Boat Tours. Scenic cruises on this beautiful mountain lake. Lake Minnewanka Drive, Box 2189, Banff, AB T1L 1B9; 403 762-3473; Fax: 403 762-3479,www.minnewankaboattours.com

- Out an' About Tours Travel Adventures. Guided tours of the City of Edmonton and Area, P.O. Box 68183 — 162 Bonnie Doon Mall, Edmonton, AB T6C 4N6; 780 909-8687, 1-888-488-8687; Fax: 780 463-0743, Email: info@outanabouttours.com, www.outanabouttours.com

- Rocky Mountaineer Railtours. Offering spectacular journeys through and around the Rocky Mountains travelling in luxury. A variety of tour packages available. 1150 Station Street, 1st Floor, Vancouver, BC V6A 2X7; 604 606-7245, 1-877-460-3200; Fax: 604 606-7250, Email: reservations@-rockymountaineer.com, www.rockymountaineer.com

- Snowy Owl Sled Dog Tours, plus guided, off-season tours of the canine team and their homes. PO Box 8039, Canmore, AB T1W 2T8; 403 678-4396, 1-888-311-6874; Fax: 403 678-6702, Email: leaddog@snowyowltours.com, www.snowyowltours.com

- Time Out for Touring. Offering various tours in Calgary and Area to unique destinations. 755 Strathcona Drive S.W., Calgary, AB T3H 1P2; 403 217-4699; Fax: 403 217-3835, Email: tourmaster@tour-time.com, www.tour-time.com

- White Mountain Adventures. Discover the mountaintops and animal habitats through hiking, x-country skiing, snowshoeing and more. 7-107 Boulder Crescent, Canmore, AB T1W 1K9; 403 678-4099, 1-800-408-0005; Fax: 403 678-5187, Email: info@whitemountainadventures.com, www.whitemountainadventures.com

ACCOMMODATION

In all parts of Alberta there are a multitude of lodgings available, from luxury resorts to log cabins and tepees. They reflect the various faces of Alberta, everything from large cosmopolitan cities to mountainous back country.

What follows is a cross-section of the hotels, bed and breakfasts and budget establishments to be found in each city and area described. Prices indicated are approximate, based on the costs quoted at the time of publishing, for two people staying in a double room (excluding taxes) during peak season: $ = $50-$90; $$ = $90-$180; $$$ = above $180. Many establishments offer special Internet rates and online reservation services. The Web site www.explorealberta.com is a free service offering information on many Travel Alberta approved lodgings and services.

CALGARY

Accommodations in Calgary are very spread out with many located in the downtown core, near the airport and around the University of Calgary. Most facilities offer all amenities required in a large city.

- 5 Calgary Downtown Suites, 618 - 5th Ave. S.W., Calgary, AB T2P 0M7, 403 451-5551, 1 877 451-5551; Fax: 403 262-9991, Email: reservations@5calgary.com, www.5calgary.com. Onsite spa, business centre, and cheap long-distance phone calls. $$.
- Best Western Suites Downtown, 1330 8th St. S.W., Calgary, AB T2R 1B6; 403 228-6900, 1-800-981-2555, Email: bwsuites@shaw.com, www.bestwesternsuitescalgary.com. Suite accommodation including air-conditioning, balconies and fitness room. $$.
- Calgary Mariott Hotel, 110 9th Ave. S.E., Calgary, AB T2G 5A6; 403 266-7331, 1-800-896-6878; Fax: 403 269 1961, www.mariott.com. Valet parking, connected to the Telus Convention Centre, indoor pool and exercise facilities. $$.
- Carriage House Inn, 9030 Macleod Trail South, Calgary, AB T2H 0M4; 403 253-1101, 1-800-661-9566; Fax: 403 259-2414, Email: sales@carriagehouse.net, www.carriagehouse.net. Full amenities, western hospitality, conveniently located, outdoor pool. $$.
- Delta Bow Valley, 209 4th Ave. S.E., Calgary, AB T2G 0C6; 403 266-1980, 1-877-814-7706; Fax: 403-205-5460, Email: hmelhem@deltahotels.com, www.deltahotels.com. Whirlpool, sauna, dining room and air-conditioning are among the services offered at this convenient downtown hotel. $$.
- Delta Calgary Airport, 2001 Airport Road N.E., Calgary, AB T2E 6Z0; 403 291-2600, 1-877-814-7706; Fax: 403-250-8722, Email: jsheret@deltahotels.com,

www.deltahotels.com. Connected directly to the Calgary International Airport, western hospitality, all amenities. $$.
- Econo Lodge Banff Trail, 2231 Banff Trail N.W., Calgary, AB T2M 4L2; 403 289-1921, 1-800-917-7779; Fax: 403 282-2149, Email: econobanfftrail@shaw.ca, www.econolodgecalgary.com. Comfortable motel accommodation, non-smoking rooms and air-conditioning. $.
- The Fairmont Palliser Hotel, 133 9th Ave. S.W., Calgary, AB T2P 2M3; 403 262-1234, 1-866-540-4477; Fax: 403 260-1260, Email: palliserhotel@fairmont.com, www.fairmont.com. Historic and grand hotel featuring deluxe suites and all amenities. $$$.
- Four Points Sheraton, 8220 Bowridge Crescent N.W., Calgary, AB T3B 2V1; 403 288-4441, 1-877-288-4441; Fax: 403 288-4442, Email: marketing@fourpoints-calgary.ca, www.fourpointscalgarywest.com. In-city resort atmosphere, fitness centre, waterslide and indoor pool. Fine dining. $$.
- Hotel Arts, 119-12 Ave. S.W., Calgary, AB T2R 0G8; 403 266-4611, 1-800-661-9378; Fax: 403 237-0978, Email: info@hotelarts.ca, www.hotelarts.ca. New downtown hotel with pool and poolside patio, fitness centre, business centre, restaurant and wine bar. Boutique-style or executive-style suites. $$.
- HI Calgary City Centre, 520 7th Ave. S.E., Calgary, AB T2G 0J6; 403 269-8239, 1-866-762-4122; Fax: 403 283-6503, www.hihostels.ca/alberta. Newly renovated, dorm-style accommodation in the heart of the city.
- Holiday Inn Express, 2227 Banff Trail N.W., Calgary, AB T2M 4L2; 403 289-6600, 1-800-465-4329; Fax: 403 289-6767 www.sixcontinentshotels.com. Pool, sauna, and complimentary breakfast. $$.
- Hyatt Regency Hotel, 700 Centre St. S. Calgary, AB T2G 5P6; 403 717-1234, 1-800-233-1234; Fax: 403 537-4444, www.hyatt.com. Spacious suites in a full service luxury hotel. $$$.

- Inn on Crowchild, 5353 Crowchild Trail N.W., Calgary, AB T3A 1W9; 403 288-5353, 1-800-735-7502; Fax: 403 286-8966, Email: info@innoncrowchild.com, www.innoncrowchild.com. Complimentary continental breakfast, indoor pool and exercise facilities, air-conditioning and popular pub. $$.
- Kensington Riverside Inn, 1126 Memorial Drive N.W., Calgary, AB T2N 3E3; 403 228-4442, 1-877-313-3733; Fax 403 228-9608, Email: info@kensingtonriversideinn.com, www.kensingtonriversideinn.com. Small, beautiful boutique inn with views of the Bow River, located in central and trendy Kensington. $$$.
- Mystic Springs Chalets & Hot Pools, 140 Kananaskis Way, Canmore, AB T1W 2X2; 403-609-0333, 1-866-446-9784; Fax: 403-609-0264, Email: info@mysticsprings.ca, www.mysticsprings.ca. Boutique resort featuring year-round outdoor hot pools. $$$.
- Radisson Hotel Calgary Airport, 2120 16th Ave. N.E., Calgary, AB T2E 1L4; 403 291-4666, 1-800-333-3333; Fax: 403-291-6498, Email: rhi_clgy@radisson.com, www.radisson.com. All the comforts required, conveniently located near to the Calgary International Airport. $$$.
- Sandman Hotel, 888 - 7th Ave. S.W., Calgary, AB T2P 3J3; 403 237-8626, 1-800-726-3626; Fax: 403 290-1238, E-mail: rescalgary@sandman.ca, www.sandmanhotels.com. Downtown hotel featuring high-speed internet, business centre, pool, whirlpools and fitness centre. Kitchenettes and executive rooms available. $$.
- Sheraton Cavalier Hotel, 2620 32nd Ave. N.E., Calgary, AB T1Y 6B8; 403 291-0107; Fax: 403 291-2834, Email: info@sheratoncalgary.ca, www.sheratoncavalier.com/calgary. Full service hotel located near the Calgary International Airport. Steakhouse, fitness facilities, and shuttle service. $$.
- Sheraton Suites Calgary Eau Claire, 255 Barclay Parade S.W., Calgary, AB T2P 5C2; 403 266-7200, 1-888-784-8370; Fax: 403 266-1300, Email: hotelinfo@sheratonsuites.com, www.sheratonsuites.com. Elegant accommodation on the Bow River, amenities include sauna and exercise facilities, fine dining and meeting facilities. $$$.
- The Westin Calgary, 320 4th Ave. S.W., Calgary, AB T2P 2S6; 403 266-1611, 1-800-937-8461; Fax: 403 233-7471, Email: calga.calgary@westin.com, www.westin.com. Elegant accommodation in the downtown core. Whirlpool, sauna, fine dining. $$.
- Wingate Inn Calgary, 400 Midpark Way S.E., Calgary, AB T2X 3S4; 403 514-0099, 1-888-561-7666; Fax: 403-514-0090, Email: info@wingateinncalgary.com, www.wingateinncalgary.com. Located in South Calgary near Shawnessy Shopping Centre and numerous head offices. Designed with the business traveller in mind. $$.

KANANASKIS COUNTRY

Kananaskis Village is home to the majority of hotel lodgings, with the remaining choices mainly ranch style resorts and campgrounds spread throughout the area. Canmore offers the range from B&B's and budget to luxury resorts and condos.

- Assiniboine Lodge, Mt. Assiniboine B.C. Provincial Park, Box 8128, Canmore, AB T1W 2T8; 403 678-2883; Fax: 403 678-4877, Email: info@assiniboinelodge.com, www.assiniboinelodge.com. A spectacular setting for this rustic but comfortable lodge accessible only by helicopter, skiing or hiking. Guided adventure programs offered. $$$.
- Creekside Country Inn, 709 Benchlands Trail, Canmore, AB T1W 2S8; 1-866-609-5522, Email: info@creeksidecountryinn.com, www.creeksidecountryinn.com. Relaxed and luxurious mountain inn with excellent views. $$.
- Delta Lodge at Kananaskis, Kananaskis Village, AB T0L 2H0; 403 591-7711, 1-866-432-4322; Fax: 403 591-7770, Email: kan.reservations@deltahotel.com, www.deltahotels.com. Everything that you could ever need from a spa to nature at your doorstep in a spectacular environment. $$.

- Executive Resort at Kananaskis, Kananaskis Village, P.O. Box 10, AB T0L 2H0; 403 591-7500; Fax: 403 591-7893, 1-888-388-3932, Email: resortinfo@royalinn.com, www.executivehotels.net. A luxurious resort including deluxe suites and lofts, fitness centre and workshop facilities. $$$.
- Four Points By Sheraton Canmore, 1 Silver Tip Trail, Canmore, AB T1W 2Z7; 403 609-4422, 1-888-609-4422; Fax: 403 609-0008, Email: info@fourpointscanmore.com, www.fourpoints.com. Magnificent mountain views from every room. $$.
- HI Kananaskis Wilderness Hostel, Highway 40, Kananaskis, C/O Box 1358, Banff, AB T1L 1B3; 403 670-7580, 1-866-762-4122; Fax: 403 283-6503, www.hihostels.ca/alberta. Shared accommodation with laundry facilities, common fireplace, kitchen and outdoor equipment rental. $.
- Kananaskis Guest Ranch, PO Box 340, Exshaw, AB T0L 2C0; 403 673-3737, 1-800-691-5085; Fax: 403 673-2100, Email: horses@kananaskisguestranch.com, www.kananaskisguestranch.com. Perfect for retreats, weddings or just a weekend getaway, this ranch provides an authentic Western vacation with options to ride horses, raft or canoe. Breakfast and dinner included. $.
- Mt. Engadine Lodge, Kananaskis Country, Box 40025, Canmore, AB T1W 3H9; 403 678-4080; Fax: 403 678-4020, Email: lodge@mountengadine.com, www.mountengadine.com. A true back country oasis, an ideal base for experiencing the great outdoors. $$.
- Mount Kidd RV Park, PO Box 1000, Highway 40, Kananaskis, AB T0L 2H0; 403 591-7700, www.mountkiddrv.com. A full hookup R.V. park complete with activity centre and hot tub. Full service and tent sites available. $.
- Rafter Six Ranch Resort, Seebe, Exshaw, AB T0L 2C0; 403 673-3622, 1-888-267-2624; Fax: 403 673-3961, Email: vacations@raftersix.com, www.raftersix.com. Enjoy a true Western experience at this lodge complete with beautiful log cabins and private rooms. Adventure programming available along with

facilities for meetings, weddings and other special functions. $$.
- Sundance Lodges, Highway 40, Box 190, Kananaskis Village, AB T0L 2H0; 403 591-7122; Fax: 403 591-7440, Email: info@sundancelodges.com, www.sundancelodges.com. A unique family camping adventure in tepees and trapper's tents. $.

BANFF
Accommodations in the town of Banff offer everything luxurious that you could imagine, from outdoor hot tubs to complete spa treatments. Many are along Banff Avenue, or are within walking distance of it. There are also resorts and budget accommodations spread around the Park itself at popular sites.
- Banff Park Lodge Resort Hotel & Conference Centre, 222 Lynx St., Banff, AB T1L 1K5; 403 762-4433, 1-800-661-9266; Fax: 403 762-3553, Email: info@banffparklodge.com, www.banffparklodge.com. Fully equipped conference facilities in downtown Banff, pool/sauna. $$$.
- Buffalo Mountain Lodge, 700 Tunnel Mountain Road, P.O. Box 1326, Banff, AB T1L 1B3; 403 762-2400, 1-800-661-1367; Fax: 403 760-4492, Email: info@crmr.com, www.crmr.com/bml. Resort accommodations in a spectacular setting on Tunnel Mountain. Fireplaces, whirlpool and fine dining. $$$.
- Bumper's Inn, 603 Banff Ave., Banff, AB T1L 1B3; 403 762-3386, 1-800-661-3518; Fax: 403 762-8842, Email: bumpersinn@telus.net, www.bumpersinn.com. A Banff institution famous for its popular steak house. Non-smoking rooms available. $$.
- Charlton's Cedar Court, 513 Banff Ave., Banff, AB T1L 1B4; 403 762-4485, 1-800-661-1225; Fax: 403 762-2744, Email: banff@charltonresorts.com, www.charltonresorts.com/cc_home. html. Comfortable motel accommodations with kitchenettes, pool, fireplaces, cable T.V. and sauna. $$.
- Douglas Fir Resort, 525 Tunnel Mountain Road, P.O .Box 1228, Banff, AB T1L 1B2; 403 762-5591,

1-800-661-9267; Fax: 1-800-267-8774, Email: stay@douglasfir.com. www.douglasfir.com. Distinctive alpine resort including studios, lofts and rustic chalets. Indoor waterslides. $$$.

- The Fairmont Banff Springs Hotel, 405 Spray Ave., Banff, AB T1L 1J4; P.O. Box 960, Banff, AB; 403 762-2211, 1-800-257-7544; Fax: 403 762-5755, Email: banffsprings@fairmont.com. www.fairmont.com. The ultimate in luxury at this historic hotel. Restaurants and lounges, complete spa and fitness centre, spectacular rooms and service. $$$.

- HI Banff Alpine Centre, 801 Hidden Ridge Way, Tunnel Mountain, Box 1358, Banff, AB T1L 1B3; 403 762-4123; Fax: 403 762-3441, www.hihostels.ca/hostels/alberta. Excellent budget accommodation, private rooms, kitchen, fireplace, laundry. $.

- Hidden Ridge Resort, 901 Hidden Ridge Way, Box 1070, Banff, AB T1L 1H8; 403 762-3544, 1-800-661-1372; Fax: 403 762-2804, Email: reservations@bestofbanff.com, www.banffhiddenridge.com. Cabin and lodge accommodation in this intimate setting on Tunnel Mountain. Whirlpool, kitchenettes, fireplaces. $$$.

- Inns of Banff, 600 Banff Ave., Box 1070, Banff, AB T1L 1H8; 403 762-4581, 1-866-704-3693; Fax: 403 762-2434, Email: reservations@bestofbanff.com. www.innsofbanff.com. Full service hotel with balconies, kitchenettes and jetted tubs available. $$$.

- Irwin's Mountain Inn, 429 Banff Ave., P.O. Box 1198, Banff, AB T1L 1B2; 403 762-4566, 1-800-661-1721; Fax: 403 762-8220, Email: info@irwinsmountaininn.com. www.irwinsmountaininn.com. Comfortable rooms, restaurant, fireplaces, whirlpool, conveniently located. $$.

- Johnston Canyon Resort, P.O. Box 875, Banff, AB T1L 1A9; 403 762-2971, 1-888-378-1720; Fax: 403 762-0868, Email: info@johnstoncanyon.com. www.johnstoncanyon.com. Cabin accommodation complete with fitness facilities and restaurants at this world-famous natural attraction. $$.

- The Juniper, P.O. Box 3449, Banff, AB T1L 1A2; 403-762-2281, 1-877-762-2281; Fax: 403-762-8331, Email: info@thejuniper.com, www.thejuniper.com. Intimate boutique hotel just outside Banff township with stunning mountain views. $$.

- Red Carpet Inn, 425 Banff Ave., P.O. Box 1800, Banff, AB T1L 1B6; 403 762-4184, 1-800-563-4609; Fax: 403 762-4894, Email:info@banffredcarpet.com, www.banffredcarpet.com. Pets accepted. $$.

- The Rimrock Resort Hotel, Mountain Ave., P.O. Box 1110, Banff, AB T1L 1J2; 403 762-3356, 1-888-746-7625; Fax: 403 762-4132, Email: info@rimrockresort.com, www.rimrockresort.com. The ultimate in luxury and elegance at this full service resort in a spectacular setting. $$$.

- Rocky Mountain Bed & Breakfast, P.O. Box 2528, Banff, AB T1L 1C3; 403 762-4811; Fax: 403 762-4811, Email: reservations@rockymtnbb.com, www.rockymtnbb.com. Comfortable homestyle accommodation, non-smoking rooms available. $$.

- Rocky Mountain Resort, 1029 Banff Ave., P.O. Box 100, Banff, AB T1L 1A2; 403 762-5531, 1-800-661-9563; Fax: 403 762-5166, Email: info@rockymountainresort.com, www.rockymountainresort.com. Conference & meeting services, health & fitness club with tennis courts & playground, shuttle service to Banff town centre. $$$.

- Rundlestone Lodge, 537 Banff Ave., Box 489, Banff, AB T1L 1A6; 403 762-2201, 1-800-661-8630; Fax: 403 762-4501, Email: reservations@rundlestone.com, www.rundlestone.com. Full service mountain lodge and cabin accommodation including health club and fireplaces. $$.

- Sunshine Inn, Sunshine Village Ski Resort, P.O. Box 1510, Banff, AB T1L 1J5; 403 762-6500, 1-877-542-2633; Fax: 403-762-6557, Email: reservations@skibanff.com, www.skibanff.com. Full service resort at the doorstep of fantastic downhill skiing. $$.

LAKE LOUISE

- Fairmont Chateau Lake Louise, 111 Lake Louise Drive, Lake Louise, AB T0L 1E0; 403 522-3511; Fax: 403 522-3834, Email: chateaulakelouise@fairmont.com, www.fairmont.com. Luxurious rooms and services in a spectacular setting on the shores of Lake Louise. $$$.
- HI Hostel Lake Louise, Village Road, Box 115, Lake Louise, AB T0L 1E0; 403 522-2202; Fax: 403 283-6503, www.hihostels.ca/hostels/ Alberta. Home to the Canadian Alpine Centre, family and dorm accommodation, laundry, internet and kitchen. $.
- The Post Hotel, 200 Pipestone Rd., P.O. Box 69, Lake Louise, AB T0L 1E0; 403 522-3989, 403 265-4900, 1-800-661-1586; Fax: 403 522-3966, Email: info@posthotel.com, www.posthotel.com. Classic mountain hotel with relaxing atmosphere. Evening entertainment, balconies, swimming pool and steam room. $$$.

COLUMBIA ICEFIELD

Accommodations are limited along the Icefield Parkway, as most people stay in Jasper, Banff or Lake Louise. However, there are a few good options and several campgrounds along the way.

- Columbia Icefield Chalet, top floor of Icefield Centre, Icefield Parkway; 403 762-6700, 1-877-423-7433; Fax: 1-877-766-7433, Email: icefield@brewster.ca, www.columbiaicefield.com/hotel.asp. Spacious rooms, panoramic view of Athabasca Glacier. $$.
- Hostelling International hostels along the Icefield Parkway: Athabasca Falls Hostel, Mt. Edith Cavell Hostel, Beauty Creek Hostel, Hilda Creek Hostel, Rampart Creek Hostel, Mosquito Creek Hostel; 1-866-762-4122. www.hihostels.ca/Alberta. $.

JASPER

Jasper offers a broad spectrum of accommodations, all of which get booked up early for the high season, so it is advisable to book ahead.

- Amethyst Lodge, 200 Connaught Drive, P.O. Box 1200, Jasper, AB T0E 1E0; 780 852-3394, 1-888-852-7737; Fax: 780 852-5198, www.mpljasper.com/amethyst. Newly renovated, family specials, close to downtown. $$$.
- Alpine Loghouse, 920 Pyramid Lake Road, P.O. Box 585, Jasper, AB T0E 1E0; 780 852-4420, 1-888-437-2483; Fax: 780 852-5466. Email: patmarrek@hotmail.com, www.visitjasper.com/AlpineLoghou se.html. Bed & breakfast accommodation, fireplace, no pets. $.
- The Athabasca Hotel, Box 1420, 510 Patricia St., Jasper, AB T0E 1E0; 780 852-3386, 1-877-542-8422; Fax: 780 852-4955, Email: info@athabascahotel.com, www.athabascahotel.com. Newly renovated Victorian-style hotel in the heart of Jasper. $$.
- Becker's Chalets, Hwy. 93, South Icefields Parkway, Jasper, AB T0E 1E0; 780 852-3779; Fax: 780 852-7202, Email: info@beckerschalets.com, www.beckerschalets.com. Family-run, cabin-style accommodation, playground, fishing, fine dining. $$.
- Chateau Jasper, P.O. Box 1418, 96 Geikie St., Jasper, AB T0E 1E0; 780 852-5644, 1-800-661-1315; Fax: 780 852-4860, Email: info@chateaujasper.com, www.decorehotels.com/chateau. Award-winning housekeeping, fine dining, heated indoor pool and whirlpool, seasonal ski shuttle. $$$.
- The Fairmont Jasper Park Lodge, Old Lodge Rd., P.O. Box 40, Jasper, AB T0E 1E0; 780 852-3301; Fax: 780 852-5107, Email: jasperparklodge@fairmont.com, www.fairmont.com. A modern resort with charming cabins, boutiques, a world class golf course and gourmet dining facilities. Worth a visit for afternoon tea. $$$.
- HI Jasper International Hostel, Box 387, Jasper, AB T0E 1E0; 780 852-3215, 1-877-852-0781; Fax: 480 852-5560, www.hihostels.ca/hostels/Alberta. Comfortable family and dorm accommodation. Information, internet, laundry and kitchen facilities available. $.
- Jasper Inn Alpine Resort & Restaurant, 98 Geikie Street, P.O. Box 879, Jasper, AB T0E 1E0; 780 852-4461, 1-800-661-1933; Fax: 780 852-5916, Email: reservations@jasperinn.com,

www.jasperinn.com. Full resort amenities including pool, whirlpool, kitchenettes and dining. Pets allowed. $$$.

- Maligne Lodge, 900 Connaught Drive, Box 757, Jasper, AB T0E 1E0; 780 852-3143, 1-800-661-1315; Fax: 780 852-4789, Email: info@malignelodge.com www.decorehotels.com/maligne/index.html. Indoor pool and whirlpool, outdoor hot tub, spacious rooms for family accommodation. $$.

- Marmot Lodge, 86 Connaught Drive, Jasper, AB T0E 1E0; 780 852-4471; Fax: 780 852-3280, Email: marmotlodge@mtn-park-lodges.com, www.mtn-park-lodges.com. Full service lodge, designer-styled rooms, some with kitchenettes. $$$.

- Miette Hot Springs Bungalows, P.O. Box 907, Jasper, AB T0E 1E0; 780 866-3750; Fax: 780 866-2214. Cabin style accommodation in spectacular setting. Kitchenettes, playground, laundry facilities and fireplaces. $$.

- Mount Robson Inn, 902 Connaught Drive, P.O. Box 88, Jasper, AB T0E 1E0; 780 852-3327, 1-800-587-3327; Fax: 780 852-5004, Email: info@mountrobsoninn.com, www.mountrobsoninn.com. Family run, recently renovated, shuttle service to bus & train stations, outdoor whirlpools. $$$.

- Park Place Inn, 623 Patricia St., P.O. Box 2112, Jasper, AB T0E 1E0; 780 852-9770, 1-866-852-9770; Fax: 780 852-1180, Email: info@parkplaceinn.com, www.parkplaceinn.com. Centrally located locally-owned intimate and luxurious heritage inn. $$$.

- Pine Bungalows, P.O. Box 7, Jasper, AB T0E 1E0; 780 852-3491; Fax: 780 852-3432. Email: pinebung@telusplanet.net. www.pinebungalows.com. Quaint cabin accommodation, no pets. $$.

- Pyramid Lake Resort, P.O. Box 388, Jasper, AB T0E 1E0; 780 852-4900, 1-888-962-2522; Fax: 780 852-7007, Email: reservations@pyramidlakeresort.com, www.pyramidlakeresort.com. Luxurious cabins overlooking Pyramid Lake, family suites, kitchenettes and bike and boat rentals available. $$$.

- Tekarra Lodge, P.O. Box 669, Jasper, AB; 780 852-3058, 1-888-962-2522; Fax: 780 852-4636, Email: reservations@TekarraLodge.com, www.tekarralodge.com. Rustic cabins in spectacular setting, wood burning fireplaces, pets allowed, balconies, playground. $$.

- Tonquin Inn, 100 Juniper St., Box 658, Jasper, AB T0E 1E0; 780 852-4987, 1-800-661-1315; Fax: 780-852-4413, Email: info@tonquininn.com, www.decorehotels.com/tonquin/index.html. Luxury and economy rooms, some with fireplace, private sauna and balcony. $$$.

EDMONTON

Edmonton is host to a wide variety of budget to luxury accommodations. Most are located on the South Side, in the Downtown Core or close to the West Edmonton Mall.

- Coast Edmonton Plaza Hotel, 10155 105th St., Edmonton, AB T5J 1E2; 780 423-4811, 1-800-716-6199; Fax: 780 423-3204, www.coasthotels.com. Full service hotel including health fitness centre, deluxe suites, and shuttle service downtown. $$.

- Crowne Plaza Chateau Lacombe, 10111 Bellamy Hill N.W., Edmonton, AB T5J 1N7; 780 428-6611, 1-800-661-8801; Fax: 780 425-6564, Email: cpcl@chateaulacombe.com, www.chateaulacombe.com. Downtown hotel overlooking the River Valley. Home of the revolving restaurant La Ronde. $$.

- Econo Lodge Downtown, 10209 100th Ave., Edmonton, AB T5J 0A1; 780 428-6442, 1-800-613-7043; Fax: 780 428-6467, Email: reservations@econolodgeedm.com, www.econolodgeedm.com. Restaurant & bar, whirlpool, pets allowed. $.

- The Fairmont Hotel MacDonald, 10065 100th St., Edmonton, AB T5J 0N6; 780 424-5181, 1-866-540-4468; Fax: 780 429-6481, Email: hotelmacdonald@fairmont.com, www.fairmont.com. Historic and luxurious hotel located in downtown Edmonton. Full amenities. $$$.

- The Fantasyland Hotel at West Edmonton Mall, 17700 87th Ave.,

Edmonton, AB T5T 4V4; 780 444-3000, 1-800-737-3783; Fax: 780 444-3294, Email: info@fantasylandhotel.com, www.fantasylandhotel.com. Unique theme rooms including the Roman, Africa and Polynesian rooms. $$$.

- Four Points Sheraton Edmonton South, 7230 Argyll Road, Edmonton, AB, T6C 4A6; 780 465-7931, 1-800-368-7764; Fax: 780 469-3680, Email: info@chateauedmonton.com, www.chateauedmonton.com. Near Old Strathcona shopping district, newly renovated full service hotel and conference facility. $$.

- HI Edmonton, 10647 81st Ave., Edmonton, AB T6E 1Y1; 780 988-6836, 1-877-467-8336; Fax: 780 988-8698, www.hihostels/hostels/Alberta. Private, family and dorm accommodation, central to Old Strathcona. Laundry, internet and kitchen facilities. $.

- Hotel Selkirk, 1920 St., Fort Edmonton Park, PO Box 2359, Edmonton, AB T5J 2R7; 780 496-7227, 1-888-962-2522; Fax: 780 431-0946, Email: reservations@hotelselkirk.com, www.maclabhotels.com. A historic hotel, destroyed by fire in 1962, now completely rebuilt in its original grand style. Open May-September for individual/family accommodation, September-May for group special events such as weddings. $$.

- Mayfield Inn & Suites, 16615 109th Ave., Edmonton, AB T5P 4K8; 780 484-0821, 1-800-661-9804; Fax: 780 481-3923, Email: info.mayfield@chipreit.com, www.mayfieldinnedmonton.com. Full amenities, 5 minutes from West Edmonton Mall, popular dinner theatre. $$.

- Ramada Inn & Waterpark, 5359 Calgary Trail (Gateway Blvd.), Edmonton, AB T6H 4J9; 780 434-3431, 1-800-272-6232; Fax: 780 437-3714, Email: ramadaes@telusplanet.net, www.ramada.com. Full amenities including family waterpark. $.

- Sandman Hotel West Edmonton, 17635 Stony Plain Rd., Edmonton, AB T5S 1E3; 780 483-1385, 1-800-726-3626; Fax: 780-489-0611,

Email: cres@sandman.ca, www.sandmanhotels.com. Full amenities including pool, restaurant and air-conditioning. $.

- Signature Suites Edmonton House, 10205 100th Ave., Edmonton, AB T5J 4B5; 780 420-4000, 1-888-962-2522; Fax: 780 420-4364, Email: reservations@edmontonhouse.com, www.edmontonhouse.com. Spacious, comfortable rooms, centrally located, shuttle service to West Edmonton Mall. $$.

- The Sutton Place Hotel, 10235 - 101 St., Edmonton, AB T5J 3E9; 780 428-7111, 1-866-378-8866 Fax: 780 441-3098, Email: info_edmonton@suttonplace.com, www.suttonplace.com. Luxurious downtown hotel connected to the underground pedway. $$.

- West Harvest Inn, 17803 Stony Plain Road N.W., Edmonton, AB T5S 1B4; 780 484-8000, 1-800-661-6993; Fax: 780 486-6060, Email: inn@westharvest.ab.ca, www.westharvest.com. Meeting & banquet facilities, deluxe rooms available, shuttles to West Edmonton Mall and Airport, full amenities. $$.

WATERTON
Home to one of the most famous hotels in the Rockies, The Prince of Wales Hotel, Waterton offers several good options for accommodation during the high season. Places fill early; be sure to book ahead.

- The Bayshore Inn, 111 Waterton Ave., P.O. Box 38, Waterton Park, AB T0K 2M0; 403 859-2211, 1-888-527-9555; Fax: 403 859-2291, Email: info@bayshoreinn.com, www.bayshoreinn.com. Deluxe rooms and suites, fine dining and conference facilities. $$.

- Chief Mountain Lodge Bed & Breakfast, Box 101, Waterton Park, AB T0K 2M0; 403 653-1617, Email: chiefmountainlodge@hotmail.com, www.ssdirect.com/cml. Intimate accommodations, no pets. $.

- HI Waterton Alpine Centre, Cameron Falls & Windflower Ave., P.O. Box 4, Waterton, AB T0K 2M0; 403 859-2151; Fax: 403 859-2229, www.hihostels.ca/hostels/Albertaindex.html. Excellent dorm and family accommodation, full services including swimming, laundry and internet. $.

- The Prince of Wales Hotel, Waterton, AB T0K 2M0; 403 859-2231; Fax: 403 859-2630, www.princeofwaleswaterton.com. Majestic location and historic hotel. Spectacular views overlooking Upper Waterton Lake, no TV. $$$.
- Waterton Lakes Lodge, 101 Clematis Avenue, P.O. Box 4, Waterton Park, AB T0K 2M0; 403 859-2150, 1-888-985-6343; Fax: 403 859-2229, Email: reservations@watertonlakeslodge.com, www.watertonlakeslodge.com. Resort facilities with individually themed accommodations and complete health and spa club. $$$.

DRUMHELLER
Drumheller offers several comfortable options for accommodation, with many B&B's waiting to serve you.

- Best Western Hotel Jurassic Inn, 1103 Hwy 9 South, P.O. Box 3009, Drumheller, AB T0J 0Y0; 403 823-7700, 1-888-823-3466; Fax: 403 823-5002, www.bestwestern.com/reservations/ca/ab/main.html. Comfortable family accommodation, pool, whirlpool, non-smoking rooms. $$.
- Drumheller Travelodge, P.O. Box 2350, Drumheller, AB T0J 0Y0; 403 823-5302, 1-800-578-7878; Fax: 403 823-5342, www.travelodge.com. Most amenities including kitchenettes, pool, and air-conditioning. Pets allowed. $$.
- Newcastle Country Inn, 1130 Newcastle Trail, Drumheller, AB T0J 0Y2; 403 823-8356, 1-888-262-4665; Fax: 403 823-2373, Email: newcastl@telusplanet.net, www.virtuallydrumheller.com/nci. Meeting and conference facilities, no pets. $$.
- Super 8 Motel, #600, 680 2nd St. S.E., Drumheller, AB T0J 0Y0; 403 823-8887, 1-888-823-8882; Fax: 403 823-8884, www.super8.com. Continental breakfast included, pool and air-conditioning. $$.

DINING

Restaurants in Alberta are as varied as the people who live here. There are options to satisfy every inclination, and of course plenty of Alberta beef to go around. The following lists a select number of the multitude of restaurants in each city. Each listing includes the approximate price range of dinner for two, including a bottle of wine (where served), taxes, and gratuity: $ = under $45; $$ = $45-$80; $$$ = $80-$120; $$$$ = $120-$180; $$$$$ = over $180. Keep in mind that many fine restaurants make a wide selection of wines available by the glass as well. Meals served are indicated as: B = breakfast; L = lunch; D = dinner; G = grazing; T-O = take-out; Late = open past midnight. The credit cards accepted by each establishment are also listed: AX = American Express; V = Visa; MC = MasterCard. For further information, www.discoveralberta.ca, offers links to restaurant reviews for many eateries within the province.

CALGARY
The *Where Calgary* magazine, published monthly, provides up-to-date restaurant reviews and recommendations.

UPSCALE & REGIONAL
- The Belvedere, 107 8th Ave. S.W.; 403 265-9595. New York stylish, creative dishes. L/D, $$$$, AX/V/MC.
- The Big Fish, 1112 Edmonton Trail N.E.; 403 277-3403. Creative seafood dishes and oyster bar. L/D, $$$, AX/V/MC.
- Catch Restaurant, 100 Stephen Ave. S.E.; 403 206-0000. Lively seafood and oyster bar. L/D, $$$, AX/V/MC.
- Centini, 160 8th Ave. S.E.; 403 269-1600. Upscale Italian food. Email: info@centini.com, www.centini.com. L/D, $$, AX/V/MC.
- Divino Wine & Cheese Bistro, 113 8th Ave. S.W.; 403 410-5555. Amazing, fresh fare in a stylish setting. Email: events@divinobistro.com, www.divinobistro.com. L/D/G, $$$, AX/V/MC.
- Fleur de Sel, 2015 4th St. S.W.; 403 228-9764. French bistro fare. Email: info@fleurdeselbrasserie.com, www.fleurdeselbrasserie.com. L/D, $$$, AX/V/MC.
- The Living Room Restaurant, 514 17th Ave. S.W.; 403 228-9830. Romantic restaurant featuring fondues, seafood and French and Italian-influenced cuisine. www.livingroomrestaurant.com. L/D/Late, $$$, AX/V/MC.

- Murrieta's West Coast Bar & Grill, 808 1st St. S.W.; 403 269-7707. Stylish seafood, pasta and flatbreads in the historic Alberta Hotel building. www.muriettas.ca. L/D, $$, AX/V/MC.
- Muse, 107 10A St. N.W.; 403 670-6873. International cuisine served in romantic setting. D/Late, $$$, AX/V/MC.
- Piato Greek House, 1114 Edmonton Trail N.E.; 403 277-3408. Modern Greek cuisine. www.piatogreekhouse.com. D, $$$, AX/V/MC.
- The Ranche, 15979 Bow Bottom Tr. S.E.; 403 225-3939. Contemporary cowboy-style menu. Email: ranche1@telusplanet.net, www.theranche.com. B/L/D, $$$, AX/V/MC.
- The River Café, Prince's Island Park; 403 261-7670. Spectacular setting for the ultimate experience in regional cuisine. Email: info@river-cafe.com, www.river-cafe.com. L/D, $$$, AX/V/MC.
- Teatro, 200 8th Ave. S.E.; 403 290-1012. Mediterranean Cuisine. Email: info@teatro-rest.com, www.teatro-rest.com. L/D, $$$, AX/V/MC.
- Wildwood, 2417 4th St. S.W.; 403 228-0100. Eclectic rocky mountain cuisine. L/D, $$, AX/V/MC.

STEAKHOUSES

- Buchanan's, 7th St & 3rd Ave. S.W.; 403 261-4646. An excellent selection of single malt scotch. L/D, $$, AX/V/MC.
- Caesar's Steak House, 512 4th Ave. S.W.; 403 264-1222. A Calgary tradition. Email: caesarssteakhouse@ks2.ca, www.caesarssteakhouse.com, L/D, $$$, AX/V/MC.
- Hy's Steak House, 316 4th Ave. S.W.; 403 263-2222. Classic steak house. www.hyssteakhouse.com. L/D, $$$, AX/V/MC.
- O.N. Bar & Grill, 4th Ave. & 3rd St. S.W. (Westin Hotel); 403 266-1611. Renovated eatery with lots of fresh local produce. www.westincalgary.com/on-bar-grill.shtml. B/L/D, $$$, AX/V/MC.
- Ranchman's, 9615 Macleod Tr. S.; 403 253-1100. The real cowboy experience. Email: wendy@ranchmans.com, www.ranchmans.com. L/D/Late, $, AX/V/MC.
- The Rimrock Dining Room at The Palliser Hotel, 9th Ave. & 1st St. S.W.; 403 260-1219. Historic spot for a steak dinner. Email: palliserhotel@fairmont.com, www.fairmont.com. B/L/D, $$$$, AX/V/MC.
- Smuggler's Inn, 6920 Macleod Tr. S.E.; 403 252-3394. Popular local spot for steak and salad bar. www.smugglers-inn.com. L/D, $$, AX/V/MC.

EASYGOING AND ETHNIC

- Anpurna Curry Pot, 175B 52nd St. S.E.; 403 235-6028. Vegetarian paradise. L/D, $, V.
- The Barley Mill, 201 Barclay Parade S.W.; 403 290-1500. Pub fare. L/D/Late, $, AX/V/MC. Closed Mondays.
- Brava Bistro, 723 17th Ave. S.W.; 403 228-1854. Contemporary cuisine. Email: info@bravabistro.com, www.bravabistro.com. L/D/T-O/G, $$, AX/V/MC.
- Brewsters Brew Pub, 834 11th Ave. S.W.; 403 265-2739. Several locations. Email: info@brewstersbrewingco.com, www.brewstersbrewingco.com. L/D/Late, $, AX/V/MC.
- Buddha's Veggie Restaurant, 5802 Macleod Tr. S.W.; 403 252-8830. Chinese food favourites. www.buddhasveggie.com. L/D/G, $$, V/MC. Closed Tuesdays.
- Café de Tokyo, 630 1st Ave. N.E.; 403 264-2027. Sushi, noodles and tempura. L/D, $, V/MC.
- Cilantro, 338 17th Ave. S.W.; 403 229-1177. California-inspired cuisine. L/D, $$, AX/V/MC.
- Clay Oven, 349-3132 26 St. N.E., 403 250-2161. Authentic East Indian cuisine, extensive wine list. L/D, $$, AX/V/MC.
- Da Guido, 2001 Centre St. N.W.; 403 276-1365. Italian delights. L/D, $$, AX/V/MC.
- Diner Deluxe/Urban Baker, 804 Edmonton Trail N.E.; 403-276-5499. Funky retro diner fare. B/L/D/T-O, $$, V/MC.
- Earl's, 315 8th Ave. S.W.; 403 265-3275. Several locations, casual dining. www.earls.ca. L/D, $$, V/MC.
- Good Earth Café, Eau Claire

Market; 403 237-8684. 1502 11th St. S.W.; 403 228-9543. Several locations, light meals with healthy food choices. www.goodearthcafes.com. B/L/G/T-O, $, V.

- Grumans Delicatessen, 1000 7 Ave. S.W.; 403 261-6750. Delicatessen and full-service restaurant. B/L/D/T-O, $, AX/V/MC.
- Il Sogno, 24 4th St. N.E.; 403 232-8901. Influenced by the flavours of Napoli. Email: ilsogno@shaw.ca, www.ilsogno.org. L/D, $$, AX/V/MC.
- Indulge Catering and Gourmet Foods, 620 8th Ave. S.W.; 403 229-9029. Email: indulge@telusplanet.net, www.indulgecatering.com. L/D, $$, V/MC
- James Joyce Irish Pub, 114 8th Ave. S.W.; 403 262-0708. Traditional Irish meals. Email: info@jamesjoycepub.com, www.jamesjoycepub.com. L/D/Late, $, AX/V/MC.
- Joey's Only Seafood, 514 42 Ave. S.E.; 403 243-4584. 9250 Macleod Trail S.E.; 403 252-7060. Several locations, seafood for the family. www.aroundcalgary.com/joeysonly/dsc2.html. L/D, $, AX/V/MC.
- Joey Tomato's Kitchen, 208 Barclay Parade S.W.; 403 263-6336. Several locations, fun atmosphere. L/D, $$, AX/V/MC.
- Lina's Italian Market & Cappuccino Bar, 2202 Centre St., 403 277-9166. Italian groceries, prepared meals and pastries. Also features a wine bar. L/T-O, $, AX/V/MC.
- Mango Shiva Indian Bistro and Chai Bar, 507 8th Ave. S.W.; 403 290-1644. Eclectic East Indian fusion fare. L/D/Late, $$, AX/V/MC.
- Manuel Latruwe Belgian Patisserie, 1333 1 St. S.E.; 403 261-1092. B/L/G, $, AX/V/MC.
- The King and I, 822 11th Ave. S.W.; 403 264-7241. Upscale Thai cuisine. www.kingandi.ca. L/D, $$, AX/V/MC.
- Misai Japanese Restaurant, 7, 1915 32 Ave. N.E.; 403 250-1688. Japanese fare including innovative appetizers and very fresh sushi. L/D, $$, AX/V/MC.
- The Orchid Room, 513 - 8 Ave. S.W.; 403 263-4457. Vietnamese, Thai and French fusion. L/D, $$, AX/V/MC.
- Palace of Eats, 1411 11th St. S.W.; 403 244-6602. Montreal smoked meat and bagel shop. Email: info@palaceofeats.ca, www.palaceofeats.ca. L/T-O, $, V/MC.
- Ship & Anchor Pub, 534 17th Ave. S.W.; 403 245-3333. Popular with the 20-something crowd. www.shipandanchor.com. L/D/Late, $, V/MC.
- Silver Dragon, 106 3rd Ave. S.E.; 403 264-5326. Dim Sum lunch. Brunch/L/D, $$, V/MC.
- Spolumbo's Deli, 1308 9th Ave. S.E.; 403 264-6452. Gourmet Italian sausage sandwiches. Email: info@spolumbos.com, www.spolumbos.com. L/D, $, AX/V/MC.
- The Siding Café, 111, 100 7 Ave. S.W.; 111, 403 262-0282. "Slow food" café, featuring all-day breakfast. B/L, $, AX/V/MC.
- Sun Chiu Kee, #6, 1423 Centre Street N.W.; 403 230-8890. Busy Asian restaurant with extensive menu and generous portions. L/D/Late, $, AX/V/MC.
- Thi Thi Vietnamese Submarine, 209 1st St. S.E.; 403 265-5452. Satay sandwiches. B/L/D, $.
- Trong Khanh Restaurant, 1115 Centre St. N.W.; 403 230-2408. Fresh, authentic Vietnamese food. L/D/T-O, $, AX/V/MC.
- Uoza Sushi, 919 Centre St. N.W.; 403 276-8008. Japanese. L/D/T-O, $, AX/V/MC.

BANFF
- Aurora Restaurant, 110 Banff Ave.; 403 760-5300. Large, modern nightclub. D/Late, $, V/MC.
- The Baker Creek Bistro, The Baker Creek Chalets, P.O. Hwy 1A, Bow Valley Parkway, Lake Louise; 403 522-2182. A popular bistro. Email: bakerinfo@bakercreek.com. www.bakercreek.com/Dining.html. L/D, $$, AX/V/MC.
- The Balkan Restaurant, 120 Banff Ave.; 403 762-3454. Generous portions of Greek food. www.banffbalkan.com. L/D, $$, AX/V/MC.
- Banffshire Club, Banff Springs Hotel, 405 Spray Avenue; 403 762-6860. Contemporary North American cuisine served in exclusive and

luxurious dining room with views of Sulphur Mountain. D, $$$$$, AX/V/MC. Hours and days of operation based on season.

- Barbary Coast, 119 Banff Ave.; 403 762-4616. California-style menu. Email: barbary@telusplanet.net. L/D/Late, $$, AX/V/MC.
- Barpa Bill's Souvlaki, 223 Bear St.; 403 762-0377. Known for its budget-priced, takeout Greek fare. L/D/T-O, $, V/MC.
- Le Beaujolais, 212 Buffalo St.; 403 762-2712. Award-winning French cuisine. Email: restaurant@lebeaujolaisbanff.com, www.lebeaujolaisbanff.com. D, $$$$, AX/V/MC.
- Buffalo Mountain Lodge, Tunnel Mountain Road; 403 762-2400. The finest in Rocky Mountain cuisine. crmr.com/diningbuffalo.php. B/L/D, $$$$, V/MC.
- Bumper's Beef House, 603 Banff Ave.; 403 762-2622. Known for its Alberta beef and salad bar. Email: bumpersbeef@banff.net, www.bumpersinn.com/beefhouse.htm. D, $$, AX/V/MC.
- Café Soleil, 208 Caribou St.; 403 762-2090. Mediterranean meals, wines and tapas. B/L/D, $$$, AX/V/MC.
- The Cake Company, Bear Street Mall; 403 762-8642. Friendly service and a wide selection of desserts, coffees and pastries. L/L/T-O, $, V/MC.
- Caramba!, 337 Banff Ave.; 403 762-3667. Mediterranean-inspired, featuring B.C. seafood and Alberta beef. www.bestofbanff.com/bpi/caramba.html. D, $$$, AX/V/MC.
- Cilantro Mountain Café, Tunnel Mountain Rd., The Buffalo Mountain Lodge; 403 760-3008. Rocky Mountain cuisine. L/D, $$$, AX/V/MC.
- Coyotes, 206 Caribou St.; 403 762-3963. Award-winning southwestern cuisine. www.dininginbanff.com/restaurants/coyotes.shtml. B/L/D, $, AX/V/MC.
- Earls, 299 Banff Ave., 403 762-4414. Trendy and fun restaurant and bar. www.earls.ca. L/D, $, AX/V/MC.
- Eden, Rimrock Resort Hotel, 100 Mountain Ave.; 403 762-1865. French-influenced cuisine served in a luxurious dining room.

www.rimrockresort.com. D, $$$, AX/V/MC.
- El Toro, 429 Banff Ave.; 403 762-2520. Offers authentic Mediterranean dishes. www.dininginbanff.com/restaurants/eltoro.shtml. B/D, $$, AX/V/MC.
- Evelyn's Coffee Bar, 9 Town Centre Mall; 403 762-0352. Coffee and treats. B/L/T-O/G, $, MC.
- Giorgio's Trattoria, 219 Banff Avenue; 403 762-5114. Very popular choice for Italian. www.giorgiosbanff.com. D, $$, V/MC.
- Grizzly House, 207 Banff Ave.; 403 762-4055. Specializes in fondues and an extensive variety of meats. Email: fondue@shawcable.com, www.banffgrizzlyhouse.com. L/D, $$$, AX/V/MC.
- Guido's, 116 Banff Ave.; 403 762-4002. An Italian tradition. D, $$, AX/V/MC.
- Joe Btfsplk's Diner, 221 Banff Ave.; 403 762-5529. For the old-fashioned diner experience. B/L/D, $, V/MC.
- Jump Start the Coffee & Sandwich Place, 206 Buffalo St.; 403 762-0332. B/L/T-O/G, $.
- The Keg, 521 Banff Ave.; 403 762-4442. 117 Banff Ave.; 403 760-3030. Family-style steakhouse, two locations. www.bestofbanff.com/bcl/keg.html. L/D, $$, AX/V/MC
- The Kiln, Donald Cameron Hall, The Banff Centre, St. Julien Rd.; 403 762-6141. European-style café. B/L/D, $, V/MC.
- Melissa's Steak House, 218 Lynx St.; 403 762-5511. Famous for steak and more. www.melissasrestaurant.com. B/L/D, $$, AX/V/MC.
- Miki, 600 Banff Ave.; 403 762-0600. Japanese/Asian fare in the Inns of Banff. D, $$, AX/V/MC.
- The Primrose at the Rimrock Resort Hotel, Mountain Ave.; 403 762-3356. Canadian and international dining. Email: comments@rimrockresort.com. www.rimrockresort.com/primrose.htm B/D, $$$$, AX/V/MC.
- The Rose and Crown Pub, 202 Banff Ave.; 403 762-2121. Traditional English fare. Email: info@roseandcrown.ca, www.roseandcrown.ca. L/D, $, AX/V/MC.

- The Rundle Lounge, the Banff Springs Hotel; 403 762-2211. Email: banffsprings@fairmont.com, www.fairmont.com/banffsprings. L/G, $, AX/ V/MC.
- Saltlik, 221 Bear St.; 403 762-2467. Upscale steakhouse. L/D, $$, AX/V/MC.
- St. James Gate, 205 Wolf St; 403 762-9355 Popular Irish pub. L/D/G, $$, AX/V/MC.
- Suginoya, 225 Banff Ave.; 403 762-4773. Upscale Japanese. L/D, $$, AX/V/MC.
- Sushi House, 304 Caribou St.; 403 762-4353. Japanese/sushi. L/D, $$, AX/V/MC.
- Ticino, 415 Banff Ave.; 403 762-3848. Offering fine Swiss-Italian cuisine. Email: info@ticinorestaurant.com, www.ticinorestaurant.com. D, $$, V/MC.
- Tommy's Neighborhood Pub, 120 Banff Ave.; 403 762-8888. A popular spot for locals. L/D/Late, $, V/MC.
- Tony Roma's, 138 Banff Ave.; 403 762-3331. Specializes in baby back ribs, AAA Alberta steaks and slow roasted BBQ chicken, beef and pork. Email: info@mountroyalhotel.com, www.tonyromas.com. B/L/D, Late, $$, AX/V/MC.
- Typhoon, 211 Caribou St.; 403 762-2000, Eclectic Asian. www.dininginbanff.com/restaurants/typhoon.shtml. D/Late, $$, AX/V/MC.
- The Upper Hot Springs Café, Mountain Road; 403 760-6686. Take a break after a relaxing soak. B/L/G, $, AX/V/MC.
- Waldhaus Restaurant, Banff Springs Hotel, 405 Spray Avenue; 403 762-6860. A Bavarian cottage-style restaurant serving authentic Swiss and German dishes. D, $$$, AX/V/MC. Hours and days of operation based on season.
- Wild Bill's, 201 Banff Ave.; 403 762-0333. Famous for chicken and rib combos. Email: Info@wbsaloon.com, www.wbsaloon.com. L/D, $$, AX/V/MC.

LAKE LOUISE

- Brewster Cowboy's BBQ & Dance Barn — Lake Louise; 403 762-5454. Live western music and entertainment. www.brewsterlake-louisestables.com/sleighrides_dinner.html. Brunch/D, $$, AX/V/MC.
- Glacier Saloon, Chateau Lake Louise; 403 522-3511. Entertainment and dancing, light meals. www.fairmont.com/lakelouise. L/D/Late, $, AX/V/MC.
- The Post Hotel, 200 Pipestone Rd.; 403 522-3989. Known for superbly presented regional cuisine. L/D, $$$$, V/MC.
- Walliser Stube, Chateau Lake Louise; 403 522-3511. Swiss Fondue. www.fairmont.com/lakelouise. D, $$$, AX/V/MC.

COLUMBIA ICEFIELD

- Icefield Centre Snack Bar, Cafeteria and Dining Room, 1-877-423-7433. Good selection of hot and cold food. B/L/D, $, V/MC.

JASPER

- Becker's Gourmet, Becker's Chalets, Icefields Parkway; 780 852-3535. Fine continental-style dinners. www.beckerschalets.com/Documents/restaurant.htm. B/D, $$$$, AX/V/MC.

EDMONTON

FINE DINING

- Hardware Grill, 9698 Jasper Ave.; 780 423-0969. Excellent food with wines priced quite reasonably. www.hardwaregrill.com. L/D, $$$, AX/V/MC.
- Hy's Steak Loft, 10013-101A Ave. N.W.; 780 424-4444. The best of Alberta beef. www.hyssteakhouse.com. L/D, $$$, AX/V/MC.
- Jack's Grill, 5842 111 St. N.W.; 780 434-1113. An intimate restaurant. Email: jacksnet@telusplanet.net, www.jacksgrill.ca. D, $$$, V/MC.
- La Ronde, the Chateau Lacombe, 10111 Bellamy Hill N.W.; 780 428-6611. Rotating restaurant offering Alberta specialties. www.chateaulacombe.com/laronde.html. Brunch/D, $$$, AX/V/MC.

INTIMATE

- The Creperie, 10220 103 St.; 780 420-6656. Romantic French fare. Email: inquiries@thecreperie.com. www.thecreperie.com. L/D, $$, V/MC.
- The Red-Ox Inn, 9420 91st St.; 780 465-5727. Fine dining including

scallops, salmon and beef tenderloin. D, $$, V/MC.

ETHNIC

- Bach Dang, 7908 104th St.; 780 448-0288. Vietnamese fare, a great place for lunch. L/D, $, AX/V/MC.
- The Bulgogi House, 88th Ave. & 92nd St.; 780 466-2330. Korean Cuisine. L/D, $, AX/V/MC.
- East Bound Eatery and Sake Bar, 11248-104 Ave.; 780 428-2448. Sushi and other Japanese dishes. L/D, $, AX/V/MC.
- Fantasia Noodle House, 10518 Jasper Ave.; 780 428-0943. Heaping lunch specials. L/D, $, V/MC.
- Grub Med, 17 Fairway Dr. (119th St. & 37th Ave.); 780 436-1988. Excellent Greek restaurant. D, $$, AX/V/MC.
- The Happy Garden, 6525 111th St. N.W.; 780 435-7622. Chinese food. L/D, $, AX/V/MC.
- Julio's Barrio, 10450 82nd Ave.; 780 431-0774. Baha Mexican fare. Email: info@ juliosbarrio.com, www.juliosbarrio.com. L/D, $, AX/V/MC.
- The Mikado, 10350 109th St. N.W.; 780 425-8096. Japanese, including a sushi bar. Email: mikado@oanet.com, www.mikadorestaurant.com. L/D, $$, AX/V/MC.
- Mirama, 9431 Jasper Ave; 780 425-3888. Chinese dim-sum. L/D, $, AX/V/MC.
- New Asian Village, 10149 Saskatchewan Dr.; 780 433-3804. South Indian cuisine with lunch and dinner buffets available. www.newasianvillage.com. L/D, T-O, $, AX/V/MC.
- Sceppa's Trattoria and Deli, 10923 101st St. N.W.; 780 425-9241. Wonderful Italian feasts. L/D, $, V/MC.
- The Sherlock Holmes Pub, 10012 101A Ave.; 780 426-7784. Traditional pub grub, live entertainment. Also located at the West Edmonton Mall. www.thesherlockholmes.com. L/D, $, V/MC.

OTHER

- Barb and Ernie's, 9906 72nd Ave.; 780 433-3242. Famous for its eggs Benedict. B/L/D, $, V/MC.
- Colonel Mustard's, 10802-124 St.; 780 448-1590. Soups, sandwiches and hearty desserts. B/L/G/T-O, $.
- Earl's, 11830 Jasper Ave.; 780 488-6582. 8629 112th St.; 780 408-3914. A popular choice for burgers, pastas and stir frys. Various locations. www.earls.ca. L/D, $, V/MC.
- East Side Mario's, 2104 99th St.; 780 988-8938. A N.Y. family eatery with Italian for everyone. www.eastsidemarios.com. L/D, $, AX/V/MC.
- The High Level Diner, 10912 88th Ave.; 780 433-1317. Popular for brunch and vegetarian options. B/L/D, $, AX/V/MC.
- Joey Tomato's, 11228 Jasper Ave.; 780 420-1996. 9911 19th Avenue N.W.; 780-465-1880. Upbeat Italian menu, generous portions. www.joeysmedgrill.com. L/D, $, V/MC.
- Max's Light Cuisine, 7809 109th St.; 780 432-6241. Strictly vegetarian, many options. L/D, $, V/MC.
- The Old Spaghetti Factory, 10220 103rd St.; 780 422-6088. Always a favourite. www.oldspaghettifactory.ca. L/D, $, V/MC.
- Packrat Louie Kitchen & Bar, 10335 83 Ave. (Near 104 N.W.); 780 433-0123. Fresh market and Swiss cuisine. www.packratlouie.ca. L/D, $$, AX/V/MC. Closed Sunday and Monday.
- The Upper Crust Cafe, 10909 86 Ave. N.W.; 780 433-0810. Great desserts and sandwiches, popular with university students. B/L, $, AX/V/MC.

FAST FOOD

- Billingsgate Seafood Market, 7331 104th St. N.W.; 780 433-0091. Eat in or take out. www.billingsgate.com. L/D/T-O, $.
- Joey's Only Seafood, 12222 137th Ave.; 780 473-5639. 11308 104 Avenue N.W.; 780 421-1971. All you can eat Fish 'n' Chips on Tuesdays, various locations. L/D, $, V/MC.
- Kingsway Garden Mall, 109th St. & Kingsway; 780 477-5756. A food fair with great variety. www.kingswaymall.com. L/D/G/T-O, $.
- Mongolia Express, 10355 78th Ave. N.W.; 780 988-7282. Tasty fast Asian fare. Eat in or take out. L/D, $$.
- Southgate Centre, 11100 51st Ave.; 780 435-3721. An excellent food

fair. L/D/G/T-O, $.
- Tokyo Express, 11642 104th Ave. N.; 780 448-0849. Great food on the go. L/T-O, $.

DRUMHELLER
- Fred & Barney's Family Restaurant, 1222 Hwy 9 S.; 403 823-3803. www.virtuallydrumheller.com/fred barneys. B/L/D, $, AX/V/MC.
- Whistling Kettle, 109 Centre St.; 403 823-9997. Quaint teahouse that is famous for its homemade pies. B/L/G, $.
- The Rosebud Dinner Theatre, Hamlet of Rosebud, P.O. Box 654; 403 677-2001, 1-800-267-7553; Fax: 403 677-2390. A delicious country buffet followed by a lively performance. Email: info@rosebudtheatre.com, www.rosebudtheatre.com. L/D, $$, V/MC.
- Stavros Family Restaurant, Hwy. 9 S.; 403 823-6362. Something for everyone. B/L/D, $, AX/V/MC.

ATTRACTIONS

CALGARY

TOP ATTRACTIONS
The list that follows gives information on some of Calgary's most exciting visitor attractions.
- Calgary Farmer's Market. A year-round (Friday-Sundays) produce, food, crafts and other specialties market. Local artisans, growers plus food court and kids area. At the old Currie Barracks, hangar 6; 403 244-4548. www.calgaryfarmersmarket.ca
- Calgary Tower. Spectacular panoramic views of the city and beyond. 101 9th Ave. S.W.; 403 266-7171, www.calgarytower.com
- Calgary Stampede. A 10-day extravaganza billed as the Greatest Outdoor Show On Earth. With everything from chuckwagons and rodeo to pancake breakfasts and fireworks, this spectacular event brings out the cowboy in everyone. Box 1060, Stn. M, Calgary, AB T2P 2K8; 403 261-0101, 24-hour information line 403 261-0500, 1-800-661-1260, Email: reception3@calgarystampede.com, www.calgarystampede.com
- Calgary Zoo and Prehistoric Park. A world-class facility offering educational programs, botanical gardens, replicated natural environments for animals, nature exhibits and its renowned new Destination Africa pavilion. Memorial Drive N.E.; 403 232-9300, Email: info@calgaryzoo.ab.ca, www.calgaryzoo.org
- Canada Olympic Park. Offering everything from a trip down a bobsled or luge run to mountain biking, a ski hill and an Olympic Hall of Fame, this facility celebrating Calgary's Olympic legacy is well worth a visit. 88 Canada Olympic Road S.W.; 403 247-5452, Email: info@coda. ca, www.coda.ab.ca/cop
- Crossroads Market. Outdoor farmers market in the spring, summer and fall. Over 125 indoor vendors year round. 1235 26th Ave. S.E.; 403 291-5208, www.aroundcalgary.com/crossroads market
- Eau Claire Market. A complete shopping experience offering bistros, fresh fruit and vegetable stalls, specialty boutiques, trendy stores, movie theatres and galleries. 200 Barclay Parade S.W.; 403 264-6450, Email: info@eauclairemarket.com, www.eauclairemarket.com
- Fort Calgary Historic Park. Exhibits, interpretive programs and activities. A look at where Calgary got its start. 750 9th Ave. S.E.; 403 290-1875, Email: info@fortcalgary.com, www.fortcalgary.com
- Heritage Park. A working historical village that invites visitors to share a glance at life in the 1900's. 1900 Heritage Dr. S.W.; 403 268-8500, Email: info@heritagepark.ab.ca, www.heritagepark.ca
- Olympic Oval. Try your hand at speed skating or just enjoy watching some of the world's finest athletes train in this world class facility. Public skating and indoor running facilities available. University of Calgary; 403 220-7954, www.oval.ucalgary.ca
- Olympic Plaza. A downtown open space perfect for a picnic. Skating in the winter. Host to the 1988 Winter Olympics medal presentations. Corner 7th Ave. S.E. and Macleod Trail S.E.; 403 268-3888.
- The Pengrowth Saddledome. Home of the Calgary Flames and the Calgary Roughnecks. 555

Saddledome Rise S.E.; 403 777-2177, www.pengrowthsaddledome.com.

- Prince's Island Park. An inner city haven located on the Bow River suitable for walks, bike rides and picnics. Year-round it is home to festivals, events and recreation activities for people of all ages. 4th St. and 1 Ave. S.W., www.calgary.ca
- Shaw Millennium Park. Huge outdoor skate park. 1220 9th Ave. S.W.; 403 268-3888, www.gov.calgary.ab.ca/skatepark/pgmillenniumhome.html
- Spruce Meadows Equestrian Centre. A world-renowned show jumping facility in a spectacular setting that hosts several national and international competitions each year. Demonstrations and exhibits entertain all members of the family. RR9; 403 974-4200, Email: information@sprucemeadows.com, www.sprucemeadows.com
- TELUS World of Science. Formerly Calgary Science Centre. Exhibits and shows that help to make science exciting for all. 701 11 St. S.W.; 403 268-8300, www.calgaryscience.ca

ENTERTAINMENT

Entertainment in Calgary can be found live at clubs, theatres and arts centres around town. The best places to check for information include the Friday edition of the *Calgary Herald*, FFWD News & Entertainment Weekly, www.ffwdweekly.com, and *Where Calgary* publications, available free at most coffee shops and public locations. Ticketmaster sells tickets to most events and can be reached at 403 777-0000, or check out their web site, www.ticketmaster.ca

Music & Opera

- Calgary Opera Association, 1315 7 St. S.W.; 403 262-7286, mail: calgaryopera@calgaryopera.com, www.calgaryopera.com. Performed at the Southern Alberta Jubilee Auditorium 1415 14 Ave. N.W.; 403 205-2922.
- Calgary Philharmonic Orchestra, 403 571-0270, Email: info@cpo-live.com, www.cpo-live.com
- Epcor Centre for the Performing Arts, 205 8th Ave. S.W.; Ticketmaster, 403 299-8888, 24 Hour Show Information Line, 403 294-7455, Email: info@epcorcentre.org,

www.epcorcentre.org. Location of the superbly acoustic Jack Singer Concert Hall, home to the Calgary Philharmonic Orchestra.

- Mount Royal College Conservatory, .4825 Mount Royal Gate S.W.; 403 440-6821, www.mtroyal.ab.ca/conservatory. A hotspot for classical concerts.
- Rozsa Centre on the University of Calgary Campus, 2500 University Drive N.W.; 403 220-4900. Many recitals and local musical groups play here.

Theatre

- Epcor Centre for the Performing Arts, 205 8th Ave. S.E.; Ticketmaster, 403 299-8888, 24-Hour Show Information Line, 403 294-7444, Email: info@epcorcentre.org, www.epcorcentre.org. Home to the following three companies:
- Theatre Calgary in the Max Bell Theatre, a more conservative, traditional company. 403 294-7441, Email: info@theatrecalgary.com, www.theatrecalgary.com
- Alberta Theatre Projects in the Martha Cohen Theatre, presenting more contemporary theatre. 403 294-7475, Email: askATP@ATPlive.com, www.atplive.com
- One Yellow Rabbit Performance Theatre presents more risky and experimental theatre. 403 264-3224, Email: oyr@canuck.com, www.oyr.org
- The Globe Theatre, 617 8th Ave. S.W.; 403 262-3309. Art house movie theatre.
- Ground Zero Theatre, 144, 517 10 Ave. S.W.; 403 202-2520, Email: info@groundzerotheatre.ca, www.groundzerotheatre.ca. A local theatre company.
- Jubilations Calgary Dinner Theatre Limited; 403 249-7799, www.jubilations.ca.
- Loose Moose Theatre Company, 2nd floor of the Crossroads Market, 1235 26th Ave. S.E.; 403 265-5682, Email: mail@loosemoose.com, www.loosemoose.com. Host to a lively improvisational comedy scene.
- Lunchbox Theatre, 2nd Level, 205 5th Ave. S.W.; 403 265-4292, Email: lunchbox@cadvision.com, www.lunchboxtheatre.com. Offers entertainment while enjoying your

brown-bag lunch.
- Quest Theatre, 310-815 1st St. S.W.; 403 264-8575, Email: qtheatre@telusplanet.net, www.questtheatre.org. Ideal for family entertainment.
- Sage Theatre, 1002 37th St. S.W.; 403 264-7243, www.sagetheatre.com
- Stage West Theatre Restaurant, 727 42nd Ave. S.E.; 403 243-6642, Email: mail@stagewestcalgary.com, www.stagewestcalgary.com. Ideal for combining dinner and a show.
- Theatre Junction, 607, 815 1st St. S.W.; 403 205-2922, Email: info@theatrejunction.com, www.theatrejunction.com. Performances at the Grand Theatre, downtown Calgary.
- The Uptown Screen and Stage, 612 8th Ave. S.W.; 403 265-0120, Email: mail@theuptown.com, www.theuptown.com. Movies (first run art/international films) and live stage productions.
- Vertigo Mystery Theatre (formerly Pleiades), in the base of the Calgary Tower, 115 9th Ave. S.E.; 403 221-3707, www.vertigomysterytheatre.com. One of Canada's only mystery theatres, great for an intriguing evening.
- Yuk Yuk's, The Blackfoot Inn, 5940 Blackfoot Trail S.E.; 403 258-2028, www.yukyuks.com. Calgary's best-known venue for stand-up comedy.

Dance

- Alberta Ballet, at the Jubilee Auditorium, 1415 14 Ave. N.W.; Administration at the Nat Christie Centre, 141 18th Ave. S.W.; Ticketmaster, 403 299-8888, www.albertaballet.com. Canada's fourth-largest ballet company presenting both classical and modern works.
- Decidedly Jazz Danceworks, 1514 4th St. S.W.; 403 245-3533, Email: djd@decidedlyjazz.com, www.decidedlyjazz.com. Presenting rhythmically complex jazz choreography at various venues in the city.

Clubs

- Bamboo Tiki Room, 1201 1st St. S.W.; 403 261-6674. Intimate downtown pub with live/deejayed dance music.
- Beat Niq Jazz and Social Club, 811 1st St. S.W.; 403 263-1650, www.beatniq.com. Jazz with a local twist.
- Bruno's Hideout, 3460 17th Ave. S.W.; 403 204-2177.
- Ceili's Irish Pub and Restaurant, 126, 513 8th Ave. S.W.; 403 508-9999, www.ceilis.com. Traditional Irish libations.
- Cherry Lounge, 1219 1st St. S.W;. 403-266-2540. Centrally-located bar/lounge.
- Coyotes, 1088 Olympic Way S.E.; 403 263-5343. Huge country-themed downtown bar with spacious dance floor.
- Cowboys, 826 5th St. S.W.; 403 265-0699. A cavernous downtown bar and dance hall featuring live country bands and other acts.
- HiFi Club, 219 10th Ave. S.W.; 403 263-5222. A downtown bar featuring rap, dance and other music.
- Ironwood Stage and Grill, 1429 9 Ave. S.E.; 403 269-3031. www.ironwoodstage.ca. Live entertainment with a focus on independent, original music in a range of genres.
- The James Joyce Pub, 114 8th Ave. S.W.; 403 262-0708, www.thejoyce.ca. A popular Celtic pub presenting live music.
- Joyce on 4th, 506 24th Ave. S.W.; 403 541-9168, www.thejoyce.ca. Little brother to the original James Joyce.
- MacEwan Hall Ballroom, MacEwan Hall Student's Centre, University of Calgary Campus, 2500 University Drive N.W.; 403 210-9375. Plays host to some of the hottest touring bands and performers.
- The Night Gallery, 1209B 1st St. S.W.; 403 264-4484. A good venue for alternative music acts.
- Outlaws Nite Club, 24 7400 Macleod Trail S.; 403 255-4646, www.outlawsniteclub.com. Dance club with drink specials, popular with students.
- The Ranchman's, 9615 Macleod Trail S.; 403 253-1100, www.ranchmans.com. A genuine cowboy institution for a taste of the Wild West.
- Shamrock Hotel, 2101 11 St. S.E.; 403 290-0084. This well-worn bar near an industrial area has become the new home to blues since the famous King Eddy blues bar and hotel shut down.

- The Ship & Anchor Pub, 534 17th Ave. S.W.; 403 245-3333, www.shipandanchor.com. Very popular patio for meeting and greeting; great pub food and a hangout for the alternative music scene.
- Trappers Pub, 3919 Richmond Rd. S.W.; 403 217-7744. Live music, pool/billiards tables, NTN trivia, pub food.
- Tequila Nightclub, 219 17th Ave. S.W.; 403 209-2215, www.tequilanightclub.com. A party hotspot.
- Underground Pub, 731 10th Ave. S.W.; 403 266-6629. Live music acts.

MUSEUMS

Offering visitors much more than just a trip back in time, Calgary's museums are an exciting way to learn about the past of a city that has been shaped by many influences. Information on special shows can be found in Thursday's *Calgary Herald*, and on the museums' respective web sites.

- The Aero Space Museum, 4629 McCall Way N.E.; 403 250-3752, Email: aerospace@asmac.ab.ca, www.asmac.ab.ca. Calgary is remembered from the Second World War as a key centre for the British Commonwealth Air Training Plan. The museum looks at this past as well as allowing visitors to explore Canadian space history.
- The Glenbow, 130 9th Ave. S.E.; 403 268-4100, www.glenbow.org. A top-quality museum covering everything from the history of the settlement of the West to lives and stories of peoples from lands overseas.
- The Museum of the Regiments, 4520 Crowchild Trail S.W.; 403 974-2850, Email: regiments@nucleus.com, www.museumoftheregiments.ca. The second-largest military museum in Canada and a fantastic facility where history is brought alive with imagination and detailed displays.
- The Naval Museum of Alberta, 1820 24th St. S.W.; 403 242-0002, Email: navalweb@navalmuseum.ab.ca, www.navalmuseum.ab.ca. While Calgary may be far from the ocean, it has had an interesting past linking it with naval warfare and this past is displayed in the second largest naval museum in Canada.

PROFESSIONAL SPORTS TEAMS

- Football — The Calgary Stampeders play in the Canadian Football League (CFL) at McMahon Stadium. www.stampeders.com
- Hockey — The Calgary Flames play at the Pengrowth Saddledome. www.calgaryflames.com
- Lacrosse — The Calgary Roughnecks play at the Pengrowth Saddledome. www.calgaryroughnecks.com

BANFF

TOP ATTRACTIONS

The following are the sights not to miss during your visit to Banff National Park.

- The Banff Centre, Office of the Registrar, 107 Tunnel Mountain Drive, Banff, AB T1L 1H5; 403 762-6180, 1-800-565-9989; Fax: 403 762-6345, Email: arts_info@banffcentre.ca, www.banffcentre.ab.ca/CFA. Internationally renowned centre for the Arts.
- The Banff Springs Hotel. P.O. Box 960 Banff; 403 762-2211; Fax: 403 762-4447, Email: banffsprings@fairmont.com. www.fairmont.com. A prominent feature in Banff's history and a magnificent resort.
- Canada Place at the Banff National Park Administration Building, Box 900, Banff; 403 762-1550; Fax: 403 762-3380, Email: banff.vrc@pc.gc.ca, www.pc.gc.ca/pnnp/ab/banff/visit/visit1aE.asp. Beautiful gardens at the end of Banff High Street.
- The Cave and Basin National Historic Site. Cave Avenue, Banff; 403 762-1566, www.pc.gc.ca/lhn-nhs/ab/caveandbasin/index_e.asp. Exhibition detailing the history of Banff National Park and the hot springs.
- The Lake Louise Ski Hill Gondola, Box 5, Lake Louise AB; 403 522-3555, 1-800-258-7669; Fax: 403 522-2095, Email: questions@skilouise.com, www.skilouise.com/summer. Enjoy a trip up to the top of the Lake Louise ski area for a spectacular view. Interpretive programs offered.
- Self-Guided Historical Walking Tour, guides available from the

Whyte Museum (see below).
- Sulphur Mountain Gondola. Mountain Ave., Box 1258 Banff; 403 762-2523; Fax: 403 762-7493, Email: lift@banffgondola.com, www.banffgondola.com. A trip to the top of Sulphur Mountain for an incredible view of the Bow Valley.
- The Upper Hot Springs Pool and Spa. Mountain Ave., Banff; 403 762-1515. www.pc.gc.ca/regional/sourcesthermaleshotsprings/visit/banffe.asp. Enjoy a warm soak in the mineral-spring-fed pool or indulge at the spa.

NIGHTLIFE

The main area for nightlife in Banff is along Banff Avenue, where there is always a lot going on.
- Banff Springs Hotel Conference Centre, 405 Spray Ave.; 403 762-6892. Bowling.
- Barbary Coast, 119 Banff Ave.; 403 762-4616. Steakhouse and bar with daily drink specials and live entertainment in the weekends.
- Bumper's Lounge, 603 Banff Ave.; 403 762-2622. www.bumpersinn.com. For a quiet drink.
- Hard Rock Cafe, 137 Banff Ave.; 403 760-2347. American-themed rock & roll restaurant.
- Hoodoo Lounge, 137 Banff Ave.; 403 760-8636. www.hoodoolounge.com. Lounge/nightclub.
- King Eddy Billiards, 137 Banff Ave; 403 762-4629. Hippest pool place.
- Outabounds, 137 Banff Ave.; 403 762-8434. A dance club.
- The Rose and Crown Pub, 202 Banff Ave.; 403 762-2121. Email: info@banffroseandcrown.com, www.banffroseandcrown.com. Live entertainment.
- St. James's Gate Irish Pub, 207 Wolf St.; 403 762-9355. Pints for all.
- Wild Bill's Legendary Saloon, 201 Banff Ave.; 403 762-0333. Email: wildbills@banff.net, www.wbsaloon.com. Popular with locals.

ARTS

- The Banff Centre, 107 Tunnel Mountain Drive, Banff, AB T1L 1H5; 403 762-6100, 1-800-565-9989; Fax: 403 762-6345, Email: arts_info@banffcentre.ca, www.banffcentre.ab.ca

- The Luxe Cinema, 229 Bear St.; 403 762-8595.

MUSEUMS

There is plenty to learn in Banff about both the history of the park itself, and the history of the natural environment.
- The Banff Park Museum, 91 Banff Ave.; 403 762-1558, www.pc.gc.ca/lhnnhs/ab/banff/indexe.asp. Natural history museum, interpretive programs offered.
- The Buffalo Nations Luxton Museum, 1 Birch Avenue, Banff; 403 762-2388. Cultural museum of Native arts and daily life.
- The Whyte Museum of the Canadian Rockies, 111 Bear St., Banff; 403 762-2291; Fax: 403 762-8919, Email: info@whyte.org, www.whyte.org. Art galleries, heritage artifacts and international exhibitions.

COLUMBIA ICEFIELD

- The Icefield Centre, across from the Athabasca Glacier, Highway 93 (Icefield Parkway); 403 762-6700, 1-877-423-7433; Fax: 1-877-766-7433, www.columbiaicefield.com. Learn about glaciers and the local environment in the Parks Canada Glacier Gallery.
- SnoCoach Tours, Athabasca Glacier, 100 Gopher St., Box 1140, Banff, AB T1L 1J3; 403 762-6700, 1-877-423-7433; Fax: 1-877-766-7433, Email: icefield@brewster.ca, www.brewster.ca. Tours on the glacier in special Snow Coaches operated by Brewster.

JASPER

From coal mining town to major international tourist attraction, Jasper has had an interesting history and is a top location for outdoor recreation. Less developed than Banff, it offers many natural attractions and spectacular views.

TOP ATTRACTIONS

- Jasper Park Collieries and Pocahontas, Miette Hot Springs Road. www.worldweb.com/ParksCanada-Jasper/history. Site of a coal mining town that flourished in the early 1900s.
- Jasper Tramway, Whistler's Mountain Road, Box 418, Jasper, AB T0E 1E0; 780 852-3093; Fax: 780 852-5779, Email:

info@jaspertramway.com, www.jaspertramway.com. Unsurpassed views, interpretive exhibits and hikes await at the top of this trip up the mountain.

- Maligne Lake Road. Maligne Tours Ltd, P.O. Box 280, Jasper, AB T0E 1E0; 780 852-3370; Fax: 780 852-3405, Email: maligne@telusplanet.net, www.malignelake.com. On a 46-kilometre day trip, explore Maligne Canyon and Lake, where many outdoor activities are available.

- Miette Hot Springs. Hwy 16 to the Miette Hot Springs Road, P.O. Box 2579, Jasper, AB T0E 1E0; 780 866-3939, 1-800-767-1611; Fax: 780 866-2112, www.parkscanada.gc.ca. Indulge in a hot thermal soak.

- The Railway Station. 400 Connaught Drive, Jasper. A historic part of Jasper's past.

- Walking Tour of Jasper, from the Information Centre, 500 Connaught Drive, Jasper, AB T0E 1E0; 780 852-6177. Evenings during summer.

MUSEUMS

- Jasper's Wildlife Museum, Whistlers Inn, Connaught Drive & Miette Ave., P.O. Box 250, Jasper, AB; T0E 1E0; 780 852-3361, 1-800-282-9919; Fax: 780 852-4993, Email: info@whistlersinn.com, www.whistlersinn.com/museum.html. Experience Jasper's natural habitat, up close.

- Jasper Yellowhead Museum, 400 Pyramid Lake Road, PO Box 42, Jasper, AB; 780 852-3013; Fax: 780-852-3240, Email: jymachin@ telusplanet.net, www.jasper-alberta.com. A glimpse at Jasper's origins and the days of fur trading.

EDMONTON

The City of Festivals always has something exciting going on. The capital of the Province, and home to the University of Alberta and the famous West Edmonton Mall, Edmonton offers many attractions to entertain visitors of all ages.

TOP ATTRACTIONS

- The Alberta Legislature. Visitor Services, Government Centre, Pedway Mall, 10800 97th Ave., Edmonton, AB T5K 2N6; 780 427-7362; Fax: 780 427-0980, Email: laocommunications@assembly.ab.ca, www.assembly.ab.ca. Home to Alberta's government. Tours are available of this historic building and its grounds.

- The Arts District. City centre region that is home to the following five facilities:

- City Hall. 1 Sir Winston Churchill Square, Edmonton, AB T5J 2R7; 780 496-4000; Fax: 780 496-8297, Email: webmaster@ edmonton. ca, www. edmonton. ca. The main atrium is often host to choral events and community gatherings.

- The Art Gallery of Alberta. 2 Sir Winston Churchill Square, Edmonton, AB T5J 2C1; 780 422-6223; Fax: 780 426-3105, Email: info@edmontonartgallery.com, www.edmontonartgallery.com. A good collection of the Group of Seven.

- The Francis Winspear Centre. 4 Sir Winston Churchill Square, 99th St. & 102nd Ave., Edmonton, AB; 780 428-1414, 1-800-563-5081; Fax: 780 425-0167, Email: info@winspearcentre.com, www.winspearcentre.com. One of the finest and most acoustically perfect halls in North America.

- The Citadel Theatre. 9828 101A Ave., Shoctor Alley, Edmonton, AB T5J 3C6; 780 425-1820, 1-888-425-1820; Fax: 780 428-7194, Email: boxoffice@citadeltheatre.com, www.citadeltheatre.com. The largest theatre complex in Canada.

- Stanley Milner Library. 7 Sir Winston Churchill Square, Edmonton, AB T5J 2V4; 780 496-7000, www.epl.ca. The main branch of the Edmonton Public Library system.

- The Devonian Botanic Garden. Five kilometres north of Devon on Highway 60; 780 987-3054, www.discoveredmonton.com/ devonian. Over 190 acres of gardens and preserved areas to explore.

- Fort Edmonton Park. Fox Drive & Whitmud Drive, P.O. Box 2359, Edmonton, AB T5J 2R7; 780 496-8777; Fax: 780 496-8797, Email:

attractions@edmonton.ca, www.edmonton.ca/fort. A stroll through Edmonton's history, from the fur trade on. Canada's only on-location national historic site inn, Hotel Selkirk with its authentic LONG bar. Hotel reservations: 780 496-7227

- The Muttart Conservatory. 9626 96A St. Edmonton, AB T6C 4L8; 780 496-8755; Fax: 780 496-8747, Email: muttartquestions@edmonton.ca, www.edmonton.ca. A horticultural conservatory under four pyramid structures.
- Old Strathcona. 112th St. to 99th St. along 82nd Ave., Old Strathcona Business Association, 6, 10436 81st Ave., Edmonton, AB T6E 1X6; 780 437-4182; Fax: 780 433-4657, Email: info@oldstrathcona.ca, www.osba.ab.ca, www.oldstrathcona.ca. Centred on Whyte Avenue, this trendy area has boutiques, restaurants, bistros and an active nightlife.
- Princess Theatre. 10337 Whyte Ave. (Near 83), Edmonton, AB T6E 1Z9; 780 433-0728. A beautifully restored art house theatre.
- The River Valley. Miles of outdoor trails and venues to enjoy. www.edmonton.ca
- Telus World of Science (former Odyssium). 11211 142nd St. Edmonton, AB T5M 4A1; 780 452-9100; Fax: 780 455-5882, Email: info@odyssium.com, www.odyssium.com. An interactive facility with something for everyone, from space walks to star gazing.
- University of Alberta. 114 St. - 89 Ave., Edmonton, AB T6G 2E1; 780 492-3111, www.ualberta.ca
- West Edmonton Mall. Administration, 2472, 8882 170th St., Edmonton, AB T5T 4M2; 780 444-5200; Fax: 780 444-5223, Tourist Information, 1-800-661-8890, 780 444-5200, Email: tourism@westedmontonmall.com, www.westedmontonmall.com. The largest shopping centre in the world. Covering 48 city blocks it includes over 800 stores, an amusement park, ice rink, lagoon, theatres, hotel and attractions.

MUSEUMS
- The John Walter Museum. 9100 Walterdale Hill, PO Box 2359, Edmonton, AB T6J 2R7; 780 496-

8787; Fax: 780 496-4701, www.edmonton.ca. The story of one of Edmonton's foremost turn-of-the-century entrepreneurs, and the history of Edmonton's river valley.
- Royal Alberta Museum (formerly Provincial Museum of Alberta). 12845 102nd Ave., Edmonton, AB T5N 0M6; 780 453-9100; Fax: 780 454-6629, www.royalalbertamuseum.ca. A natural and human history museum that often hosts traveling exhibitions.

PROFESSIONAL SPORTS TEAMS
- The Edmonton Cracker-Cats baseball team plays in the Northern League at Telus Field. www.crackercats.ca
- The Edmonton Eskimos play in the Canadian Football League (CFL) at Commonwealth Stadium. www.esks.com
- The Edmonton Oilers play in the National Hockey League (NHL) at Rexall Place. www.edmontonoilers.com

DRUMHELLER
Home to one of the world's richest dinosaur deposits, Drumheller is a fascinating look back at the world before we knew it.
- Atlas Coal Mine National Historic Site. Box 521, East Coulee, AB T0J 1B0; 403 822-2220; Fax: 403 822-2225, Email: info@atlascoalmine.ab.ca, www.atlascoalmine.ab.ca. Explore a former coal mine.
- Dinosaur Provincial Park. P.O. Box 60, Patricia, AB T0J 2K0; 403 378-4342; Fax: 403 378-4247, Toll-free (Alberta only) 310-0000, www.cd.gov.ab.ca/enjoying_alberta/parks/dinosaur. A UN World Heritage Site in the Alberta Badlands.
- The Fossil Shop. 61 Bridge St., Box 1086, Drumheller, AB T0J 0Y0; 403-823-6774; Fax: 403-823-6774, Email: miles@thefossilshop.com, www.thefossilshop.com. Sells rare fossils, gifts and educational supplies.
- The Passion Play. P.O. Box 457, Drumheller, AB T0J 0Y0; 403 823-2001; Fax: 403 823-8170, Email: pplay@telusplanet.net, www.canadianpassionplay.com. July. The life and times of Christ, depicted in a natural rock amphitheatre. Sells out early.

- The Rosebud Dinner Theatre. Box 654, Rosebud, AB T0J 2T0; 403 677-2001, 1-800-267-7553; Fax: 403 677-2390, Email: info@ rosebudtheatre.com, www.rosebudtheatre.com
- The Royal Tyrrell Museum of Paleontology. Box 7500, Drumheller, AB T0J 0Y0; 403 823-7707, 1-888-440-4240; Fax: 403 823-7131, Email: tyrrell.info@gov.ab.ca, www.tyrrellmuseum.com. A world-renowned research facility housing the largest collection of dinosaur fossils in the world. Exhibits, demonstrations, interactive displays and interpretive programs will interest all ages.

WATERTON

One of Canada's most spectacular mountain destinations, Waterton is popular for its quiet town, miles of hiking and challenging outdoor adventure possibilities.

- Alpine Stables. Box 53, Waterton Lakes National Park, Waterton, AB T0K 2M0; 403 859-2462 in season, 403 653-2089 off season. Email: alpine6@alpinestables.com, www.alpinestables.com
- Peace Park Pavilion. Waterton Ave., Waterton Lakes, AB; www.parkscanada.pch.gc.ca. Discover why Waterton, together with Glacier National Park in Montana, was declared an International Peace Park.
- The Prince of Wales Hotel. Waterton, AB T0K 2M0; 403 859-2231; Fax: 403 859-2630. www.princeofwaleswaterton.com. A spectacular hotel built in 1927 that is well worth a visit for afternoon tea.
- Waterton Heritage Centre. 117 Waterton Ave., Box 145, Waterton Lakes, AB T0K 2M0; 403 859-2624, www.eidnet.org/local/wnha
- Waterton Inter-Nation Shoreline Cruise Co. Ltd. Box 126, Waterton Lakes National Park, AB T0K 2M0; 403 859-2362; Fax: 403 938-5019, Email: wscruise@telus.net, www.watertoninfo.ab.ca/m/cruise. Enjoy a scenic cruise from Upper Waterton Lake to Goat Haunt, Montana, U.S.A.
- Waterton Lakes Golf Course. Box 2000, Waterton Lakes National Park, Waterton, AB T0K 2M0; 403 859-2114.
- Waterton National History Association. Box 145, Waterton Lakes National Park, Waterton, AB T0K 2M0; 403 859-2624. Email: wnha@telusplanet.net, www.wnha.ca
- Waterton Park Chamber of Commerce and Visitor Association. Box 100, Waterton, AB T0K 2M0; 403 859-2252; Fax: 403 859-2342. www.watertoninfo.com

OUTDOOR RECREATION

There are exciting opportunities awaiting everyone who ventures out to explore Alberta and the Rocky Mountains. Be sure to obtain correct trail information before heading out, and take proper equipment. Information centres are available to offer advice, maps, guide books etc. The following are some of the major outdoor resorts and areas to be found.

KANANASKIS

- The Bow River Corridor, Access: Highway 1 between the Highway 40 overpass and Canmore; 403 673-3663.
- Bow Valley Provincial Park, Access: Highway 1 west, Highway 40 south, Highway 1X north; 403 673-3985.
- Canmore Golf and Curling Club, 2000 8th Ave., Canmore, AB T1W 1Y2; Proshop / Tee-Times: 403 678-4785, 1-888-678-4785, Fax 403 678-6616, www.canmoregolf.net
- Canmore Nordic Centre Provincial Park, Suite 100, 1988 Olympic Way, Canmore, AB T1W 2T6; 403 678-2400; Fax: 403 678-5696, Email: Ray.Andrews@gov.ab.ca, www.cd.gov.ab.ca/enjoying_alberta/ parks/featured/kananaskis/parkscan more.asp
- Elbow-Sheep Wildland Park, Forestry Trunk Road (Hwy. 40); 403 673-3985.
- Highwood to Cataract Creek Drive; 403 678-5508.
- Kananaskis Country Golf Course, Mount Kidd & Mount Lorette, Hwy. 40, P.O. Box 1710, Kananaskis Country, AB T0L 2H0; 403 591-7154, 1-877-591-2525; Fax: 403 591-7072, www.kananaskisgolf.com.
- Nakiska Ski Resort, Kananaskis Valley, AB; 403 256-8473, 1-800-258-7669; Email: info@skinakiska,

www.skinakiska.com
- Peter Lougheed Provincial Park, Highway 40; 403 591-6322.
- The Sheep River Valley. Access off of Hwy. 40; 403 949-3754.
- SilverTip Golf Course, 301 SilverTip Road, Canmore; 403 678-3110, Tee times: 1-877-877-5444, www.silvertipresort.com
- Spray Lakes Provincial Park; 403 591-6322.
- Stewart Creek Golf Course, Box 8570, Canmore, AB T1W 2V3; 1-877-993-GOLF (4653), Pro Shop: 403 609-6099; Fax: 403 609-6085, www.stewartcreekgolf.com
- William Watson Lodge, Peter Lougheed Provincial Park, P.O. Box 130, Kananaskis Village, AB T0L 0M0; 403 591-7227.

BANFF
- Abominable Ski & Sportswear, 229 Banff Ave.; 403 762-2905.
- Banff Mount Norquay, Box 1520, Banff, AB T1L 1B4; 403 762-4421; Fax: 403 762-8133, Email: info@banffnorquay.com, www.banffnorquay.com
- The Banff Recreation Centre, Mt. Norquay Rd.; 403 762-1235.
- Banff Springs Golf Course, Banff Springs Hotel, Box 690, Banff, AB T1L 1J4; 403 762-6801; Fax: 403 762-0363, www.banffsprings.com
- Lake Louise Ski Hill, Skiing Louise Ltd., Box 5, Lake Louise, AB; 403 209-3321, 1-877-253-6888, Snow Phone: 403-244-6665; Fax: 403 522-2095, Email: questions@skilouise.com, www.skilouise.com
- Mountain Magic Equipment, 224 Bear St.; 403 762-2591, www.mountainmagic.com
- Performance Ski and Sports, 208 Bear St.; 403 762-8222, www.performance-ski.com
- Sunshine Village, Highway 1 beyond Banff, Box 1510, Banff, AB T0L 0C0; 403 762-6500; Fax: 403 762-6513, Email: reservations@skibanff.com, www.skibanff.com

COLUMBIA ICEFIELD
The Parks Canada Information Booth offers advice on hiking and camping in the Icefield region, along with current field reports. Icefield Centre, Hwy 93 (Icefield Parkway).

JASPER
- Athabasca Falls. Icefield Parkway.
- Lake Edith and Lake Annette. Day use areas offering picnic sites, playgrounds, shelters and trails, including the wheelchair-accessible Lee Foundation trail.
- Marmot Basin Ski Hill, Hwy 93A, P.O. Box 1300, Jasper, AB T0E 1E0; 780 852-3816; Fax: 780 852-3533, Email: info@skimarmot.com, www.skimarmot.com
- Mount Robson Provincial Park. Yellowhead Highway 16; 250 964-2243, wlapwww.gov.bc.ca/bcparks/explore/parkpgs/mtrobson.htm
- Pyramid Lake. Follow Cedar Avenue, which becomes Pyramid Lake Road. Fishing, boating, horseback riding, sailing and skating are just a few of the choices here. Rental facilities available.
- Sunwapta Falls. Icefield Parkway, whitewater rafting available.

SHOPPING

CALGARY

DOWNTOWN
- Alberta Boot Co., 614 10th Ave. S.W.; 403 263-4623. www.albertaboot.com
- Arnold Churgin Shoes Limited, 227 8th Ave. S.W.; 403 262-3366.
- Bankers Hall, 315 8th Ave. S.W.; 403 266-8922.
- The Bay, 200 8th Ave. S.W.; 403 262-0345. www.hbc.com
- Blu's Womens Wear, 361 Bankers Hall; 403 234-7971. www.blus.com
- Calgary Eaton Centre/TD Square, 8th Ave. & 3rd St. S.W.; 403 206-6490.
- The Compleat Cook, 221 Banker's Hall; 403 264-0449.
- Glenbow Museum Shop, 130 9th Ave. S.E.; 403 268-4119. Email: bstuber@glenbow.org, www.glenbow.org/visiting/shop
- Holt Renfrew & Co. Ltd., Calgary Eaton Centre, 751 3rd St. S.W.; 403 269-7341. www.holtrenfrew.com
- La Cache, Scotia Centre; 403 263-5545.
- McNally Robinson Book Sellers, 120 8th Ave. S.W.; 403 538-1797. www.mcnallyrobinson.com
- Micah Gallery of Native Arts, 110 8th Ave. S.W.; 403 245-1340. Email: info@micahgallery.com,

- www.micahgallery.com
- Penny Lane Mall, 513 8th Ave. S.W.; 403 262-4681.
- Riley McCormick the Original Western Store, 220 8th Ave. S.W.; 403 262-1556. www.realcowboys.com
- Scotia Centre, 8th Ave. & 2nd St. S.W.; 403 206-6490.
- Smithbilt Hats Ltd., 1235 10th Ave. S.W.; 403 244-9131. www.smithbilthats.com
- Sunterra Market Bistro, 3rd Flr. 401 9th Ave. S.W.; 403 263-9759. www.sunterramarket.com
- Taschen, 315 8th Ave. S.W.; 403 262-5422. www.taschen.ca
- Winners Apparel Ltd., 128 8th Ave. S.W.; 403 262-7606. www.winners.ca

UPTOWN 17TH AVENUE

- Bernard Callebaut Chocolates, 847 17th Ave. S.W.; 403 244-1665. Email: bernardc@bernardcchocolate.com, www.bernardcchocolate.com
- Blue Light Special, Clothing/Accessories, 919 17th Ave. S.W.; 403 245-5338.
- The Cookbook Co,. 722 11th Ave. S.W.; 403 265-6066. www.cookbookcooks.com
- Eiffel Tower Bakery, 121-1013 17th Ave. S.W.; 403 244-0103. www.eiffeltowerbakery.com
- Focus Clothing, 800 16th Ave. S.W.; 403 244-4426.
- Gravity Pope, Clothing/Accessories, 524 17th Ave. S.W.; 403 209-0961.
- Janice Beaton Fine Cheese, 1708 8th St. S.W.; 403 229-0900. www.jbfinecheese.com
- Koolhaus, 724A 11 Ave. S.W.; 403 731-5665. www.koolhausdesign.com
- Lululemon, 1708 4th St. S.W.; 403 207-5858. www.lululemoncalgary.com
- Maria Tomas, 1015 11 St. S.W.; 403 233-9055. www.mariatomas.com
- Metrovino, 722 11 Ave. S.W.; 403 205-3356. www.metrovino.com
- Mount Royal Village Mall, 17th Ave. & 8th. St. S.W.; 403 228-6123. www.mountroyalvillage.ca
- Muse, 1301 17th Ave. S.W.; 403 806-0099.
- Oasis Wellness Centre & Spa, 880 16th Ave. S.W.; 403 216-2747.
- Park Avenue Boutique Ltd., 880 16th Ave. S.W.; 403 244-2746.
- Purr, 919 17th Ave. S.W.; 403 244-7877.
- The Rubaiyat Crafts Gallery, 722 17th Ave. S.W.; 403 228-7192. www.rubaiyatgallery.com
- Rustic Sourdough Bakery and Delicatessen; 1305 17th Ave. S.W.; 403 245-2113.
- Smyth and Kang, Clothing/Accessories, 1020 17th Ave. S.W.; 403 541-1717. Email: info@smythandkang.com, www.smythandkang.com
- Soho and Nada, 820 11 Ave. S.W.; 403 261-0888. www.sohonada.com

KENSINGTON

- The Galleria Arts & Crafts Gallery, 1141 Kensington Rd. N.W.; 403 270-3612. Email: galleria@shaw.ca, www.calgarycraftedgifts.com
- Honey B's, 28 12 St. N.W.; 403 283-0272.
- Ingear, 1115 Kensington Rd. N.W., 403 283-9387. www.ingearstore.com
- Janice Beaton Fine Cheese 1249 Kensington Rd. N.W.; 403 283-0999. www.jbfinecheese.com
- Joints Custom Framing, Suite 2, 1145 Kensington Cres. N.W.; 403 270-0030.
- Kensington Wine Market, 1257 Kensington Rd. N.W.; 403 283-8000. www.kensingtonwinemarket.com
- Kilian International Design, 1110 Kensington Rd. N.W.; 403 270-8800. Email: info@kilian.ca, www.kilian.ca
- Livingstone & Cavell Extraordinary Toys, 1124a Kensington Rd. N.W.; 403 270-4165.
- Pages Books on Kensington, 1135 Kensington Rd. N.W.; 403 283-6655. Email: info@pages.ab.ca, www.pages.ab.ca
- The Roasterie; 227 10th St. N.W.; 403 283-8131. 314 10th St. N.W.; 403 270-3304.
- Splash of Fashion, 200 1211 Kensington Rd. N.W.; 403 283-3353.
- Swimco for Swimwear, 1140 Kensington Rd. N.W.; 403 270-3081. www.swimco.com
- Urban Barn, 1117a Kensington Rd. N.W.; 403 270-7129. www.urbanbarn.com

INGLEWOOD

- Circa, 915 14 St. S.E.; 403 265-3637.
- Hinchcliff & Lee, 1217A 9th Ave. S.E.; 403 263-0383.
- Junktiques Ltd., 1226 9th Ave. S.E.; 403 263-0619. Email:

info@junktiques.ca,
www.junktiques.ca

MALLS, BIG BOX AND OUTLET SHOPPING

- Chinook Centre, 6455 Macleod Trail S.; 403 255-0613. www.chinookcentre.com
- Glenmore Landing Shopping Centre, 103a 1600 90th Ave. S.W.; 403 258-0091.
- Market Mall, 3625 Shaganappi Trail N.W.; 403 288-5466.
- Signal Hill Centre / Westhills Towne Centre, Sarcee Trail & Richmond Rd. S.W.; 403 245-4447.
- Southcentre, 100 Anderson Rd. S.E.; 403 225-9100.
- Winners, 5478 Signal Hill Centre S.W.; 403 246-4999. www.winners.ca
- Winners/HomeSense, 3221 Sunridge Way N.E.; 403 250-2461.

ECLECTIC, ETHNIC AND OUT-OF-THE-WAY SHOPS

- Camper's Village Outdoor Adventure Store, 7208 Macleod Trail S.E.; 403 252-3338. Email: info@campers-village.com, www.campers-village.com
- Chintz and Company, 1238 11th Ave. S.W.; 403 245-3449. www.chintz.com
- The French Connection Fine Antiques, 1221 11th Ave. S.W.; 403 283-4344.
- Home Evolution, 7133 11th St. S.E.; 403 253-5552. www.home-evolution.com
- Lee Valley Tool Ltd., 7261 11th St. S.E.; 403 253-2066. Email: customerservice@leevalley.com, www.leevalley.com
- Mountain Equipment Co-Op, 830 10th Ave. S.W.; 403 269-2420. www.mec.ca
- Pacific Plaza Mall, 999 36th. St. N.E.; 403 207-4425.
- Ribtor Sales, 318 11th Ave. S.E.; 403 262-6994. Email: sales@ribtor.com, www.ribtor.com
- Robert Sweep, 739 11th Ave. S.W.; 403 262-8525.
- T&T Supermarket Inc, 3516 8th Ave. N.E.; 403 569-6888.
- University of Calgary Outdoor Programs, 2500 University Dr. N.W.; 403 220-5038.
- Utsuwa-No-Yakata, 800 East 36th St. N.E.; 403 272-2828. Email: vc@utsuwa.com, www.utsuwa.com

BANFF

The best way to shop in Banff is to stroll Banff Avenue, enjoying the wide array of tourist and specialty shops.
- Cascade Plaza, 317 Banff Ave.; 403-762-8484. The largest mall in the Rockies.
- Welch's Chocolate Shop, 126 Banff Ave.; 403 762-3737. www.banffcandy.com.

JASPER

There are many fine stores and excellent gift shops to be found by strolling the main street in Jasper, and stopping by the many resorts.
- Alpine Experience: The Jasper Tramway Store, 640 Connaught Dr.; 780 852-3093. Email: info@jaspertramway.com, www.jaspertramway.com
- Edge Control Ski Shop, 626 Connaught Dr.; 780 852-4945. www.explorejasper.com/edgecontrol
- The Friends of Jasper National Park, Jasper Information Centre, 500 Connaught Dr.; 780 852-4767. Email: friends@incentre.net, www.friendsofjasper.com
- Jasper Camera & Gift, 412 Connaught Dr.; 780 852-3165.
- The Jasper Marketplace, Patricia & Hazel Sts.; 780 852-3152.
- Pine Cones & Pussy Willows, 308 Connaught Dr.; 780 852-5310. Email: pc-pw@telusplanet.net

EDMONTON

- The Bay, 1001 Edmonton Centre; 780 444-1550. 200 Southgate Shopping Centre; 780 435-9211. www.hbc.com
- Eaton Centre, 102nd St. & 102nd Ave. N.W.; 780 428-2243.
- Edmonton Centre, 107 Ave. N.W.; 780 424-9949.
- Holt Renfrew, 10180 101 St. N.W.; 780 425-5300. www.holtrenfrew.com
- Manulife Place, 101st St. & 101st Ave.; 780 420-6236.
- Old Strathcona, Along Whyte Avenue (82 Ave.) and 3 blocks wide. www.oldstrathcona.com
- Revillon Building, 10320 102 Ave.; 780 496-4999.
- Strathcona Farmers Market, 10310 83rd Ave. N.W.; 780 439-1844. Famous for trendy boutiques, family run stores and one-of-a-kind shops. Complete with street performers and stalls.

- West Edmonton Mall. Tourist Information, 780 444-5200, 1-800-661-8890, Email: tourism@westedmontonmall.com, www.westedmontonmall.com. Almost every retail chain is represented at this massive facility, with specialty stores in between.

BOOK SHOPS
- Athabasca Books, 8228 105th St. N.W.; 780 431-1776.
- Audrey's Books, 10702 Jasper Ave.; 780 423-3487.
- The Edmonton Book Store Ltd., 11216 76 Ave. N.W.; 780 433-1781. Email: bookmail@edmontonbookstore.com, www.edmontonbookstore.com
- Greenwoods' Bookshoppe Ltd., 7925 104th St. N.W.; 780 439-2005. Email: books@greenwoods.com, www.greenwoods.com
- Greenwoods' Small World, 7925 104th St. N.W.; 780 439-5600. www.greenwoods.com
- Indigo Books, 1837 99th St.; 780 432-4488. www.indigo.ca
- Laurie Greenwood's Volume II, 12433 102nd Ave. N.W.; 780 488-2665. www.volume2.ca
- The Wee Book Inn, 10425 Jasper Ave. N.W.; 780 423-1434. 10310 Whyte Ave. N.W.; 780 432-7230.

GROCERY SHOPS
- Debaji's Groceries, 9680-142 St.; 780 409-9911. www.debajis.com
- SunTerra Marketplace, 10150 Jasper Ave. N.W.; 780 426-3791. www.sunterramarket.com

FESTIVALS

CALGARY

SPRING
- Funny Fest Calgary Comedy Festival. 403 228-7888. www.funnyfest.com. Held at venues around the city in late April and early May, the festival features more than 70 shows.
- The Calgary International Children's Festival. 403.294.7414. www.calgarychildfest.org. A week of performances and roving entertainers including everything from dance and puppetry to face painting and storytelling. Late-May.
- Fourth Street Lilac Festival. 403 229-0902. www.4streetcalgary.com/lilacfestival. A trendy afternoon street carnival. Music, entertainment and artisans selling their wares. Last Sunday of May.

SUMMER
- Carifest. Prince's Island Park, 403 292-0310. A week-long celebration of Caribbean culture including food, music and dance. Early June.
- Canada Trust Jazz Festival. www.jazzfestivalcalgary.ca. Ten days of jazz greats and fantastic concerts. Last week of June.
- Calgary Folk Music Festival. Prince's Island Park. www.calgaryfolkfest.com. A celebration of folk music in a beautiful setting. Late July.
- Shakespeare in the Park. Prince's Island Park. www.mtroyal.ab.ca/conservatory. Free performances by theatre students from Mount Royal College. July/August, no shows on Mondays.
- Calgary Dragon Boat Race Festival. Glenmore Reservoir, North Glenmore Park. www.calgarydragonboat.com. Two spectacular days of Chinese Dragon Boat Racing, highlighted with an Asian culture celebration. August.
- Afrikadey! www.afrikadey.com. Western Canada's largest tribute to African culture. Mid-August.
- Calgary Reggae Festival. www.CalgaryReggaeFestival.com. Mid-August.
- Global Fest. www.globalfest.ca. Late August.
- Hispanic Festival. www.geocities.com/hispanicarts. Late August.

FALL
- Country Music Week. www.ccma.org. The Canadian country music industry's annual convention and awards gala. September.
- Artcity Festival. Festival of contemporary visual art, design and architecture. www.art-city.ca. Mid-September.
- The Calgary International Film Festival. www.calgaryfilm.com. This event showcases a variety of films at venues around the city. Late September.
- PanCanadian Wordfest.

www.wordfest.com. An international writer's festival. Mid-October.

- The Calgary International Organ Festival and Competition. Jack Singer Concert Hall. Staged every four years, this event attracts world class up-and-coming concert organists competing for the largest prize package in the organ world.
- The Esther Honens Calgary International Piano Competition. Jack Singer Concert Hall. www.honens.com. Occurring every three years, this world-class competition attracts many emerging pianists who compete for fame and fortune.

WINTER

- 12 Days of Christmas Festival. Heritage Park Historical Village. www.heritagepark.ca. Celebrate the festive season as they did in 1910. Held on weekends leading up to December 25th.
- Zoolights. At the Calgary Zoo. www.calgaryzoo.ab.ca. Be awed by 750,000 twinkling lights shaped into animals and festive decorations. December and early January.
- Alberta Theatre Projects playRites Festival of New Canadian Plays. Epcor Centre for Performing Arts. www.atplive.com. Celebrates risk and adventure in playwriting. January through March.
- One Yellow Rabbit Performance Theatre, High Performance Rodeo. Epcor Centre for Performing Arts. www.oyr.org. One never knows what to expect at this eclectic collection of performances. January.
- Calgary Winterfest. www.calgarywinterfest.com. A chance to take a break and enjoy Calgary as a winter wonderland. February.

KANANASKIS COUNTRY

- Canmore's Winter Festival. Canmore Special Events Bureau, Canmore, AB; 403 678-1878, www.canmore.ca. Winter family fun for all. Includes the International Sled Dog Classic at the Nordic Centre. January.
- Canmore International Ice Festival. Canmore Special Events Bureau, Canmore, AB; 403 678-1878, www.canmore.ca. Ice climbing

demonstrations and races. February.

- ArtSPeak Arts Festival. P.O. Box 8521, Canmore, AB T1W 2V3, 403 678-6436. Email: info@artspeakcanmore.com, artspeakcanmore.com. Concerts, art workshops, book readings, street performers and more. June.
- Canmore Folk Music Festival. Canmore, AB. www.canmorefolkfestival.com. A 25-year tradition that practically doubles the town's population during the first weekend in August.
- Canmore Highland Games. Box 8102, Canmore, AB T1W 2T8; 403 678-9454; Fax: 403 678-3385, Email: canmorehighlandgames@ telus.net, www.canmorehighlandgames.ca. Celtic sports, food and entertainment. Early September.
- Mozart on the Mountain. At the Stewart Creek Golf Course, Canmore, 403-678-1295, 1-866-CANMORE; Fax: 403 678-1296. Performed by the Calgary Philharmonic Orchestra. Mid-September.
- Art on the Mountain. At the Three Sisters Mountain Village, Canmore, AB T1W 2V3; 403 264-9944, 1-866 388-2877, www.threesistersmountainvillage.com/art. Local art exhibition and sale. October.

BANFF

- Banff Winter Festival. 403 762-8421. Winter events and celebrations including an ice sculpture competition. January.
- Banff Mountain Film Festival. 403 762 6100, www.banffcentre.ab.ca. A celebration of outdoor adventure films. End of October/early November.

JASPER

- Jasper in January Festival. www.discoverjasper.com. A parade and two weeks of exciting winter activities.

EDMONTON

SPRING

- International Children's Theatre Festival. 5 St. Anne St., St. Albert, AB T8N 3Z9; 780-459-1542. www.childfest.com. Theatre troupes from around the world. May.

- Dreamspeakers Festival. 8726 112 Ave., Edmonton, AB T5B 0G6 ; 780 378-9609; Fax: 780 378-9611, www.dreamspeakers.org. A celebration of Native arts. June.
- The Works Visual Arts Festival. 2 Flr., 10225 100 Ave., Edmonton, AB T5J 0A1; 780 426-2122; Fax: 780 426-4673, Email: theworks@telusplanet.net, www.theworks.ab.ca. Celebrated in local galleries and downtown foyers. June.
- Yardbird Jazz Festival. 780 432-0428, www.yardbirdsuite.com. Jazz venues spring up all over town. Late June-early July.

SUMMER

- The Street Performers Festival. #650, 7 Sir Winston Churchill Square, Edmonton, AB T5J 2V5; 780 425-5162; Fax: 780 426-0853, Email: producer@edmontonstreetfest.com, www.edmontonstreetfest.com. July.
- Klondike Days. c/o Northlands Park, Box 1480, Edmonton, AB T5J 2N5; 780 471-7210, 1-888-800-7275; Fax: 780 471-8176, Email: klondikedays@northlands.com, www.klondikedays.com. Trade show, midway and events all over town celebrating the 1890s. July.
- Heritage Days. Held at William Hawrelak Park, 9330 Groat Rd. Administration: #202, 10715 124th St., Edmonton, AB T5M 0H2; 780 488-3378; Fax: 780 455-9097, Email: info@heritage-festival.com, www.heritage-festival.com. Celebrate Edmonton's mosaic of cultures with food and entertainment. August.
- Edmonton Folk Festival. 10115 97Ave., P.O. Box 4130, Edmonton, AB T6E 4T2; 780 429-1899; Fax: 780 424-1132, www.efmf.ab.ca. A brilliant collection of folk performers from around the world. August.
- Cariwest Festival. 780 421-7800, Email: cariwest@shaw.ca, www.cariwestfestival.com. Cariwest Steel drum bands and dancing. August.
- The Fringe Festival. 10330 84th Ave. Edmonton, AB T6E 2G9; 780 448-9000; Fax: 780 431-1893, Email:

fta@fringetheatreadventures.ca, www.fringetheatreadventures.ca/ index.php/festival/. Buskers and street entertainment complement performances all over Old Strathcona. August.

FALL

- Symphony Under the Sky. Held at Hawrelak Park, 9330 Groat Rd., Edmonton. Tickets at the Winspear Centre Box Office, #4 Sir Winston Churchill Square, Edmonton, AB T5J 4X8; 780 428-1414, 1-800-563-5081; Fax: 780 425-0167, www. edmontonsymphony.com. A classical and contemporary music festival. September.
- The Edmonton International Film Festival. #201, 10816A 82 Ave., Edmonton, AB T6E 2B3; 780 423-0844; Fax: 780-447-5242, Email: info@edmontonfilmfest.com, www.edmontonfilmfest.com. Independent films and filmmakers from around the world gather to watch and host great films. October.

WINTER

- First Night Festival. New Year's Eve. A downtown celebration for the whole family.

EXCURSIONS

ELK ISLAND NATIONAL PARK

www.parkscanada.pch.gc.ca/parks/albe rta/elk_island. The beautiful home of not only elk, but over 400 head of plains bison and a herd of wood bison. Designed with accessible conservation in mind, the environment (including lakes and marshes) can be enjoyed on trails throughout.

FATHER LACOMBE CHAPEL PROVINCIAL HISTORIC SITE

Located on St. Vital Avenue just off the St. Albert Trail, in St. Albert, Alberta. Mailing address c/o 8820 112 Street, Edmonton, AB T6G 2P8; Summer (May 15 - Labour Day) phone 780 459-7663, Winter phone 780 431-2300; Fax: 780 427-0808, Email: marianne.mack@gov.ab.ca, www.cd.gov.ab.ca/enjoying_alberta/ museums_historic_sites/site_listings/ father_lacombe. Alberta's oldest building, the chapel was constructed in 1861 and became the centre of the French speaking Metis community of St. Albert.

KICKING HORSE PASS AND YOHO NATIONAL PARK

- Parks Canada Visitor Information in Field, Yoho National Park, P.O. Box 99, Field, B.C. V0A 1G0; 250 343-6783; Fax: 250 343-6012, Email: yoho_info@pch.gc.ca, www.pc.gc.ca/pn-np/bc/yoho/
- Emerald Lake Lodge & Conference Centre, P.O. Box 10, Field, B.C. V0A 1G0; 250 343-6321, 1-800-663-6336; Fax: 250 343-6724, www.emeraldlakelodge.com

KOOTENAY NATIONAL PARK

- Radium Hot Springs, PO Box 225, Radium Hot Springs, BC V0A 1M0; 250 347-9331, 1-800-347-9704; Fax: 250 347-9127, www.radiumhotsprings.com
- Visitor Information, Kootenay National Park, P.O. Box 220, Radium Hot Springs B.C. V0A 1M0; 250 347-9615; Fax: 250 347-9980, Email: Kootenay_reception@pch.gc.ca, www.pc.gc.ca/pn-np/bc/kootenay
- Fernie Golf & Country Club, Box 1507, Fairway Drive, Fernie, B.C. V0B 1M5; 250 423-7773, Email: DougRobb@golffernie.com, www.golffernie.com
- Panorama Village Resort, 1-800-663-2929, Email: paninfo@intrawest.com, www.panoramaresort.com

- Kimberly Ski Resort, 1-877-754-5462, Email: info@skikimberley.com, www.skikimberley.com
- Fernie Alpine Resort, 5339 Fernie Ski Hill Rd., Fernie, B.C. V0B 1M6; 250 423-4655, 1-866-633-7643; Fax: 250 423-6644, Email: info@skifernie.com, www.skifernie.com

REYNOLDS-ALBERTA MUSEUM

Box 6360, Wetaskiwin, AB T9A 2G1; 780 361-1351, 1-800-661-4726; Fax: 780 361-1239. Email: ram@gov.ab.ca, www.machinemuseum.net. The museum features over 8000 artifacts celebrating machinery from the 1800s to the 1970s. It includes displays such as vintage automobiles, planes and agricultural machinery, as well as special exhibitions.

UKRAINIAN CULTURAL HERITAGE VILLAGE

C/o 8820 112th St. Edmonton, AB T6G 2P8; 780 662-3640; Fax: 780 662-3273, Email: uchv@gov.ab.ca, www.cd.gov.ab.ca/enjoying_alberta/ museums_historic_sites/site_listings/ ukrainian_heritage_village; www.collections.ic.gc.ca/ukranian. An open air museum celebrating the unique history of Ukrainian Settlers. A Provincial Heritage Site.

PHOTO CREDITS

Legend: Top - T; Center - C; Bottom - B

All photos contained in this book were taken by Shannon Oatway or Corey Hochachka, and are copyright James Lorimer & Co., with the following exceptions:

Alberta Ballet: 24T; Assiniboine Lodge: 46B (B. Renner); Robert Black: 162B; Brian Brennan: 11C, 13B, 20, 22T, 24B, 25B, 26T, 27, 28B, 29, 30T; Brewster: 76C, 77B, 104B, 107T&B; Calgary Downtown Association: 9B; Calgary Folk Music Festival: 35, 36C; Calgary Opera: 21B; Calgary Stampede: 10C, 38, 39, 40B; Calgary Stampeders: 10T; Canadian Badlands Passion Play: 160B; Canadian Mountain Holidays: 64B; Canmore Nordic Centre: 47T; Anthony Cooney: 158B, 159, 160T&C, 161, 162T, 163, 164T; The Creperie, 149C; Cultural Image (Brad Zipursky): 36T; Sean Dennie: 36B; Eau Claire Market: 24B; Edmonton Economic Development: 141B, 147T, 151T, 152T&B; Fairmont Hotels: 62B, 63T, 71T, 84C, 88B, 122B, 140B; Fort Calgary: 12B; Glenbow Museum: 31T, 32; Jasper-Yellowhead Museum: 111T&B, 112 T&B, 113T, 114T&B; Lunchbox Theatre: 24C; Janice MacDonald: 136B, 138, 139B, 140B, 144B, 145T, 146T, 149T, 153T; Susan Marr: 50; Marmot Basin: 61B, 127, 128B (Hugh Lecky), 128T (Sean Miller); Richard McDowell 21T; Chris Morrison: 165, 167T; Museum of the Regiments: 33; One Yellow Rabbit: 22B; Denise Onysko: 83, 97B; Parks Canada: 57T, 130T&C, 156T; Petro-Canada: 15B; Provincial Archives of Alberta: 14T (E. Brown Collection), 14B (H. Pollard Collection); Provincial Museum of Alberta: 145B; Reynolds-Alberta Museum: 156T; Rimrock Resort Hotel: 74B; River Café: 28T; Ken Saunders: 63B, 88T, 134C, 168T; Karen Scolding: 53T, 103T, 164B, 167B, 168B; Mac Slipek: 46T, 64T, 66C, 123T, 134T; Sunshine Village: 51 (Ian Tomlinson), 61T (Malcolm Carmichael), 62T (Dan Hudson); Alana Thibault: 80T, 86B ; Travel Alberta: 5T, 7, 8, 9, 11T&B, 12T, 13T, 16, 17, 18T, 19, 31B, 34B, 37T, 40T; Troglodyte Photography (www.trogphoto.com): 56C, 58T, 59T, 66T, 68B, 75C, 100B, 102B, 105, 108B, 126T&C, 133T, 142C, 154T; Trudie Lee Photography: 23; Ukrainian Cultural Heritage Village: 156C&B; Dave Volk: 42C, 54B, 55B, 65B, 78T, 79C, 80C&B, 84B, 91B, 101, 113C, 120T, 121B, 130B; West Edmonton Mall: 144T; The Works Visual Arts Festival: 151B; Wild Bill's: 74T; Yoho-Burgess Shale Foundation: 96C&B.

Maps: Peggy McCalla and Maggie Pitts.

INDEX

Abbot Pass, 86
Abominable Ski & Sportswear, 79, 197
Aero Space Museum, 34, 192
Afrikadey!, 36, 200
Akamina Parkway, 167–68
Alamo car rental, 174
Alberta Ballet, 21, 24, 191
Alberta Boot, 26, 197
Alberta House, 145
Alberta legislature, 138, 139, 145–46, 194
Alberta Motor Association (AMA), 173
Alberta Theatre Projects, 23, 36, 190
Alpine Circuit, 97
Alpine Club of Canada, 134
Alpine Experience: The Jasper Tramway
    Store, 199
Alpine Loghouse, 180
Alpine Stables, 196
Alta Liebe, 94
Amethyst Lodge, 180
Angel's Staircase, 96
Anpurna Curry Pot, 30, 184
Anthracite trail, 81
Arnold Churgin Shoes Limited, 197
Artcity Festival, 36, 200
Art Gallery of Alberta, 146, 194
Art on the Mountain, 50, 201
Arts District (Edmonton), 146–147, 194
ArtSpeak Arts Festival, 50, 201
Ashlar Ridge, 132
Assiniboine Lodge, 177
Astley, Willoughby, 84
Athabasca Books, 142, 200
Athabasca Falls, 101, 122, 197
Athabasca Glacier, 106–8
Athabasca Hotel, 180
Athabasca Pass, 112
Atlas Coal Mine National Historic Site,
    159, 195
Audrey's Books, 142, 200
Aurora Restaurant, 73, 185
Avalanche Bulletin, 172
Avis car rental, 174
Aylmer Pass and Lookout, 59

Bach Dang, 149, 188
Back Country Jack's, 94
Badlands, 164
Baker Creek Bistro, 74, 185
Balkan Restaurant, 72, 185
Balkiston Falls, 167
Bamboo Tiki Room, 24, 191
Banff Centre, 75, 78–79, 192
Banff Heritage Passport, 77
Banff Mountain Film Festival, 201
Banff Mount Norquay, 63, 64, 197
Banff National Park, 86, 88, 95
    entrance fee, 54
    history, 55–57
    hot springs, 56–57
    weather, 54, 171–72
    wildlife, 53–54
Banff Park Lodge Resort Hotel &
    Conference Centre, 178
Banff Park Museum, 76–77, 193
Banff Recreation Centre, 79, 197
Banff self-guided historical walking
    tour, 78, 192
Banffshire Club, 73, 185
Banff Springs Hotel, 57, 69–71, 74, 82,
    192
Banff Springs Hotel Conference Centre,
    75, 193
Banff Sundance Lodge, 64
Banff (town), 68–82
Banff Upper Hot Springs, 57, 81
Banff Weather Office, 172
Banff Winter Festival, 201
Bankers Hall, 25–26, 197
Bankhead Interpretive Trail, 82
banking, 170–171

Barb and Ernie's, 150, 188
Barbary Coast, 72, 75, 186, 193
The Barley Mill, 30, 184
Barpa Bill's Souvlaki, 73, 186
Barrier Lake Information Centre, 43, 172
Bathhouse Theatre, 76
Bayshore Inn, 182
The Bay (Calgary), 25, 197
The Bay (Edmonton), 199
bears, 45, 54, 89, 93, 102, 125–26, 128
Bear's Hump trail, 167
Beat Niq Jazz and Social Club, 24, 191
Becker's Chalets, 118, 180
Becker's Gourmet, 118–19, 187
Beehive paths, 86
The Belvedere, 183
Berg Lake Trail, 134
Bernard Callebaut Chocolates, 26, 198
Best Western Hotel Jurassic Inn, 183
Best Western Suites Downtown
    (Calgary), 176
The Big Fish, 30
Big Hill, 92
Big Secret Theatre, 21
Billingsgate Seafood Market, 150, 188
Blackfoot Market, 20
Blakiston Creek, 167
Blue Light Special, 26, 198
Blue Moose Tours, 98
Blu's Womens Wear, 26, 197
Boom Lake, 59
bootlegging, 12, 32
Boulder Pass, 86
Boundary Pass, 86
Bourgeau Lake, 60
Bow River, 66, 79, 80
Bow River and Hoodoos trail, 80–81
Bow River Corridor, 196
Bow River Loop interpretative trail, 85
Bow Valley, 44–45, 55
Bow Valley Parkway, 58, 60
Bow Valley Provincial Park, 44–45
Bow Valley Square mall, 23
Bragg Creek, 47
Brava Bistro, 30, 184
Brewster Cowboy's BBQ and Dance
    Barn, 90, 187
Brewster Ice Explorer tour, 107
Brewster Rocky Mountain Adventures,
    174
Brewsters Brew Pub, 30, 184
Brewster Transportation and Tours, 104, 174
Brisebois, Ephrem, 12
British Commonwealth Air Training
    Plan, 15, 34
Bruno's Hideout, 24, 191
Buchanan's, 29, 184
Buddha's Veggie Restaurant, 30, 184
Budget car rental, 174
Buffalo Mountain Lodge, 72, 73, 178, 186
Buffalo Nations Luxton Museum,
    77–78, 193
Bulgogi House, 149, 188
Bumper's Beef House, 72, 186
Bumper's Inn, 178
Bumper's Lounge, 75, 193

Caesar's Steak House, 29, 184
Café de Tokyo, 30, 184
Café Soleil, 74, 186
The Cake Company, 74, 186
Calgary
    economy, 9, 13–15
    history, 12–15
    weather, 8–9
Calgary City Hall, 21
Calgary Dragon Boat Race Festival, 36,
    200
Calgary Eaton Centre, 25, 197
Calgary Exhibition and Stampede. See
    Calgary Stampede
Calgary Farmer's Market, 20, 189
Calgary Flames, 10, 192
Calgary Folk Music Festival, 19, 36, 200

Calgary Hitmen, 10
Calgary International Airport, 170
Calgary International Children's
    Festival, 18, 35, 200
Calgary International Film Festival, 36,
    200
Calgary International Organ Festival
    and Competition, 36, 201
Calgary Mariott Hotel, 176
Calgary Opera Association, 21, 22, 190
Calgary Philharmonic Orchestra, 22, 190
Calgary Pro Musica Society, 22
Calgary Reggae Festival, 36, 200
Calgary Roughnecks, 10, 192
Calgary Stampede, 14, 37–40, 189
    grandstand show, 39–40
    parade, 38–39
    rodeo, 40
Calgary Stampeders, 15, 192
Calgary Tower, 9, 10, 189
Calgary Transit system, 10, 173
Calgary Winterfest, 201
Calgary Zoo, 14
Calgary Zoo and Prehistoric Park, 17,
    36, 189
Calgary Zoo Botanical Gardens, 17
Cameron Creek campground, 166
Cameron Falls, 168
Cameron Lake, 167, 168
Camper's Village Outdoor Adventure
    Store, 27, 199
Canada Olympic Park, 18, 189
Canada Place at the Banff National
    Park, 78, 192
Canada Trust Jazz Festival, 35, 200
Canada West Tours and Adventures, 174
Canadian Mountain Holidays, 64
Canadian National Railway (CNR),
    114, 115, 116, 119–20
Canadian Northern Railway, 114
Canadian Pacific Railway (CPR), 13,
    32, 56–57, 78, 91, 120
Canadian Rockies Rafting Company, 174
Canadian Ski Museum West, 75–76
Canmore, 49–50, 64
Canmore Folk Music Festival, 50, 201
Canmore Golf and Curling Club, 50, 196
Canmore Highland Games, 50, 201
Canmore Nordic Centre Provincial
    Park, 46–47, 88, 196
Canmore's International Ice Festival,
    50, 201
Canmore's Winter Festival, 49, 201
Caramba!, 72, 74, 186
Carifest, 35, 200
Cariwest Festival, 153, 202
Carrot Creek trackset trail, 63
Cascade Dance Hall, 78
Cascade Fire Road trackset trail, 63
Cascade Mountain, 60, 82
Cascade Plaza, 75, 199
Cascadia Gardens, 78
Castle Mountain Group Campground, 89
Catch Restaurant, 29, 183
Cathedral Crags, 92
Cave and Basin Centennial Centre, 80
Cave and Basin National Historic Site,
    57, 76, 192
Cave and Basin trackset trail, 63
Cavell, Edith Louise, 121
Cavell Meadows, 122
Cedar Street Bridge, 13
Chamber of Commerce & Visitors
    Association (Waterton), 173
Chancellor Peak campground, 98
Charlton's Cedar Court, 178
Chateau Jasper, 180
Chateau Lacombe, 148
Chateau Lake Louise, 84, 180
Cherry Lounge, 24, 191
Chief Mountain Lodge Bed &
    Breakfast, 182

Chinatown, 11, 27, 30
Chinese Cultural Centre, 11
Chinook Centre, 199
chinooks, 8–9
Chintz and Company, 27, 199
chuckwagon races, 39
Cilantro, 30, 184
Cilantro Mountain Café, 72, 186
Circa, 27, 198
Citadel Pass, 59
Citadel Theatre, 146, 194
City Centre Mall (Edmonton), 147
City Hall, 194
Clay Oven, 30, 184
C-Level Cirque trail, 81
Coast Edmonton Plaza Hotel, 181
Coleman, A.P., 113
Collie, Norman, 113
Colonel Mustard's, 150, 188
Columbia Icefield, 60, 105–8
Columbia Icefield Chalet, 102–3, 180
Commonwealth Games, 140
Compleat Cook, 26, 197
Consolation Lakes, 86
Continental Divide, 46, 59, 87, 100
The Cookbook Co., 26, 198
Cory Pass hike, 60
Cosmic Ray Station, 77
Country Music Week, 200
Cowboys Dance Hall, 24, 191
Coyotes (club), 24, 191
Coyotes (restaurant), 73, 186
Cranbrook, 93
Crandell campground, 166–67
Crandell Lake, 167
Creative Journeys, 174
Creekside Country Inn, 177
The Creperie, 149, 187
Crescent Heights, 13
Crooks Meadow Group Campground, 94
Crossroads Market, 20, 189
Crowfoot, 12
Crowne Plaza Chateau Lacombe, 181
Crypt Lake trail, 167
C-Train, 10
Currie, Philip, 161
Currie Barracks, 15
Curries Guiding/Beyond the Beaten
    Path, 174
customs, 171

Da Guido, 30, 184
Deadman's Flat, 79
Deane House, 16
Death Trap, 86
Debaji's Groceries, 142, 200
Decidedly Jazz Danceworks, 24, 191
Delta Bow Valley, 176
Delta Calgary Airport, 176
Delta Lodge at Kananaskis, 45, 177
Devonian Botanical Garden, 138, 156, 194
Diner Deluxe/Urban Baker, 30, 184
dinosaur fossils, 140, 158
Dinosaur Provincial Park, 164, 195
Discover Banff Tours Ltd., 174–75
Divino Wine & Cheese Bistro, 29, 183
Dr. Robert Thirsk Communications
    Centre, 34
Dorothy Harvie Garden, 18
Douglas Fir Resort, 178
Dreamspeakers Festival, 151, 202
drivers' licences, 173
Drumheller, 158–164
Drumheller, Samuel, 159
Drumheller Regional Chamber of
    Development & Tourism, 172
Drumheller Travelodge, 183
Dupres, Charley, 128

Earl's, 30, 73, 150, 184, 186, 188
East Asian Village, 150, 188
East Bound Eatery and Sake Bar, 149, 188
East Side Mario's, 150, 188
Eaton Centre (Calgary), 25, 197

Eaton Centre (Edmonton), 142, 199
Eau Claire Market, 20, 189
Eckhardt-Gramatté Hall, 22
Econo Lodge Banff Trail, 176
Econo Lodge Downtown (Edmonton), 181
Eden, 73, 186
Edge Control Ski Shop, 199
Edith Pass Trail, 60
Edmonton, 135–153
Edmonton Book Store Ltd., 142, 200
Edmonton Centre, 142, 199
Edmonton City Hall, 146, 195
Edmonton Cracker-Cats, 195
Edmonton Eskimos, 140, 195
Edmonton First Night Festival, 153, 202
Edmonton Folk Festival, 152, 202
Edmonton Fringe Theatre Festival, 144,
    153, 202
Edmonton Heritage Days, 152, 202
Edmonton International Airport, 136, 170
Edmonton International Children's
    Theatre Festival, 151, 202
Edmonton International Film Festival,
    153, 202
Edmonton Oilers, 140, 195
Edmonton Tourism, 172
Edmonton Trappers, 140
Eiffel Lake, 86
Eiffel Tower Bakery, 26, 198
Elbow-Sheep Wildland Park, 47–48, 196
Elk Island National Park, 138, 154–55,
    202
El Toro, 72, 186
Elveden House, 9
Emerald Lake, 83, 92, 96
Emerald Lake Lodge & Conference
    Centre, 203
Enbridge playRites Festival of New
    Canadian Plays, 23, 36, 201
Engineered car rental, 174
Enmax Wildlights, 36, 201
Enselwood, John, 84
Enterprise car rental, 174
Epcor Centre for the Performing Arts,
    10, 21, 23, 190
Ester Honens Calgary International
    Piano Competition, 36, 201
Evelyn's Coffee Bar, 74, 186
Executive Resort at Kananaskis, 45,
    177–78
Exploring Holidays Inc., 175

Fairmont Banff Springs Hotel, 69–71,
    179. See also Banff Springs Hotel
Fairmont Chateau Lake Louise, 84, 180
Fairmont Hotel MacDonald, 181–82
Fairmont Hot Springs, 92
Fairmont Jasper Park Lodge, 120, 180
Fairmont Palliser Hotel, 176
Fairview Lookout Trail, 85
Fairview Mountain, 84, 85, 86
Fantasia Noodle House, 149, 188
Fantasyland Hotel at West Edmonton
    Mall, 181
Father Lacombe Chapel Provincial
    Historic Site, 156, 202
Fenland trail, 82
Fernie, 94
Fernie Golf & Country Club, 203
Festival of Quilts, 17
Fiddle Valley, 129, 130
Fish Creek Park, 29
5 Calgary Downtown Suites, 176
Flemming, Sir Sanford, 56–57
Fleur de Sel, 29, 183
Focus Clothing, 26, 198
Foothills Brass, 22
Forefield Trail, 108
foreign currency exchange, 170–171
Fort Brisebois, 12
Fort Calgary, 12
Fort Calgary Historic Park, 16–17, 194
Fort Edmonton Park, 138, 143, 194
Fossil Shop, 160, 195

Four Points By Sheraton Canmore, 178
Four Points By Sheraton Edmonton, 182
Four Points Sheraton, 176
Fourth Street Lilac Festival, 35, 200
Francis Winspear Centre, 146, 194
Fred & Barney's Family Restaurant, 160, 189
French Connection Fine Antiques, 27, 199
The Friends of Jasper National Park,
    116–17, 118, 123, 199
Funny Fest Calgary Comedy Festival,
    35, 200
fur trade, 32, 56, 111–12

Galleria Arts & Crafts Gallery, 26, 198
Gallery District (Edmonton), 142
Geo-Spirit Tours, 175
Giorgio's Trattoria, 73, 186
Glacier National Park (Montana), 166, 167
glaciers, 105–8
Glacier Saloon, 90, 187
Glenbow Museum, 31–33, 192
Glenbow Museum Shop, 26, 197
Glenmore Landing Shopping Centre, 199
Glenmore Reservoir, 17
Global Fest, 36, 200
The Globe Theatre, 11, 190
golf, 50, 94, 120, 196, 197, 203
Good Earth Café, 30, 184
Goods and Services Tax (GST), 171
Grain Exchange Building, 14
Grand Culturehouse, 22
Grand-Maître, Jean, 24
Grand Theatre, 191
Grand Trunk Pacific Railway, 16, 114,
    120, 131
Gravity Pope, 26, 198
Greenwoods' Bookshoppe Ltd., 142, 200
Greenwoods' Small World, 142, 200
Greyhound bus, 170
Grizzly House, 74, 186
Ground Zero Theatre, 23, 190
Grub Med, 150, 188
Grumans Delicatessen, 30, 184–85
Guido's, 73, 186

Happy Garden, 149, 188
Hard Rock Cafe, 75, 193
Hardware Grill, 148, 187
Harvey Pass, 60
Healy Pass, 59
Heart Mountain Trail, 44
Hector, James, 56, 91
helicopter sightseeing, 79
helicopter skiing, 64, 79
Henry, William, 112
Henry House, 112, 124
Herbert Lake, 84
Heritage Days (Edmonton), 152, 202
Heritage Park, 189
Hertz car rental, 174
HI Banff Alpine Centre, 179
HI Calgary City Centre, 176
Hidden Ridge Resort, 179
HI Edmonton, 182
HiFi Club, 24, 191
The High Level Diner, 149, 188
Highline Trail, 86
Highway 1, 170
Highway 2, 137, 170
Highway 16, 170
Highwood Road Corridor Wildlife
    Sanctuary, 48
Highwood to Cataract Creek Drive, 196
HI Hostel Lake Louise, 180
HI Jasper International Hostel, 180
HI Kananaskis Wilderness Hostel, 45,
    178
Hinchliff & Lee, 27, 198
Hispanic Festival, 36, 200
HI Waterton Alpine Centre, 182
H.J. Moberly Bridge, 119, 132
Holiday Inn Express, 176
Holt Renfrew & Co. Ltd. (Calgary),
    25, 197

Holt Renfrew & Co. Ltd. (Edmonton), 142, 199
Home Evolution, 27, 199
Home Sense, 27, 199
Honey B's, 26, 198
Hoodoo Creek, 97
Hoodoo Lounge, 75, 193
Hostelling International hostels, 180
Hotel Arts, 176
Hotel Selkirk, 143, 182
Howard Douglas Lake, 59
Howling Dog Tours, 64, 175
Hudson's Bay Company, 56, 119, 139
Hummer Tours, 175
Hyatt Regency Hotel (Calgary), 176
Hydra River Guides, 175
Hy's Steak House, 29, 184
Hy's Steak Loft, 148, 187

IceFest (Canmore International Ice Festival), 201
Icefield Centre, 102–3, 107, 108, 193, 197
Icefield Centre Snack Bar, Cafeteria and Dining Room, 187
Icefield Highway, 115
Icefield Information Centre, 106
Icefields Parkway, 100–4
Il Sogno, 30, 185
Indigo Books, 142, 200
Indulge Catering and Gourmet Foods, 11, 185
Ingear, 26, 198
Inglewood, 27
Ink Pots, 58–59
Inn on Crowchild, 177
Inns of Banff, 179
International Children's Theatre Festival, 151, 201
International Peace Park, 166
International Sled Dog Classic, 49, 201
Invermere, 92, 94
Ironwood Stage and Grill, 24, 191
Irwin's Mountain Inn, 179

Jack's Grill, 148, 187
Jack Singer Concert Hall, 22, 24
James Joyce Irish Pub, 24, 30, 185, 191
Janice Beaton Fine Cheese, 26, 27, 30, 198
Jasper backcountry camping, 125–126
Jasper-Banff Highway, 114
Jasper Camera & Gift, 199
Jasper campgrounds, 126
Jasper House, 112–13
Jasper Information Centre, 116, 172
Jasper in January Festival, 128, 201
Jasper Inn Alpine Resort & Restaurant, 180
Jasper Market place, 199
Jasper National Park, 111–14, 117
Jasper Park Collieries, 113, 131–32, 193
Jasper Park Lodge, 114, 117, 119–20, 128
Jasper Railway Station, 117, 194
Jasper's Wildlife Museum, 117, 194
Jasper (town), 115–22
Jasper Tramway, 119, 193-94
Jasper-Yellowhead Museum, 117, 194
Jewell Pass, 44
Joe Btfsplk's Diner, 72–73, 186
Joey's Only Seafood (Calgary), 30, 185
Joey's Only Seafood (Edmonton), 150, 188
Joey Tomato's (Edmonton), 150, 188
Joey Tomato's Kitchen (Calgary), 30, 185
Johnson Lake trackset trail, 63
Johnson Lake trail, 81
Johnston Canyon, 58–59
Johnston Canyon Resort, 179
Johnston's Canyon Campground, 89
John Walter Museum, 195
Joints Custom Framing, 26, 198
Jones, Robert Trent, 50
Joyce on 4th, 24, 191

Jubilations Dinner Theatre, 23, 190
Jubilee, 22, 24
Julio's Barrio, 150, 188
Jumpingpound Demonstration Forest, 47
Jump Start the Coffee & Sandwich Place, 74, 186
The Juniper (Banff), 179
Junktiques, 27, 198

Kananaskis Country, 41–48
Kananaskis Country Golf Course, 45, 50, 196
Kananaskis Guest Ranch, 178
Kananaskis Ranch Golf Course, 50
Kananaskis River, 45
Kananaskis Valley, 45
Kananaskis Village, 45
Kane, Paul, 113, 143
The Keg, 72, 187
Kensington Riverside Inn, 177
Kensington Sinfonia, 22
Kensington Wine Market, 27, 198
Kicking Horse campground, 98
Kicking Horse Pass, 91–92, 203
Kilian International Design, 26, 198
The Kiln, 74, 186
Kimberley, 94
The King and I, 30, 185
King Eddy Billiards, 75, 193
King Edward Hotel, 24
Kingsway Garden Mall, 150, 188
Klondike Days, 152, 202
Koolhaus, 27, 198
Kootenay Lodge, 95
Kootenay National Park, 92–95, 203
Kootenay Parkway, 93

La Cache, 26, 197
Lac des Arcs, 44
Laidlaw Transit, 87
Lake Agnes, 86
Lake Edith and Lake Annette, 197
Lake Louise, 60, 62–63, 64, 83–90
Lake Louise Campground, 88–89, 90
Lake Louise Ski Hill, 87–90, 197
Lake Louise Ski Hill Gondola, 192
Lake Louise Visitor Centre, 90, 172
Lake Minnewanka, 59, 82
Lake Minnewanka Boat Tours, 82, 175
Lake Oesa, 97
Lake O'Hara, 97
Lakeshore and Bertha Lake trail, 167
Lakeshore Trail, 84–85
Larch Valley, 86
La Ronde, 148, 187
Laughing Falls, 96
Laurie Greenwoods' Volume II, 142, 200
Leacock Theatre, 22
Le Beaujolais, 73, 186
Lee Foundation Trail, 119
Lee Valley Tool Ltd., 27, 199
Lina's Italian Market & Cappuccino Bar, 30, 185
Lincoln Park, 15
Lineham Lake, 168
Linnet Lake loop path, 167
The Living Room Restaurant, 30, 183
Livingstone & Cavell Extraordinary Toys, 26, 198
Loose Moose Theatre Company, 190
Lululemon, 26, 198
Lunchbox Theatre, 23, 190
Luxe Cinema, 75, 193

MacEwan Hall Ballroom, 24, 191
Mackay, Don, 15
Macleod, James F., 12
Maligne Lake, 133
Maligne Lake Road, 132–33, 194
Maligne Lodge, 180–181
Mango Shiva Indian Bistro and Chai Bar, 30, 185
Manuel Latruwe Belgian Patisserie, 30, 185

Manulife Place, 142, 199
Marble Canyon Campground, 94
Marble Creek Trail, 94
Maria Tomas, 27, 198
Market Mall, 199
Marmot Basin, 127–28
Marmot Lodge, 181
Marsh Loop, 80
Martha Cohen Theatre, 21, 190
Max Bell Theatre, 21, 190
Max's Light Cuisine, 150, 188
Mayfield Inn & Suites, 182
McArthur Valley-Cataract Brook, 97
McCabe, Franklin, 57
McCardell, Thomas, 57
McCardell, William, 57
McLean Creek Off-Highway Zone, 47
McLeod Meadows Campground, 93–94
McNally Robinson Book Sellers, 26, 197
Medicine Canyon, 132
Medicine Lake, 133
Medicine River, 132
Melissa's Steak House, 72, 186
Memorial Drive, 14
Mercantile Building, 160
Metrovino, 26, 198
Micah Gallery of Native Arts, 26, 197
Miette Hot Springs, 114, 129–30, 194
Miette Hot Springs Bungalows, 129, 130, 181
Mikado, 150, 188
Miki, 74, 186
Millennium Music Foundation, 22
Mincuk, Roberto, 22
Mirama, 149, 188
Misai Japanese Restaurant, 30, 185
missionaries, 12, 32
Mistaya Canyon, 101
Moberly, Henry, 119
Monach campground, 98
Mongolian Express, 150, 188
Moraine Lake, 60, 86, 88
Moraine Lake Trail, 86
Mosquito Lake Campground, 89
Mount Assiniboine, 60
Mount Bourgeau, 60
Mount Cory, 60
Mount Edith, 60
Mount Edith Cavell, 121–22
Mt. Engadine Lodge, 45, 46, 178
Mt. Kidd golf course, 50, 197
Mount Kidd RV Park, 45, 178
Mount Lefroy, 86
Mt. Lorette golf course, 50, 197
Mount Ogden, 92
Mount Robson Inn, 181
Mount Robson Provincial Park, 134, 197
Mount Royal College Conservatory, 22, 190
Mount Royal Village Mall, 26, 198
Mount Rundle, 56, 60
Mt. Shark Trailhead, 45–46
Mt. Stephen Fossil Beds, 97
Mount Temple, 86
Mount Victoria, 86
Mount Whitehorn, 87
Mount Yamnuska, 60
Mountain Equipment Co-op, 27, 199
Mountain Magic Equipment, 79, 197
Mozart on the Mountain, 50, 201
Murdoch, Mayor, 12
Murrieta's West Coast Bar & Grill, 29, 183
Muse (restaurant), 30, 184
The Muse (store), 26, 198
Museum of the Regiments, 33, 192
Muttart Conservatory, 138, 147, 195
Mystic Springs Chalets & Hot Pools, 177

Nakiska, 48
Nakiska Ski Resort, 196-97
National Car Rental, 174
National Parks Act, 114
National Park Warden Service, 172

Natural Bridge, 92, 96
Naval Museum of Alberta, 33–34, 192
New Asian Village, 150, 185
Newcastle Country Inn, 183
The Night Gallery, 24, 191
Northover Ridge, 46
North Saskatchewan River, 137, 140
North West Company, 112–13, 139
North West Mounted Police (NWMP), 12, 32

Oasis Wellness Centre & Spa, 26, 198
oil economy, 15
Odaray-Highline Trail, 97
Old Fort Point Trail, 123, 124
Old Post Office (Edmonton), 144
Old Salzburg, 94
The Old Spaghetti Factory, 150, 188
Old Strathcona, 141–142, 144, 195, 199
Old Time Fall Fair, 17
Olympic Hall of Fame and Museum, 18
Olympic Oval, 18–19, 189
Olympic Plaza, 18, 189
Olympic Plaza Cultural District, 21
Olympic Winter Games, 15
O.N. Bar & Grill, 29, 184
One Yellow Rabbit Performance
    Theatre, 23, 36, 190
One Yellow Rabbit Performance
    Theatre High Performance Rodeo,
    36, 201
Opabin Plateau, 97
The Orchid Room, 30, 185
Ottertail Valley campgrounds, 98
Outabounds, 75, 193
Out an' About Tours Travel Adventures,
    175
Outlaws Nite Club, 24, 191
Overlanders, 113

Pacific Northern Railway, 168
Pacific Plaza Mall, 27, 199
Packrat Louie Kitchen & Bar, 149, 188
Pages Books on Kensington, 26, 198
Palace of Eats, 30, 185
Palliser, John, 42, 56
Palliser Expedition, 113
Palliser Hotel, 14, 29
Palliser Square, 23
PanCanadian Wordfest, 36, 200-01
Paradise Valley, 86
Park Avenue Boutique Ltd., 26, 198
Parker Ridge Trail, 108
Park Place Inn, 181
Parks Canada Glacier Gallery, 107
Parks Canada Visitor Information
    Centre (Waterton), 172–73
Passion Play, 160, 195
passports, 171
Patricia Lake, 124
Peace Park Pavilion, 196
Pengrowth Saddledome, 10, 189-90
Penny Lane entertainment district, 11
Penny Lane Mall, 198
Performance Ski and Sports, 79, 197
Peter Lougheed Provincial Park, 45–46,
    88, 197
Petro-Canada, 10
Peyto Lake, 101
Phillips, Donald "Curly," 114
Piato Greek House, 30, 184
Pine Bungalows, 181
Pine Cones & Pussy Willows, 199
Plain of Six Glaciers, 85, 86
Plain of Six Glaciers Trail, 86
Plus-15 Walkway system, 10–11, 25
Pocahontas, 113, 126, 131–132, 194
Point Lace Falls, 96
Post Hotel, 88, 90, 180, 187
Prairie View, 44
Primrose at the Rimrock Resort Hotel,
    73, 186
Prince of Wales Hotel, 168, 183, 196
Prince's Island, 28

Prince's Island Park, 19, 35, 36, 189
Princess Theatre, 144, 195
Protection Mountain Campground, 89
Provincial Institute of Technology and
    Art, 15
Provincial Sales Tax, 171
public transit systems, 173
    Calgary, 10, 173
    Edmonton, 138, 173
Punchbowl Falls, 132
Purr, 26, 198
Pyramid Bench, 120
Pyramid Lake, 120–21, 124, 197
Pyramid Lake Bungalows, 121
Pyramid Lake Resort, 181
Pyramid Mountain, 120

Quaite Valley, 44
Queen Elizabeth Highway, 137, 170
Quest Theatre, 23, 191

Radisson Hotel Calgary Airport, 177
Radium Hot Springs, 92, 93, 203
Rafter Six Ranch Resort, 178
Railway Days, 17
Ramada Inn & Waterpark, 182
Rampart Creek, 89
The Ranche, 28–29, 184
ranching, 12–13
The Ranchman's, 24, 29, 184, 191
Red Carpet Inn, 179
Red Crow, 12
Red-Ox Inn, 149, 187-88
Red Rock Canyon, 167
Red Rock Parkway, 167
Redstreak Campground, 93
remittance man, 12
Revillon Building, 199
Reynolds, Stanley G., 156
Reynolds-Alberta Museum, 155–56, 203
Ribtor Sales, 27, 199
Riley & McCormick the Original
    Western Store, 26, 198
The Rimrock Dining Room at the
    Palliser Hotel, 29, 184
Rimrock Resort Hotel, 179
River Café, 28, 184
The River Valley, 147, 195
Road Rocket, 18
The Roasterie, 27, 198
Robertson Glacier, 46
Robert Sweep, 27, 199
Robin Hood Flour Mills, 14
Rockbound Lake Trailhead, 59
Rock Wall Trail, 94
Rocky Mountain Bed & Breakfast, 179
Rocky Mountaineer Railtours, 175
Rocky Mountain House, 112
Rocky Mountain Resort, 179
Rogers, A.B., 56
The Rose and Crown Pub, 73–74, 75,
    186, 193
The Rosebud Dinner Theatre, 160, 189,
    196
Ross Lake, 97
Rouleauville, 12, 13
Rowand, John, 143
Rowe Lake, 168
Royal Alberta Museum, 138, 140, 145,
    195
Royal Tyrrell Museum of Paleontology,
    159, 161–63, 196
Royal Winnipeg Ballet, 24
Rozsa Centre, 22, 190
Rubaiyat Crafts Gallery, 26, 198
Rundle, Robert, 56
Rundle Lounge, 187
Rundlestone Lodge, 179
Rustic Sourdough Bakery and
    Delicatessen, 26, 198

Saddleback Trail, 85, 86
Sage Theatre, 23, 191

St. James's Gate Irish Pub, 74, 75, 187,
    193
Saltlik, 72, 186–87
Sandman Hotel, 177
Sandman Hotel West Edmonton, 182
Sanson, Norman, 76, 77
Saskatchewan Glacier, 108
Saskatchewan River Crossing, 104
Saskatoon preserves, 142
Sceppa's Trattoria and Deli, 150, 188
Scotia Centre, 25, 198
Self-Guided Historical Walking Tour, 192-93
Shadow Lake Lodge, 64
Shakespeare in the Park, 36, 200
Shamrock Hotel, 24, 191
Shaw Millennium Park, 20, 190
Sheep River Valley, 47, 48, 197
Sheraton Cavalier Hotel, 177
Sheraton Suites Calgary Eau Claire
    Hotel, 177
Sherbrooke Lake, 97
Sherlock Holmes Pub, 150, 188
Ship & Anchor Pub, 24, 30, 185, 191-
    92
Sibbald Lake, 47
Siding Café, 30, 185
Signal Hill Centre/Westhills Towne
    Centre, 199
Signature Suites Edmonton House, 182
Silver Dragon, 30, 185
SilverTip Golf Course, 50, 197
Silverton Falls, 59
Simpson, George, 140
Sinclair, James, 93
Sir Winston Churchill Square, 146, 152
skiing, 43, 45, 46, 47, 48, 62, 63–64,
    87–88, 121, 127–28
Skoki Lodge, 64
Smithbilt Hats, 26, 198
Smith-Dorrien Trail, 46
Smuggler's Inn, 29, 184
Smyth and Kang, 26, 198
SnoCoach Tours, 193
Snowy Owl Sled Dog Tours, 64, 175
Soho and Nada, 27, 198
Southcentre, 199
Southern Alberta Institute of
    Technology, 15
Southgate Centre, 188–89
Southgate Mall, 150
speed limits, 174
Spiral Tunnels viewpoint, 91–92
Spirit Island, 133
Splash of Fashion, 26, 198
Spolumbo's Deli, 30, 185
Spray Lakes Provincial Park, 46, 197
Spray River trackset trail, 63
Springs at the Radium, 94
Spruce Meadows Equestrian Centre, 19,
    190
Stage West Theatre Restaurant, 23, 191
Stanley Milner Library, 147, 194
Stavros Family Restaurant, 160, 189
Stephen Avenue pedestrian mall, 26, 29
Stewart Creek Golf Course, 50, 197
Stoney Squaw Mountain, 82
Strathcona Farmers Market, 140, 142, 199
Street Performers Festival, 152
Suginoya, 74, 187
Sulphur Mountain Gondola, 77, 79, 193
Sun Chinese greenhouses, 81
Sun Chiu Kee, 30, 185
Sundance Canyon, 76
Sundance Lodges, 45, 178
Sundance trackset trail, 63
Sundance trail, 80
The Sunroom at the Banff Springs
    Hotel, 74
Sunshine Inn, 179
Sunshine Village, 59, 62, 64, 197
Sunterra Market Bistro, 26, 198
SunTerra Marketplace, 142, 200
Sunwapta Falls, 101, 133, 197
Sunwapta Lake, 108

Sunwapta Pass, 115
Super 8 Motel, 183
Sushi House, 187
Sutton Place Hotel, 182
Swimco for Swimwear, 26, 198
Symphony Under the Sky, 153, 202

Takakkaw Falls, 92, 96
Takakkaw Falls campground, 96, 98
Talisman Centre for Sports and
    Wellness, 10
Taschen, 26, 198
taxes, 171
Teatro, 29, 184
Tekarra Lodge, 181
Telus World of Science (formerly the
    Calgary Science Centre), 20, 190
Telus World of Science (formerly The
    Odyssium), 138, 195
Ten Peaks, 86
Tequila Nightclub, 24, 192
Theatre Calgary, 23, 190
Theatre Junction, 22, 23, 191
Thi Thi Vietnamese Submarine, 30, 185
Thompson, David, 112
Thompson, Stanley, 120
Thrifty car rental, 174
Ticino Swiss-Italian Restaurant, 74, 187
Time Out for Touring, 175
time zones, 171
Tokyo Express, 150, 189
Tommy's Neighborhood Pub, 74, 187
Tonquin Inn, 181
Tony Roma's, 73, 187
Tourism Calgary, 172
Tourism Canmore, 172
Trail Rider Store, 79
TransCanada Highway, 170
Trappers Pub, 24, 192
Travis, Jeremiah, 12
Treaty #7, 12
T-Rex, 159
Trong Khanh Restaurant, 30, 185
T&T Supermarket, 27, 199
Tunnel Mountain, 80
Tunnel Mountain camping facilities, 89
Tunnel Mountain trail, 81–82

Turner Valley oil field, 15
12 Days of Christmas Festival, 12, 36,
    201
Twin Falls, 96
Two Jack Lakeside Campground, 89
Two Jack Main Campground, 89
Typhoon, 74, 187
Tyrell, Joseph Burr. 161

Ukrainian Cultural Heritage Village,
    138, 155, 203
Underground Pub, 24, 192
University of Alberta, 195
University of Calgary, 15
    Department of Music, 22
    Outdoor Programs, 27, 199
Uoza Sushi, 30, 185
The Upper Crust Cafe, 149, 188
Upper Hot Springs Café, 74, 187
Upper Hot Springs Pool and Spa, 76, 193
The Uptown Screen and Stage, 11, 191
Urban Barn, 26, 198
Utsuwa-No-Yakata, 27, 199

Valemount (B.C.), 134
Valley of Five Lakes, 125
Van Horne, William Cornelius, 56, 70
Vasanji, 52, 208
Vertigo Mystery Theatre, 23, 191
Victoria Glacier, 86, 87

Wabasso campground, 126
Wainwright Hotel, 17
Walcott, Charles D., 95
Waldhaus Restaurant, 73, 187
Walking Tour of Jasper, 194
Walliser Stube, 90, 187
Wall Lake trailhead, 168
Walter, John, 140
Walterdale Bridge, 140
Wapiti Campground, 123, 126
Wapta Falls, 97–98
Wapta Lake, 97
Waterfowl Lake Campground, 89
Waterton campgrounds, 166
Waterton Heritage Centre, 196
Waterton Inter-Nation Shoreline Cruise

    Co. Ltd., 196
Waterton Lakes Golf Course, 196
Waterton Lakes Lodge, 183
Waterton Lakes National Park, 165–68
Waterton National History Association,
    196
Waterton Park Chamber of Commerce
    and Visitor Association, 196
Wee Book Inn, 142, 200
Weeping Wall Viewpoint, 101
Welch's Chocolate Shop, 75, 199
West Edmonton Mall, 138, 141,
    143–44, 195, 200
West Harvest Inn, 182
Westin Calgary, 177
Where Calgary magazine, 183
Whistler campground, 126
Whistlers, 125
Whistler's Inn, 117–18
Whistling Kettle, 189
White Mountain Adventures, 59, 175
Whyte Museum of the Canadian
    Rockies, 57, 77, 78, 193
Wilcox, Walter, 113
Wild Bill's Legendary Saloon, 74, 187,
    193
Wilderness Pass, 126
Wildwood, 29, 184
William Watson Lodge, 45, 197
Willows Stream, 70–71
Wilson, Tom, 83, 85
Windermere, 92, 94
Wingate Inn Calgary, 177
Winners Apparel Ltd., 27, 197, 199
Winners/HomeSense, 199
Woolley, Herman, 113
The Works Visual Arts Festival, 151, 202
World Track and Field Games, 140
World Universiade Games, 140

Yardbird Jazz, 151, 202
Yellowhead Highway, 137
Yellowhead Pass, 112, 115
Yoho National Park, 95–98, 203
Yoho Valley campgrounds, 98
Yuk Yuk's, 191

Formac Publishing Company Limited recognizes the support of the Province of Nova Scotia
through the Department of Tourism, Culture and Heritage. We acknowledge the financial support
of the Government of Canada through the Book Publishing Industry Development Program
(BPIDP) for our publishing activities

Library and Archives Canada Cataloguing in Publication

The Canadian Rockies : a colourguide / edited by Brian Brennan. -- 2nd ed.

(Colourguide series)
Includes index.
ISBN 10: 0-88780-692-9 ISBN 13: 978-0-88780-692-6

1. Rocky Mountains, Canadian (B.C. and Alta.)--Guidebooks. 2. Calgary
(Alta.)--Guidebooks. 3. Edmonton (Alta.)--Guidebooks. I. Brennan, Brian, 1943-
II. Series.

FC219.C35035 2005   917.123'3044   C2005-907378

Formac Publishing Company
5502 Atlantic Street
Halifax, Nova Scotia B3H
1G4
www.formac.ca

Printed and bound in China

Distributed in the
United States by:
Casemate
2114 Darby Road, 2nd Floor
Havertown, PA 19083

Distributed in the
United Kingdom by:
Portfolio Books Limited
Unit 5, Perivale Industrial Park
Horsenden Lane South,
Greenford, UK UB6 7RL